A HISTORY OF
THE PLYMOUTH
LIFEBOATS

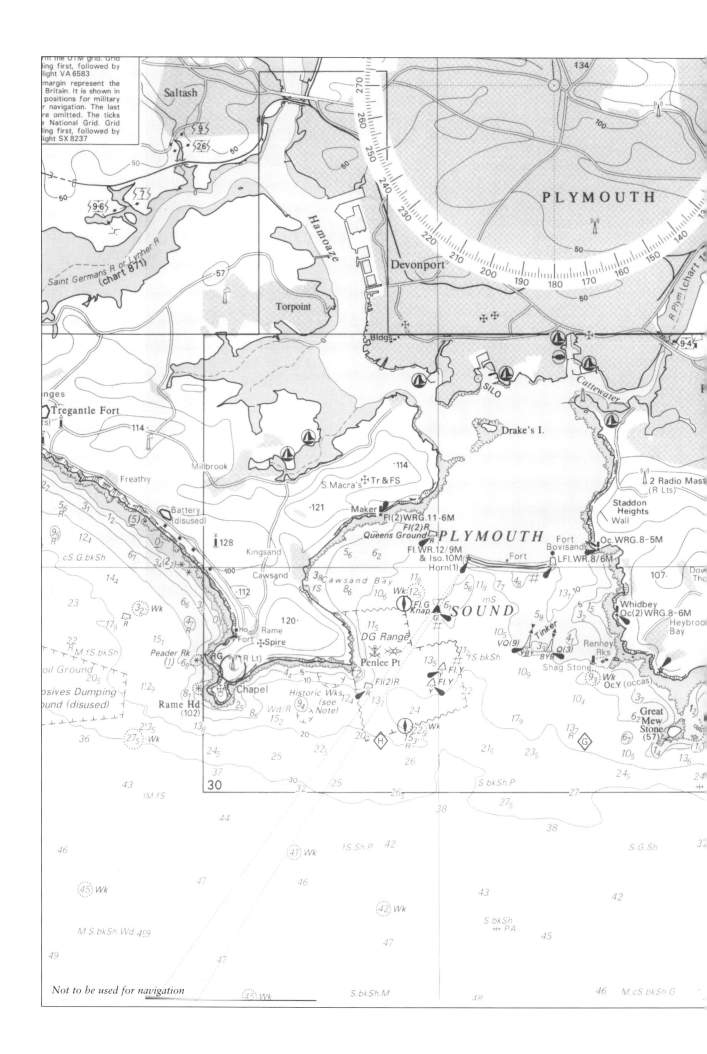

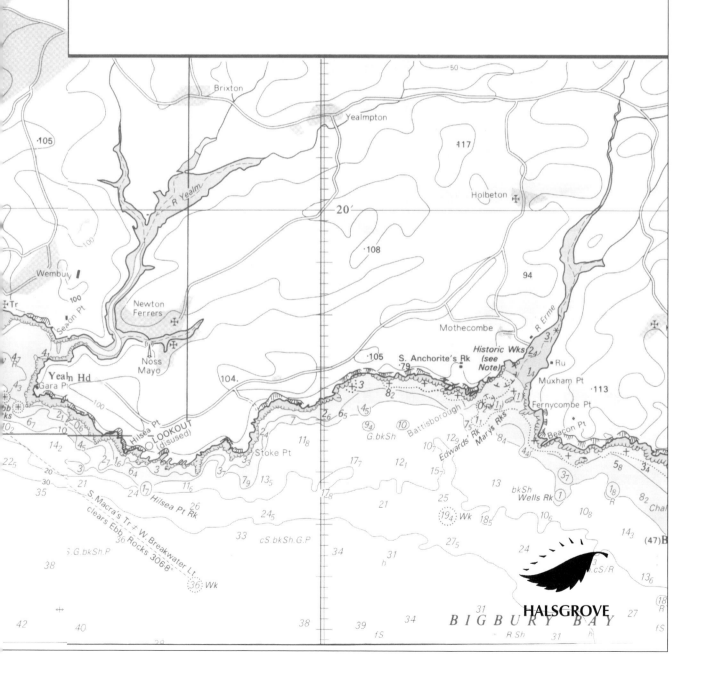

A HISTORY OF
THE PLYMOUTH
LIFEBOATS

200 YEARS OF COURAGE
ALAN SALSBURY

HALSGROVE

First published in Great Britain in 2003

British Library Cataloguing-in-Publication Data
A CIP record for this title is available from the British Library

ISBN 1 84114 275 1

HALSGROVE

Halsgrove House
Lower Moor Way
Tiverton, Devon EX16 6SS
Tel: 01884 243242
Fax: 01884 243325
email: sales@halsgrove.com
website: http://www.halsgrove.com

Frontispiece image: *Reproduced from the Admiralty chart 1613 by permission of the Controller of
Her Majesty's Stationary Office and the UK Hydrographic Office (www.ukho.gov.uk).*

Printed and bound in Great Britain by Bookcraft Ltd, Midsomer Norton

FOREWORD

by Sir Robin Knox-Johnson

Britain has the longest coastline in Europe. Although Iceland, the Faroes and Norway can lay claim to worse weather conditions, the British Isles, particularly in winter, are frequently battered by a series of gales and storms that put vessels and their crews at considerable risk. In the past, if the crew of distressed vessels could not take to their own boats, or jump or wade ashore, the chances of drowning were great. At the height of Britain's maritime power, when more than half the world's commercial shipping fleet flew the British Ensign, losses were frequent, and the loss of life appalling. Rescue for the crew of a vessel in distress was a very haphazard affair.

So it is perhaps a little surprising that an important port like Plymouth did not organise some form of life saving until the Napoleonic Wars when the first lifeboat was presented to the three towns of Devonport, Stonehouse and Plymouth by P. Langmead, Esq., MP, and arrived in Sutton Harbour on Wednesday 20 July 1803. She was one of 31 boats constructed to a design by William Wouldhave of South Shields. These lifeboats were 30 feet in length with a beam of 10 feet. No records exist of the number of lives saved, but she remained in service for 22 years and was replaced by a new boat designed by William Plenty of Newbury, Berkshire. The Plenty had a length of 26' 0" and a beam of 8' 6", it pulled ten oars and was built purely as a rowing boat. This boat was placed on station by the National Institution for the Preservation of Life from Shipwreck. Again no records are available of the services rendered and lives saved.

The Plymouth station lapsed between 1840–62 and then the first RNLI lifeboat was commissioned, a 34-foot self-righting boat, the *Prince Consort*, which came into service on 24 February 1862. The RNLI has maintained a lifeboat at Plymouth ever since. Up until 1926 these were powered by muscle or sails, when the first motor lifeboat was introduced, a 60-foot Barnett Class, the *Robert and Marcella Beck*. She remained on station until 1952 apart from war service when she carried out convoy rescue duties in Icelandic waters. During her absence, she was temporarily replaced by the *Minister Anseele*, a vessel belonging to the Belgian Government, which had been found abandoned in the English Channel.

Since the RNLI took over the station, 11 lifeboats have been in service at Plymouth and have saved a total of 593 lives. Plymouth's last lifeboat, the *City of Plymouth*, was one of the highly successful Arun Class fleet of fast rescue craft. The *City of Plymouth* was recently replaced by a new boat, one of the even faster Severn Class vessels, the *Sybil Mullen Glover*. Over the years the services have changed. When the lifeboats were first introduced their services were almost entirely to commercial and Naval vessels. This remained the case until quite recently when the dramatic reduction of the fishing fleet, Merchant and Royal Navies, and the huge expansion in yachting, has inevitably meant that a greater proportion of services these days are for pleasure craft.

The type of casualty may have changed but the sea is still as dangerous as ever. Whatever the reason for being at sea, a vessel in distress means humans at risk and this is what the lifeboats are for. Lifeboat crew are a special breed of people. When others are heading into shelter the men and women who man the boats know that this is when their services are most likely to be required. They never pause or flinch for they know that speed may mean all the difference between a life lost or saved. Their experience and willingness to risk their own lives demand everyone's respect, but particularly from those of us who carry out our business at sea.

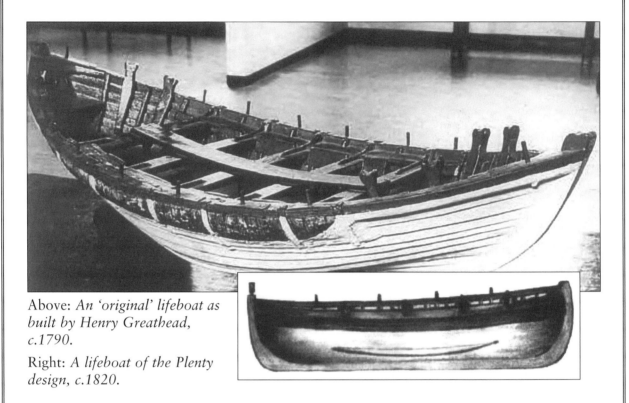

Above: *An 'original' lifeboat as built by Henry Greathead, c.1790.*

Right: *A lifeboat of the Plenty design, c.1820.*

The crew of the Escape, *1 April 1887. The crew included: John Lucock (First Coxswain), C. Mumble (Coxswain), W. Hooper, W. Cowles, John Mumford, J. Penny, James Bennett, D. Mumford, Joe Mumford, T. Crocker and J. Amery.* WESTERN MORNING NEWS

ACKNOWLEDGEMENTS

In compiling this book, I wish to acknowledge the help and assistance that I have received from the following: the staff of the Royal National Lifeboat Institution, Poole, Dorset; Claire Bright, Area Organiser, Devon; David Nicoll, Area Organiser, Cornwall; the *Western Morning News*; the *Western Evening Herald*; the Plymouth City Museum & Art Gallery; Nigel Overton, Maritime Heritage Officer; the Plymouth City Library Services; Bartley's Magic Lantern Collections; Devon and Cornwall Police, Air Operations Unit.

I convey my sincere appreciation, and respect, to those persons who have put up with many months of my constant barraging and intrusion into their homes. My thanks are extended, in particular, to the following individuals for their advice, knowledge, guidance and support, together with their photographs and memorabilias: Cyril Alcock, Derek Allen, Peter Crowther, John Dare, Malcolm Flintoff, Peter Helmore, Sean Marshall and Frances Zisimides.

Last, but by no means least, I thank those without whom a story such as this could not be told. I thank and wish God's speed to the coxswains and crews, past, present and future, of the Royal National Lifeboat Institution, Plymouth Station.

Alan Salsbury
March 2003

The aftermath of the Christmas hurricane, 1912. Stranded in Jennycliffe Bay are, left to right: the dismasted schooner Guild Mayor, *the schooner* Ottawa, *the lifeboat* Eliza Avins *and the Brazilian river steamer* Goyaz.

Mechanic Bill Rogers and a crewman of the Thomas Forehead and Mary Rowse *demonstrate equipment to a group of visiting schoolchildren, 1960s.*

52-40 City of Plymouth

Contents

The crew of the Robert and Marcella Beck, *1939–43.* Left to right, back: *Bert Sleeman, Walter Crowther (Coxswain), Arthur Banham (Mechanic), Arthur Foot;* centre: *Fred Fowler, Walter Lillicrap, Len Holmes;* front: *George Stanbury, John Hignett, Ernie Curtis.*

Left to right: *Raymond Jago, John Dare, Cyril Alcock and Keith Rimmer proudly display their Bravery Awards following the service to the* St Simeon, *15 February 1985.*

INTRODUCTION

Poets, authors, songwriters and philosophers have described her from time immemorial. Each has reflected upon her varying moods, romantic, enticing or volatile, unforgiving and dangerous. She means all things to all men, a provider of food, recreation and, for many, the sustainer of life itself. She is also the final resting place of countless souls. She covers two-thirds of the surface of the earth, and remains one of the great forces of Mother Nature, one that man may harness, but cannot tame – she suffers no fools – she is the sea.

Visitors to Plymouth cannot fail to be magnetically drawn towards the maritime history of this great city and port. Meandering around areas of the Barbican, Sutton Harbour and The Hoe, lasting impressions are forever imprinted upon the memory. While wandering along these historic waterfronts and side streets, steeped in history and tradition, one can almost sense the presence of Hawkings, Gilbert and Raleigh, together with that of the most famous son of Plymouth, Sir Francis Drake. No doubt every schoolboy can recount the story of that famous game of bowls which Drake allegedly played on Plymouth Hoe in 1588, whilst awaiting the approach of the Spanish Armada. They will also recall the sailing of the *Mayflower*, from Plymouth in 1620, as it carried the Pilgrim Fathers to America. In latter years they may also remember the arrival, at Plymouth in 1967, of the yachtsman Francis Chichester as, in *Gypsy Moth IV*, he completed

Left to right: *the Looe lifeboat*, Boy's Own No.1, ON 45, *the Yealm lifeboat* Darling, ON 163 and the Plymouth lifeboat (either the Escape or the Eliza Avins). *The Pier Pavilion and the Belvedere indicate a date of c.1891.*
BARTLEY'S MAGIC LANTERN COLLECTIONS

his single-handed circumnavigation of the world.

The maritime history of Plymouth, both ancient and modern, is inextricably linked with the Royal Navy. A Naval base was first established in Plymouth during the reign of Edward I. Devonport Dockyard, which stands on the Hamoaze (the name for the waters of that particular part of the River Tamar), was originally known as Plymouth Dock. The dockyard dates from 1693 when both wet and dry docks were built. This yard was developed further with the provision of workshops, stores, and the construction of additional docks, which subsequently formed the area known as South Yard. The dockyard was extended with the addition of the Morice Yard, which provided ordnance, powder and shot to the fleet, and was further extended with the addition of the Steam Yard in 1844.

Devonport Dockyard played an extremely important role in both world wars and is now the largest Naval dockyard in Western Europe. Amongst other functions, the dockyard of today boasts modern frigate refit sheds and has facilities to accommodate and refit nuclear submarines. The area now occupied by the Royal Navy is known as the Plymouth Naval Base. Most of the former dockyard is now in private hands, Devonport Management Limited, as a commercial enterprise. In more recent years DML has played a leading role in assisting the Royal National Lifeboat Institution with the development of the new generation of Fast Slipway

11

lifeboats. In January 2003 DML launched the first Severn Class lifeboat, which the yard had fitted out on behalf of the Institution.

The unsung heroes of the city's maritime history are undoubtedly the men and women of the Royal National Lifeboat Institution. Although the Institution is perhaps of less prominence to the individual, the lifeboat service of today continues to maintain a long and proud tradition. Plymouth's first purpose-built lifeboat was placed at Sutton Pool in 1803.

Over the last two decades Plymouth, in common with most coastal resorts, has experienced a vast increase in the number of leisure craft using the facilities of the harbours. To some extent this has changed the nature of the services which the lifeboats of the RNLI provide. Some individuals venturing out to sea have little or no regard for their own safety, let alone the safety of others; likewise they show little or no respect for the sea. It is reassuring and gratifying to know that when assistance is required, whatever the circumstances and whoever the casualty, without judgement of the individual and with unquestionable bravery and dedication, help is

readily at hand from the brave men and women of the lifeboat service. In this short history it is clearly not possible to chronicle, in detail, every launch of every lifeboat during the 140-plus years that the RNLI has served the seafarers of Plymouth. Only in a small way is it the author's intention to record some of the acts of heroism and bravery of the crews of the Royal National Lifeboat Institution's Plymouth Station.

Right: *Smeaton's Eddystone Lighthouse on the Reef before it was replaced by the present Douglass Lighthouse, c.1880.*
PLYMOUTH CITY MUSEUM & ART GALLERY

Main image: *'The wreck of the Dutton.'*

1

THE LOSS OF THE DUTTON

1796

Since man first desired to navigate the great waters of this planet and pit his wits against the forces of both seas and weather, there have been shipwrecks and loss of life. In the years before the formation of the RNLI, one particular disaster in the South Devon area which deserves special mention is the loss, in 1796, of the ship the *Dutton*.

On Tuesday 26 January 1796, the man-o'-war, *HMS Indefatigable*, was lying in the Hamoaze; her captain was Sir Edward Pellew. On the same day, a large East Indiaman, the *Dutton*, which was carrying members of the 2nd, or Queen's Regiment, was driven into Plymouth by the prevailing gale-force winds. The vessel had been at sea for a full seven weeks, bound for the West Indies, when weather conditions forced her captain to return to Plymouth. Throughout that Tuesday afternoon the gale, which increased in ferocity, was accompanied by ever-worsening conditions at sea. Late in the afternoon the captain of the *Dutton* set a course to seek out the somewhat greater safety of the Cattewater. Unbeknown to the crew of the *Dutton*, the buoy that marked the extremity of the Mount Batten reef had been ripped from its mooring by the raging sea, thus leaving the navigable channel unmarked. With this loss of warning, the *Dutton* ran onto the Mount Batten reef and, in consequence, lost her rudder. Now out of control, she fell off and was driven aground under the Citadel where she lay rolling heavily, broadside-on to the pounding waves. It was reported that the force of the waves was such that, with only the second roll, the *Dutton* lost all masts overboard.

On this day, Sir Edward and Lady Pellew were to dine with the vicar of Charles Church, Dr Hawker. Pellew had been a lifelong friend of Hawker, the two men having served together as surgeons to the Marines at Plymouth. Sir Edward, having noticed the crowds running to The Hoe, learned of the impending disaster and ran with the throng. Upon arriving at The Hoe, Pellew realised that, in the absence of someone to direct a rescue attempt, the loss of the *Dutton*, together with the estimated 500 men, women and children aboard, would be inevitable. Pellew himself took command of the situation and, upon seeing that the ship's senior officers had left their posts and reached the safety of the shore, urged them to return to their vessel and assist those whose lives remained in danger. His appeal was in vain as were his attempts to offer payment to local pilots and seamen, all deeming the circumstances too dangerous to warrant any attempt at rescue. His appeals having failed, Pellew reportedly exclaimed 'Then I will go myself!'

The only contact between the *Dutton* and the shore was a single rope by means of which the ship's officers, and a few other persons, had landed. Using this rope, Pellew was hauled through the surf and debris to the stricken vessel. As he was dragged through the waves Sir Edward was dragged under the mainmast and sustained a back injury, for which he was subsequently confined to bed for a week. At the time, however, he disregarded his injury, boarded the East Indiaman, and in identifying himself to those on board, assumed command of the vessel. He was greeted with three hearty cheers, which were echoed by the spectators on The Hoe. Sir Edward Pellew's reputation preceded him and his orders were unquestionably obeyed by those left on board the stricken ship.

The coat of arms of Sir Edward Pellew, incorporating the wreck of the Dutton.

women, children and the sick were the first to be taken off, including a three-week-old baby, and it was recorded that:

... nothing in the whole transaction impressed Sir Edward more strongly, than the struggle of the mother's feelings before she would entrust her infant to his care, or afford him more pleasure than the success of his attempts to save it.

The soldiers were the next to be taken ashore, followed by the ship's company. Every person aboard the *Dutton* was saved, and finally, in true seafaring tradition, Sir Edward Pellew left his 'command'.

Within a very short period of time the once proud vessel surrendered to the relentless pounding of the sea and was dashed to pieces. Sir Edward Pellew was honoured with the Freedom of Plymouth and, in the following year, was made a Baronet, subsequently being granted an augmentation to his coat of arms, which depicted, 'Upon waves of the sea the wreck of the 'Dutton', East Indiaman, upon a rocky shore off Plymouth garrison, all Proper.' In 1814 Pellew was created Viscount Exmouth of Canonteign.

Unaware of his presence on the *Dutton*, the officers of the *Indefatigable* attempted their own rescue mission with the ship's boat and barge. Their attempts to manoeuvre alongside the wreck failed, but a boat belonging to a merchant vessel was more fortunate in its attempt. Mr Edsell, Signal Midshipman to the Port Admiral, and Mr Coghlan, mate of the vessel, succeeded in bringing their boat alongside. At great personal risk, two additional hawsers were taken ashore and Pellew constructed cradles, which were slung upon them, with ropes attached by which they could be pulled back and forth between the ship and the shore.

As this activity was taking place, with great difficulty in the gale-force conditions, a cutter from Plymouth Pool and two boats from the dockyard, under the command of Mr Hemmings, the master-attendant, made their respective ways to the scene of the disaster. By exercising great skill and seamanship the two smaller boats approached the *Dutton* and took off the sick and injured, transferring them to the cutter. Sir Edward Pellew, who stood with his sword drawn to preserve order (as the soldiers on board had located the spirit store and were, for the most part, intoxicated), oversaw the proceedings. The

THE FOLLOWING, APPARENTLY UNATTRIBUTED, VERSE WAS WRITTEN IN COMMEMORATION OF THE CONDUCT OF SIR EDWARD PELLEW.

*While o'er the reeling wreck the savage storm
Pour'd all its lightning's, thunders, blasts, and hail;
And every horror in its wildest form
Smote the firm heart, that never knew to fail.*

*'Twas thine, Pellew, sublimely great and good!
For man, thy brother man, distress'd, to dare
The dreadful passage of the raging flood,
And join the frantic children of despair.*

*There it was thine, in comfort's balmy tone,
To soothe their sorrows 'mid the tempest's roar;
To hush the mother's shriek – the sick man's groan,
And bear the sufferers trembling to the shore.*

*So when this mighty orb, in dread alarm,
Shall crash in ruins, at its God's decree;
May thy Redeemer, with triumphant arm,
From the vast wreck of all things – rescue thee.*

2

THE FIRST PLYMOUTH LIFEBOAT
1803

The latter part of the eighteenth century, and the early years of the nineteenth century, saw considerable interest in the development of a purpose-built lifeboat. In 1789 a major sea tragedy occurred when, in a storm, the collier *Adventure* ran aground on the River Tyne. To attempt a rescue mission in such weather conditions would have meant almost certain death for the rescuers. Several thousand onlookers are reported to have watched in horror as all the crew of the stricken vessel drowned. The tragedy so struck the members of a Gentlemen's Club in South Shields that they sponsored a competition to provide a design for a lifeboat, offering a reward of two guineas. William Wouldhave, the Parish Clerk of South Shields, drew up the winning design which, modified by the judges, was given to Henry Greathead to use in the construction of the first purpose-built lifeboat, *The Original*. The boat was launched on Saturday 30 January 1790. Some 30 feet in length and 10 feet wide, she was non-self-righting and was propelled solely by 12 oars. Her high-rise design, at the bow and stern, provided cases that contained 7 cwt. of cork buoyancy, the hull was lined with cork and a cork rail provided additional buoyancy. *The Original* served for 40 years on the River Tyne, while 30 other vessels, built to the same specifications, were placed throughout Britain.

Local harbour authorities throughout the land received financial assistance from the Lloyd's Corporation in order to obtain one of the 31 lifeboats that were built to Greathead's specifications. Plymouth was one of the first ports to receive such a lifeboat.

Trewman's Exeter Flying Post, of Thursday 27 January 1803, carried the following entry:

Friday. P. Langmead, Esq. M.P. for this borough, by letter to the Treasurer of the merchants' seamen's hospital at this port, has informed him, that for the use of the port of Plymouth, and its dependencies, he has purchased one of the celebrated life-boats, for the preservation of shipwrecked and drowning seamen, in gales of wind, and in violent seas, of Mr. Greathead, which, when furnished, he shall present to the borough, for their use, free of any expense; an attention to the welfare of this borough very much to the credit of P. Langmead, Esq.

The lifeboat arrived at Sutton Pool at 18.00 hours on the evening of Wednesday 20 July 1803, to a 21-gun salute. The Mayor and Corporation, accompanied by local merchants, ship-owners and inhabitants of the borough, gathered at Barbican Pier Head to formally welcome the arrival of the lifeboat.

An account of its arrival in Plymouth is recorded in *Felix Farley's Bristol Journal*:

Yesterday afternoon a good procession of boats, decorated with colours, streamers, &c. rowed and sailed to Hamoaze to visit and conduct the Life Boat to Plymouth. It was received at the entrance of the harbour with a band of music, playing 'God Save the King', and was rowed, the rowers dressed in white shirts, black velvet caps, decorated with blue ribbands, by ten seamen. As the boat passed the shipping, it was saluted and also received a royal salute from Mr. T. Lockyer's Battery, Teat's Hill, of 21 guns. The Mayor, accompanied by the principal merchants and inhabitants, proceeded to the Prince George Tavern, and partook of a very elegant cold collation and dessert of fruit, wines, &c. and the evening concluded with the greatest festivity.

Following the inauguration of the Plymouth lifeboat, it would appear that little use was made of it, despite the fact that severe winter weather and storms continued to lash the coastline of South Devon with the resultant loss of numerous lives and vessels.

A major long-term project to protect shipping was identified by Admiral Earl St Vincent when, in 1806, he was placed in command of the Channel Fleet. Vincent's proposal was for the construction, in Plymouth Sound, of a breakwater. Following a survey, formal proposals were made for a central breakwater with piers extending from the shore. The plan, however, was not brought to fruition.

There were multiple losses sustained in the many gales that afflicted South Devon during the period 1803–25. On Christmas Day, Sunday 25 December 1803, several vessels were driven ashore including the captured privateer, the *Cosmopilite*. A brigantine from the town of Dartmouth, and the *Les Amis*, a prize vessel taken by HMS *Malta*, were lost in the Cattewater. The gale that swept Plymouth on the night of Thursday19–Friday 20 January 1804 resulted in the loss, also in the Cattewater, of the Plymouth vessel, the *British Tar*, the captured French privateer, the *L'Effronteur*, and two fishing vessels. The Swedish vessel, the *Gustaf Sophia*, was dismasted and the Dutch galliot, *Jong Backe*, was driven ashore. The armed brig *Fearless* was driven ashore at Cawsands, whilst the frigate, *La Loire*, lost her spars in the Sound. The *Jane*, bound from Plymouth for Liverpool, was lost off the Mew Stone with all hands.

In the gales of January 1806 a boat, carrying 45 persons and belonging to the *Hibernia*, was driven ashore near the Shag Stone. On this occasion there were 26 lives lost. A violent storm which blew from the west-north-west on Saturday 19 November 1808 wrought havoc on shipping in Stonehouse Pool. On this occasion a complete tier of vessels broke adrift and several ships grounded and were lost.

In 1811 the proposal for a central breakwater was revisited and on 22 June 1811 an Order in Council was made authorising the commencement of the scheme. Just over one year later, on Wednesday 12 August 1812, the first stone of the new breakwater was laid, at Shovel Rock. The commencement of the construction coincided with the onset of the autumn and the winter gales. On the night of Sunday 18–Monday 19 October 1812, a violent south-westerly gale saw nine vessels driven ashore, one of which was the *Providence* of Dartmouth.

By early 1814 the construction of the breakwater had progressed sufficiently to give an element of protection to shipping, although this was not sufficient to prevent further disasters. In 1844 the lighthouse became operational on the west end of the structure, and the beacon at the east end was built the following year. An iron ball that could shelter ten men, in case of shipwreck, surmounted the beacon.

On Monday 12–Tuesday 13 December 1814, in a south-westerly gale, a further six vessels were lost in the waters off Plymouth. South-south-westerly hurricane-force winds, a raging sea and an extremely high tide combined to cause major damage to the stonework of the breakwater on the night of Saturday 18–Sunday 19 January 1817. This particularly tragic night saw the loss, in Deadman's Bay, of the *Princess Mary*, together with the vessel's master, his wife and two children, and members of the crew. The 14-gun sloop-of-war, *Jasper*, was lost near Mount Batten. Some 72 men from a crew of 76 lost their lives.

It is an enigma that nowhere in the brief accounts of these incidents is reference made to the use, or indeed the existence, of a Plymouth lifeboat. Indeed, to date, no records have been traced to indicate that this Plymouth lifeboat was ever used for the saving of life.

At that time, many lifeboats were operated independently. A man with great foresight, Colonel Sir William Hillary, a member of the Douglas lifeboat crew, Isle of Man, readily identified the need for a coordinated approach to saving life at sea, and the requirement of a national regulating body. In 1823 Sir William Hillary published his paper with the rather unwieldy title:

An Appeal to the British Nation on the Humanity and Policy of Forming a National Institution for the Preservation of Lives and Property from Shipwreck

In this he highlighted the shortfalls which he perceived in the existing provision of lifeboat cover and outlined his recommendations for a national lifeboat service. His paper enjoyed widespread support and there was much sympathy for victims of shipwreck. On 4 March 1824, at a meeting in the City of London Tavern, the National Institution for the Preservation of Life from Shipwreck (NIPLS) was formed. King George IV became Patron of the Institution, the Prime Minister, Lord Liverpool, became the President, and Thomas Wilson, MP, was made the Secretary. Hillary's Institution sought to alleviate the nation's loss and misery caused by shipwreck. Sir William Hillary became the holder of no less than three RNLI Gold Medals, the lifeboat man's VC, a feat equalled only by the legendary Henry Blogg, GC, BEM, a former crew member and Coxswain of the Cromer, Norfolk, lifeboat. Appropriately, Hillary's family motto was 'With courage, nothing is impossible.'

Upon the foundation of the Institution, a set of Captain Manby's mortar apparatus, by means of which lines could be fired to ships in distress, was placed at Plymouth.

Initially the Institution received annual Government funding but this soon fell by the wayside. Subsequent to 1827, HM Customs, or Revenue, were primarily responsible for rescuing and saving the lives of shipwrecked mariners. The boats used by the Revenue were not of a specific design but were of a model and colour that reflected and blended in with those used in the local community, thus proving advantageous for the detection of Revenue evasion.

In these formative years of the RNLI there was not an active lifeboat at Plymouth; nevertheless, the Institution continued to recognise bravery shown by individuals in rescuing and preserving life from shipwreck. The Institution acknowledged such acts of bravery by the presentation of Gold or Silver Medals, and subsequently, from 1917, Bronze Medals

During the great gale of Monday 22 November–Wednesday 24 November 1824, the barometric pressure reportedly fell to 28.19 inches as the tide rose to 21' 2". The gale was described in the local newspaper as being 'the most disastrous in recent times'. In the short distance between the Citadel and the Cattewater, 25 ships were driven ashore, 16 within 30 yards of Deadman's Bay. A correspondent for the *Western Daily Mercury* reported that:

The desolation on our shores is of the most melancholy description, nothing but wrecks are to be seen in every direction, and valuable property lies floating about on the water without an owner. The ruin has extended far and wide; and every creek and inlet is a scene of destruction without parallel in this part of the world.

The *Plymouth and Devonport Weekly Journal* listed the following vessels as being amongst those lost that day:

Zephyr – *brig – from London to Oporto with coals – crew saved.*
City of Rochester – *ship – for Calcutta*
Colonist – *ship – for Bombay – (both driven ashore at Teat's Hill)*
Retrench – *brig – from Canary Islands – ashore Millbay – total wreck*
Female – *brig – parted her cables in the Sound – considerable damage*
Percy – *ship – for St. Vincent's – general cargo – grounded between the piers – crew saved*
Star – *brig – for Buenos Ayres – ashore Deadman's Bay – crew saved*
Coromandel – *ketch – considerable damage*

LIFE BOAT.

THE

Merchants, Ship-Owners, and Inhabitants

Of PLYMOUTH, are informed,

THAT THE

Life Boat,

PURCHASED BY

PHILIP LANGMEAD, Efq.

One of the Reprefentatives of the Borough,

And by him fo liberally prefented to the Inhabitants, for the Prefervation of the Lives of Seamen and others, in Tempefts, will be brought into

Sutton-Pool, on Wednefday Evening next,

at Six o'Clock; and that in Compliance with a general Wifh, the Worfhipful the MAYOR, accompanied by the *Merchants, Ship-Owners,* and *Inhabitants* of the Borough, will attend at the *Barbacan Pier Head,* at the Time above-mentioned, to greet the Reception of fo truly patriotic and valuable a Donation.

ROBERT FUGE,

Treafurer to the Merchants Hofpital.

Plymouth, Monday, July 18, 1803.

HAYDON, Printer, Stationer, &c. No. 75, Market-Place, Plymouth.

Sceptre – *brig – wrecked in Deadman's Bay – crew saved*

Loyalty – *brig – for Trieste – went to pieces in Deadman's Bay – crew saved*

Lapwing – *total wreck in Deadman's Bay*

George Canning – *schooner – from Alicant [sic] – driven on shore – cargo of dry fruit landed – master of vessel washed overboard off Start Point*

Margaret – *ship (American) – on shore at Deadman's Bay but expected to be got off*

Caledonia – *bound for Grenada – total wreck in Deadman's Bay*

The brig, *Hibernia*, which was bound for Waterford with a cargo of hemp and tallow, was wrecked beneath the Citadel with the loss of five of her six hands.

Not surprisingly, from the chaos and tragedy of that day stemmed individual acts of outstanding bravery. In his book, *Wrecks and Rescue on the Coast of Devon*, the late Grahame Farr recounts a report carried by a contemporary newspaper, which unfortunately cannot now be traced. The report read:

MOST EXTRAORDINARY PRESERVATION

The Coromandel *while a short distance to the S.E. of Eddystone under close reefed topsail and stay foresail was struck by a sea, and five minutes more another took her under the bilge whilst rolling and upset her, precipitating the unfortunate watch (two men) into the sea. The master (John Renton), two of the crew and a passenger who were in the cabin, felt themselves thrown down and almost smothered with the cabin furniture which was piled upon them. While groping in the frightful darkness the master accidentally seized the scuttle hatch which was now above their heads. He and his companions crept into the coal hole and there remained in dreadful anxiety for one hour before the water reached them. After a miserable lapse of six hours when the water had reached their chins, they felt the ship strike – the water receded – she struck again – light issued from below and shortly after the rejoicing prisoners crept from their retreat and landed on the breakwater, a huge projecting mass of which had pierced the vessel and held her fast.*

Richard Eddy, a Cawsand pilot, together with his crew of six, showed great skill and personal courage in approaching the *Coromandel* with the pilot's skiff and taking off the crew. The newly formed Royal National Institution for the Preservation of Life from Shipwreck awarded Eddy their Silver Medal.

The RNIPLS also awarded a Silver Medal for an outstanding act of heroism to James Craggs, who rescued the wife of the captain of the ship, the *John*. All officers and crew of the ship were lost. Another medal was awarded to John Miller for the rescue of seven of the crew of the ship, the *Harmonie*. Six members of the crew lost their lives.

Following this terrible storm, interest was reawakened in establishing a lifeboat station and, in order to coordinate matters, a local branch committee of the RNLI was formed in Plymouth. *Trewmans Exeter Flying Post (Plymouth & Cornish Advertiser)*, of 14 April 1825, reported the following:

ROYAL NATIONAL INSTITUTION FOR THE PRESERVATION OF LIFE FROM SHIPWRECK

A meeting took place at the Guildhall, Plymouth on Thursday last for the purpose of establishing a Branch Society of the above lamentable institution at this port. Admiral Sir James Saumarez presided and opened the business of the meeting.

After some remarks by Sir William Elford, E. Lockyer, H. Woollcombe, Esqrs. and other gentlemen, the resolutions were carried unanimously and a liberal subscription entered into.

In 1825, a new lifeboat was sent to the station. The lifeboat, which was kept at Cawsand, was a vessel of the Plenty design, taking its name from the designer and builder, William Plenty of Newbury, Berkshire. Plenty established his reputation as a builder of lifeboats in the 1820s, supplying many vessels to the Admiralty and Coastguard. The NIPLS also commissioned Plenty to supply boats to their newly established lifeboat stations.

The Plenty had a length of 26' 0" and a beam of 8' 6", it pulled ten oars and was extremely robust. Built purely as a rowing boat, it was often described as 'a boat within a boat', with the space between the two skins of the hull being watertight, thus providing greater buoyancy. Part of the outer hull was covered in cork, further adding to the buoyancy, and a gap below the gunwale was used to drain any excess water taken in by the craft.

During the ensuing years the coastline and waters off Plymouth were assaulted by numerous gales and atrocious weather patterns, which once again culminated in acts of outstanding bravery, as ships floundered and lives were saved from the unrelenting sea.

ON NO LESS THAN EIGHT OCCASIONS, BETWEEN 1825 AND 1840, THE INSTITUTION AWARDED SILVER MEDALS FOR ACTS OF BRAVERY IN SAVING LIVES FROM SHIPWRECK IN THE IMMEDIATE VICINITY OF PLYMOUTH:

A Silver Medal was awarded to Lt J.W. Blake, RN, for saving the lives of seven passengers and sixteen crewmen from the vessel, the Mary Ann, *from St Kitts at Bovisand Bay on Sunday 13 January 1828.*

On Wednesday 20 February 1833 the brig Erin *was wrecked on the breakwater. For leading three boats and saving the lives of the ship's master and nine members of the crew, Silver Medals were awarded to Francis Strong, Thomas Huss and Augustus May of HMS* Spartiate.

To Lt A.T. Mann, RN, for the rescue, with the use of a Coastguard boat, of two men from a barge, the James, *and four men from a boat; both vessels having capsized on Friday 26 April 1833.*

A second Silver Medal, and a silver boat, was awarded to Richard Eddy for his rescue, on Monday 13–Tuesday 14 January 1834, of the crew of ten from the ship the Koningsberg.

Lt Thomas Holman was awarded the Institution's Silver Medal for rescuing, on Wednesday 14 February 1838, by boat, the crew of six from the ship the Thetis.

Mr J.S.W. Grandy, of the Revenue Cutter, the Harpy, *received his award for the rescue, on Wednesday 28 November 1839, of the crew of five from the French brig,* Le Collosse.

The master of the Revenue Cutter, the Stork, *Andrew Gillespie, was awarded a Silver Medal for his part in the rescue of the four crewmen from the sloop, the* Ann, *on Saturday 23 March 1839.*

The eighth award was made following the wreck, on Sunday 22 October 1843, of the schooner, the Norman, *at Bovisand. The recipient on this occasion was Lt John Cornish, RN.*

Medal awarded to Lieutenant A.T. Mann for saving the lives of six men on 26 April 1833. PETE HELMORE

In all of these cases, irrespective of the award of a Silver Medal to an individual, the Institution made monetary rewards to the remaining members of the crew.

Unfortunately, once again, there are no records of the lifeboat being used in a life-saving capacity. In 1840 the lifeboat station lapsed, the Plenty was withdrawn from Plymouth and transferred to the Isles of Scilly. As with the RNLI of today, the NIPLS became reliant upon legacies and public donations, which in turn were most prevalent in the wake of a maritime disaster. One such incident, which served to raise public awareness, occurred on 7 September 1838 when in a storm the SS *Forfarshire*, on passage from Hull to Dundee, struck rocks in the Farne Islands. The vessel carried about 60 persons. Nine of the crew and one passenger escaped in the only lifeboat and many of the passengers, who had been in their cabins below deck, drowned. The storm continued in all its ferocity and as day dawned the lighthouse keeper of the Longstone lighthouse and his daughter spotted nine remaining survivors, five crew and four passengers, clinging to rocks. Battling against the storm and treacherous seas, the young girl, aided by her father, rowed out to sea to save the lives of the nine survivors. The young girl became a national heroine; her name was Grace Darling. Tragically, Grace died of consumption only three years after this heroic rescue. A memorial in St Cuthbert's Chapel, on the Farne Islands, includes the following inscription to her:

Pious and pure,
modest and yet so brave,
though young so wise,
though meek so resolute.

The plight of the National Institution for the Preservation of Life from Shipwreck was again highlighted in 1849 when, in the December gales, the River Tyne lifeboat *Providence* was lost together with a number of her crew. The lifeboat had been launched to go to the assistance of the *Betsey*, which had run aground on the Herd Sands, at the mouth of the Tyne. The crew of the *Providence* had skilfully laid the lifeboat alongside the *Betsey* when a freak wave ran between the two vessels and overturned the lifeboat. One member of the lifeboat crew was pulled to safety by the crew of the *Betsey* whilst a further three crew members could be seen clinging to the upturned hull of the lifeboat. The crowds ashore immediately assisted in launching the *Tyne*, she successfully landed the crew of the *Betsey* and the four lifeboat men, and then assisted her sister boat, the *Northumberland*, in searching for the *Providence* and her crew. The *Providence* was located and towed into shallow waters where the crowd waded in, thigh deep, to right her. The boat was completely empty, 20 of her crew of 24 had been lost.

In 1851, the Fourth Duke of Northumberland, then First Lord of the Admiralty, became President of the Institution. He identified the pressing need for advancement and instigated a national competition to elicit a new design for a lifeboat. From the 280 designs submitted to the Northumberland Prize Committee, six came from South Devon designers; they were J. Christophers of Heavitree, ? Gilley of Torquay, William Sparke of Exeter (who had the foresight to design a sliding keel), George Turner of Devonport Dockyard, R. Westaway of Plymouth and Commodore Lord John Hay, CB, RN, Superintendent of HM Dockyard (whose design was not eligible). The winning design, scoring 84 points, was that of James Beeching, a boat builder of Great Yarmouth. The boat was designed with a low waist and high cases at the bow and stern, which provided stability and, together with the fact that the vessel was fast-draining, also gave it self-righting capabilities in the case of capsize. Beeching built several lifeboats to this design before it was subsequently improved upon and modified by James Peake, Master Shipwright of the Royal Naval Dockyard, Woolwich. The self-righting boat, modified to Peake's design, became the accepted standard for lifeboats throughout Britain.

Over the years the Institution's name had become shortened to the National Shipwreck Institution and, in 1854, was changed to the Royal National Lifeboat Institution for the Preservation of life from Shipwreck, this in turn being shortened to the Royal National Lifeboat Institution.

When the National Institution for the Preservation of Life from Shipwreck was founded in 1824, there were no lifeboat stations on the coast of Devon, those at Exmouth and Plymouth having already fallen into disuse. With financial support from local businessmen and gentry, the first true lifeboat on the Devon coast was founded at Bideford, North Devon, in October 1854. As public interest in the lifeboat service grew, a station was established at Ilfracombe; the Institution took over responsibility for the station at Appledore and increased funding allowed for the establishment of further stations at Lynmouth and Clovelly. Today eight RNLI lifeboat stations, namely Exmouth, Teignmouth, Torbay, Salcombe, Plymouth, Clovelly, Appledore and Ilfracombe, serve the coasts of Devon.

The first lifeboat to be stationed in Plymouth under the auspices of the Royal National Lifeboat Institution entered service on Monday 24 February 1862. The lifeboat, which was named in honour of a Vice-President of the Institution, was the *Prince Consort*.

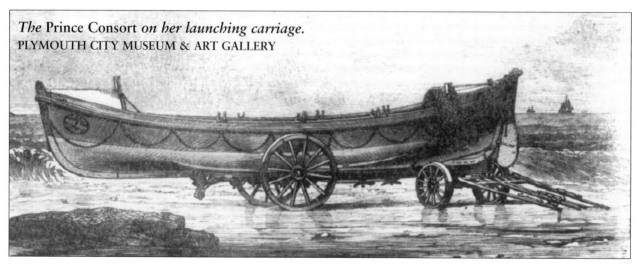

The **Prince Consort** *on her launching carriage.*
PLYMOUTH CITY MUSEUM & ART GALLERY

3

THE *PRINCE CONSORT*

24 *FEBRUARY 1862–8 DECEMBER 1872*

Type: *Self-Righting*   **Propulsion:** *Pulling*   **Oars:** *10*   **Crew:** *12*

Length: *34' 0"*   **Beam:** *7' 1"*   **Displacement:** *1^T 18^{Cwt}*

Built: *1862*   **Builder:** *Forrestt, Limehouse*

Service Launches: *11*   **Lives Saved:** *60*

Coxswain: *William Teel*

During 1861 the campaign by local dignitaries to replace the Plymouth lifeboat culminated in a meeting, which was held on Wednesday 16 October at St George's Hall, Stonehouse, and presided over by Admiral Kingecombe.   Also present were: Messrs W. Radmore, T. Restarick, Dr Rolston, Thomas Stevens, John Greenwood, Henry J. Waring, Thomas Peake, A. Norman, E.W. Cole, Francis Brent, J. Shepheard, Samuel Triscott, John Webber, Captain Puckford, RN, and Captain Gilpin.   The meeting of 'the supporters and friends of this most desirable and humane object' were addressed by Mr T. Stevens who then read the following report:

Those engaged in canvassing for donations and annual subscriptions for the life-boat, for the information of the subscribers and public, beg to say that the result of their labour has been most satisfactory both as to the amount sub-scribed, and the willing and kind manner in which it has been given, proving thereby that the inhabitants of the Three Towns and neigh-bourhood, were desirous the Port should be no longer without a life-boat well established and properly maintained.   The winter approaching rapidly necessitated prompt action with respect to obtaining the life-boat, and also a suitable site whereon to build a house to receive it; our labours in this respect were very much light-ened through the kindness of Capt. Thompson,

R.N., the Queen's Harbour Master, and the Directors, Secretary, and Dock Master, Great Western Docks.   A spot under Long Room Hill, the west side of Millbay, is considered after due examination and survey by nautical men, to be the best position and the site for the life-boat house, affording an incline to the water inside or outside the bounds, as may be required.   The sanction of the Board of Ordnance, and also the Lords of the Admiralty will be necessary before we can commence building.   It is anticipated that their leave will soon be obtained.   There is good reason to expect the lifeboat will be down in the course of next month; and if the house is not ready for its reception the Directors of the Great Western Docks will provide a safe place for its temporary occupation.

Captain Puckford, RN, moved:

That the report just read be received and adopted, and that the Port of Plymouth Lifeboat Branch being now established, the rules and regulations of the Royal National Lifeboat Institution for the arrangement of their lifeboats be strictly adhered to.

In moving the resolution, he said that a boat's crew and a coxswain would be appointed.   The only paid man on the establishment would be the coxswain, and he would receive £8 per year, and be considered the responsible person. He could take the boat out at any time without asking the permission of a committee man. The rule of the Society required that the boat should be tried and exercised four times a year, without which no payment would be made. Mr H.J. Waring seconded the motion. In answering questions put by several gentlemen, Captain Puckford added:

... bona fide, the boat would be the property of the society. The crew were paid at the follow-ing rates when they put out in their boat: On a fine day, 3s; if it blows a gale, 5s; and if they went out to a wreck, 10s. They had not the power to give any more, but if the conduct of the men was brave, they would draw up a petition to the society, asking them to award what sum they thought would be sufficient.

Mr Restarick informed the meeting that he had received an offer from Mr James Hingston, block-maker, of Richmond Walk, Devonport, 'to supply the oars for the Plymouth lifeboat, and keep good the stock.' Mr Restarick read a letter from Mr Lewis, the Secretary of the Royal National Lifeboat Institution, in which he said that the offer of Mr Hingston 'was a very kind and liberal one'. Following a lengthy discussion, the motion was put to the meeting and carried unanimously.

In November 1861, Miss Burdett Coutts, a well-known philanthropist of London and Torquay, offered financial assistance to help fund the new Plymouth lifeboat. The Local Board accepted her kind and generous offer. Born Angela Burdett, the daughter of Sir Francis and Lady Sophia Burdett, she added her mother's maiden name in order to assert her independence as a woman. She became Angela Burdett Coutts and thus kept alive the memory of her grandfather, the famous banker, Thomas Coutts. Miss Coutts was later to become Baroness Burdett Coutts.

In 1862 the first purpose-built lifeboat, under the direct authority of the Royal National Lifeboat Institution, was placed at Plymouth. She was built to the 'Peake' specification at a cost of £180.0s.0d. The lifeboat was originally fitted for seven oars, single banked, but subsequently altered to accommodate ten oars, double banked. The lifeboat was kept at a boat-house in the tidal basin of the Millbay railway dock. The construction of the boat-house cost £159.0s.0d.

The lifeboat had been carried from London on Friday 21 February by the express goods trains of the Great Western, Bristol and Exeter, and South Devon railway companies, free of charge, arriving in Plymouth the following day.

The *Western Daily Mercury* of Tuesday 25 February 1862 reported on the event as follows:

INAUGURATION OF THE PLYMOUTH LIFE-BOAT

The exertions made during the past twelve months by a committee of gentlemen belonging to the Three Towns, with Mr. Thomas Stevens, of Plymouth, and Mr. Alderman Restarick, of Devonport, at their head, have at length been successful in obtaining for Plymouth an efficient life-boat. A procession was formed yesterday morning at the South Devon Terminus, Millbay, for the purpose of carrying the boat round the Three Towns by way of inauguration. The formation was in the following order:

Mr Dunbar, inspector of boats, mounted and acting as pioneer.
A party of twelve men and twelve boys from HMS Cambridge.
The Royal Marine Band, in a large van.
A body of County Police.
THE LIFE-BOAT,
Borne upon its carriage, drawn by six

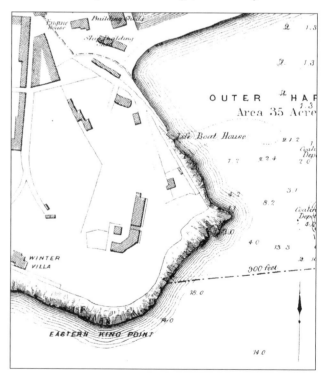

Map, c.1864, showing the site of the first Plymouth's Lifeboat Station, before the construction of the West Wharf and Camber.
PLYMOUTH CITY MUSEUM & ART GALLERY

Plymouth's first RNLI lifeboat, the Prince Consort, *is paraded along Union Street, 24 February 1862.* ILLUSTRATED LONDON NEWS

splendid horses, lent by W. Derry Esq., the Mayor, the crew at their quarters, and the flag flying.
Four carriages, with postilions; the committee and other gentlemen occupying the carriages.
A party of merchant seamen carrying Naval flags.
Several vans, and a dense crowd of people.

In this order the boat was taken along Millbay-road, through Little Durnford-street, up Durnford-street to the Bridge, over Stonehouse Hill, through Mount Wise, George-street (Devonport), St. Aubyn-street, Fore-street, through the Archway, and round the boundaries of the Park to St. Michael's Church, through Navy-row to Penlee, over Mill bridge, past the No Place Inn, along the North-road into Plymouth, down Tavistock-road, Tavistock-street, Old Town-street, Treville-street, Briton Side, round to the Parade, up St. Andrew's-street, through Bedford-street, George-street, and Union Street, into

Stonehouse again, then down Durnford-street from the Quay, to the Royal William Victualling Yard, where the boat was left for the night. It was in the first instance intended to go down Newpassage Hill, but it was found that the drawbridge arch would not admit of the boat's being taken through, and the route was consequently altered.

The procession halted in front of the Government House on Mount Wise and the band played the National Anthem. Major-General Hutchinson came out and was loudly cheered. A similar compliment was paid to Admiral Sir Houston Stewart, who greeted the promoters of the movement with a hearty "Success to you."

The ships in the several harbours were gaily dressed out for the day; and at every point along the way the public turned out to give the life-boat an ovation.

The boat is 34 feet in length and 7 in width, and as our readers will know, was the present of Miss Burdett Coutts. It was built by Messrs

Forrestt, of Limehouse, and is said to possess every quality that can make it valuable. The carriage upon which it was drawn was made by Mr. Robinson, of Camden Town. The boat is appropriately named "The Prince Consort." It was gratuitously conveyed to Plymouth by the Great Western, the Bristol and Exeter, and the South Devon railway Companies. Mr. Finemore has liberally offered to keep it painted, and the flag was given by Mr. Shapcott. The funds subscribed by the Three Towns have been laid out in the erection of a suitable boathouse at the Great Western Docks, Millbay, upon a site provided by the Company and liberal subscriptions will be needed to defray the constant necessary expenses of the Life-boat Establishment.

Tomorrow, at ten o'clock, the boat will be launched at the Victualling Yard, at eleven it will be under Mount Wise; and at two under the Hoe. Its qualities will be put to the test during the day.

The inauguration dinner took place at the Globe Hotel at 5 o'clock that evening, presided over by Captain Puckford, RN. After the removal of the cloth, Captain Puckford rose and in proposing the toast, 'The Queen, Albert Edward Prince of Wales, and all the Royal family', paid tribute to the memory of the late Prince Consort, whose name he was unhappily obliged to omit from the toast. Following a toast to 'the Army, the Navy and the Volunteers', the Chairman proposed the toast 'The National Lifeboat Institution'. It would, he could not help feeling, be something like presumption on his part to enlarge upon this toast in the presence of the secretaries of the institution. He would, however, say that the presence of both these gentlemen was a mark of peculiar honour and distinction conferred on Plymouth. With the present toast he would couple the name of Miss Burdett Coutts – (hear, hear) – and he really wished he had the ability to speak of that bountiful lady as she deserved and as he felt. He was sorry that Admiral Kingcome was unable to attend and officiate as chairman on that occasion, for he himself felt that he was deficient in oratorical powers – (cries of 'No, no'). Before calling on them to drink the toast he had given, he would read a letter which had been received from Miss Burdett Coutts in reply to a letter thanking her for her munificent present. He then read the following letter:

Holly Lodge. Highgate. Feb. 22nd. 1862.

SIR, I regret that a slight indisposition has caused a delay in my acknowledgment of your letter on the 14th inst, but I hope the message I sent will have avoided any inconvenience. I was anxious to write in reply myself in order to express how fully it was in accordance with my own feelings that the life-boat should be named after the beloved and honoured Prince so recently called to rest from his many labours of love amongst us.

Indeed, I had intended, in the event of my being asked to name the boat, to call it after the Prince Consort, as I thought it would be grateful to all our feelings, and that its associations would strengthen and encourage its brave crew in their hours of difficulty and danger in the service of humanity.

I am extremely glad to hear that the lifeboat house has been built, and that the prospects of the funds of the branch for its first-year's expenses, and for the parent institution, are so flourishing.

I need not add with what great pleasure I find myself associated in the lifeboat work with the port of Plymouth, and with the inhabitants of Plymouth, Devonport, and Stonehouse.

I beg to thank you for your kind note and its message.

I am, Sir, yours faithfully.

Burdett Coutts.

To Admiral Kingcombe.

Mr. Lewis (Secretary of the National Lifeboat Institution), in responding to the last toast, spoke in the highest terms of commendation of the charitable and kindly spirit which had prompted Miss Coutts to acts of the most praiseworthy benevolence. The present was the fourth lifeboat which she gave to the Institution, and the universality of her acts of charity indicated that she considered that if God had given her much, she was bound to distribute much for the benefit of her fellow creatures. With respect to the Committee of the Institution, he felt bound to say that they were most self-sacrificing in the discharge of their duties.

On Wednesday 26 February 1862 the *Western Daily Mercury* reported on the launch and trial of the *Prince Consort*:

Yesterday morning, between 10 and 11 o'clock, the interesting ceremony of launching the lifeboat, and testing its qualities, took place.

The boat was launched from the quay of the Royal William Victualling Yard, at a point 22 feet from the water, in perpendicular height. On reaching the water she barely half filled, and the seas thus shipped were, by the self-action of the boat, ejected in 10 seconds. An interesting test of the fitness of this remarkable vessel for the purpose to which she is to be devoted was that of placing 17 men on one of her gunwales, in order to ascertain approximately the force necessary to capsize her. This great and uncounter-balanced weight was barely sufficient to bring the gunwale to the water's edge. She was afterwards taken to the Admiral's tender and appliances were put in requisition to capsize her. Upon this being done it was found she righted herself in 20 seconds. The great stability of this vessel in the water was thus satisfactorily demonstrated, and the impossibility of her being upset by any sea whatever was clearly established. After these searching ordeals the lifeboat and her crew were exercised (about 3 o'clock) under Mount Wise and the Hoe, in the presence of some 6,000 or 7,000 applauding spectators as she passed the Devil's Point, in her course for the Hoe, in excellent style, in the teeth of a strong breeze; and the unanimous verdict of the nautical men who were present to watch the various experiments was that she had proved herself a most excellent lifeboat.

The *Illustrated London News*, of Saturday 8 March 1862, also carried an account of the arrival, in Plymouth, of the new lifeboat:

Monday week was a day that will be long remembered in Plymouth and its neighbourhood, and well deserves, says a local journal, to be marked with a white stone in the annals of the Three Towns. It is calculated that nearly 70,000 people turned out on that day to witness the splendid life-boat which Miss Burdett Coutts had presented through the National Lifeboat Institution to the Port of Plymouth. The boat, mounted on her transporting-carriage, had arrived in Plymouth on Saturday afternoon, the Great-Western and other railway companies having liberally brought her down by express goods-train free of any charge.

In accordance with the wishes of Miss Coutts, the life-boat is named "The Prince

Consort," and beneath the words on the boat has been painted "National Life-boat Institution, supported by voluntary contributions."

About eight minutes after ten the van of the procession moved from the arrival yard into the station road, windows, the terraces, the balconies and even the tops of some of the houses, being crowded with spectators. Preceded by a detachment of blue-jackets and the band of the Royal Marines came the spectacle of the day, the life-boat itself, on its transporting-carriage, drawn by six magnificent horses, their heads gaily decorated with rosettes. The boat was filled by its double crew furnished with their cork jackets and life-buoys, wearing on their hats the badge "Royal National Lifeboat Institution," and working their oars in imitation of rowers at sea. From the stern of the boat where the Coxswain stood waved a flag bearing the inscription similar to that on the hats of the men. From the centre floated the Union Jack and from the prow floated the flag handsomely presented by Mr. Shapcott inscribed lifeboat in white letters on a blue background.

The bells of the parish churches rang merry peals at intervals throughout the day. The line of march extended over a distance of 12 miles and was densely crowded in every part. Most frequently deafening and enthusiastic cheers rose as in a torrent from the vast concourse which lined the streets. The accompanying view of the procession passing through Union Street [see page 23] is from a sketch by Mr. John J. Offard of Plymouth. In the evening there was a public dinner at the Globe Hotel. The chair was occupied by Captain Puckford, R.N., supported on his right by William Derry, Esq., the Mayor of Plymouth, and on his left by John William Walter Ryder, Esq., the Mayor of Devonport. The vice-chair was taken by Thomas Restarick, Esq., one of the hon. Secretaries of the Plymouth branch, supported on his right by W.B. Cuming, Esq., Lloyds surveyor at this port, and on his left by Thomas Stevens, Esq., hon. Secretary of the Plymouth branch. Several toasts were given and duly honoured; and Mr. Lewis, the secretary of the National Life-boat Institution, entered into a detailed and interesting statement of the invaluable benefits rendered by this society. Remarking on the list of local subscriptions, he said the list from Plymouth was without a parallel in the United Kingdom.

On the following day the life-boat was launched from the wharf of the Royal William Victualling Yard, at an altitude of 22ft. from the sea, having been previously christened by Mrs. Curry, wife of the Captain Superintendent of the yard. In this desperate "header" she took in some water, which she ejected in a few seconds. She was subsequently severely tested by being upset off Mount Wise and Plymouth Hoe, and proved her stability, buoyancy, and selfrighting power in every instance.

The National Life-boat Institution has now life-boats at the following places on the Devonshire and Cornish coasts – viz., Exmouth, Teignmouth, Appledore and Braunton, in Devon; and Fowey, Lizard, Penzance, Sennen Cove, St. Ives, Newquay, Padstow and Bude Haven in Cornwall.

Some of these lifeboats have within the last three or four years been instrumental in rescuing the following shipwrecked crews:- Brig Gonslave, 7; schooner Caroline, 5; schooner Clifton, 5; schooner Frederick William, 5; brig North Esk, 6; a dismasted barge, 2; smack Wonder, 2; brigantine Nancy, 9; schooner Druid, 5; brigantine Nugget, 5; schooner Hurrell, 4; making a total of 55 persons rescued from a watery grave. For the important services the institution has paid £115.11s.8d. to the crews of the life-boats.

Mr. T. Restarick, of Devonport, and Mr. T. Stevens, of Plymouth, have been indefatigable in their exertions in the establishment of the Plymouth life-boat. Admiral Kingcome and Captain Puckford, R.N., and other gentlemen, have also cordially co-operated in the formation of this undertaking.

William Teel was appointed Coxswain of the lifeboat. Nine months passed before the first recorded service, provided by the *Prince Consort*, took place on Saturday 6 December 1862. The casualty requiring assistance was the Dutch galliot, *Aremana*. The vessel had entered Whitsand Bay, in a south-westerly gale and, being unable to point high enough to the wind, found herself unable to beat out around Rame Head. Her captain ordered her anchors to be dropped, intending to ride out the storm, but the anchors failed to hold and the galliot started to drift towards the shore. The alarm having been raised, and the lifeboat crew alerted, the harbour-master,

Commander J.R. Aylen, RN, set out for the stricken vessel aboard the Admiralty tug, *Confiance*, with the *Prince Consort* in tow. Upon reaching the *Aremana* it was found that there was an insufficient depth of water for the tug to approach the casualty; however, drawing a lesser draft, the lifeboat was able to approach the galliot and secure a hawser between the vessel and the tug. The *Confiance* then towed both the *Aremana* and the *Prince Consort* to the safety of the Sound and harbour respectively.

On Saturday 13 December 1862, the Norwegian brig *Imanuel* became stranded on the Batten Shoal. The *Prince Consort* was launched but her services were not required.

The shoreline of Plymouth was constantly lashed by a gale, which blew from the west-south-west, from Wednesday 22–Saturday 25 November 1865. Contemporary newspaper reports claimed that: 'Forty years had elapsed since Plymouth experienced such tempestuous weather.' The *Western Morning News* carried the headline: 'TWELVE VESSELS ASHORE AT PLYMOUTH. EIGHT SERIOUSLY INJURED.' The Sound was described as being 'one mass of boiling foam – wild and grand in the extreme.' In all, some 30 vessels were driven onto the shoreline off Plymouth. During the Wednesday and Thursday, the principal casualties were foreign vessels, namely the French ship *Paulista*, of Havre, 609 tons register, commanded by Captain Loyer and bound for Rio; the 273-ton Swedish brig *Jules II*, commanded by Captain Hüglund, from Havre in ballast to Cardiff, and the Belgian brigantine *Espoir*, commanded by Captain Duraud. Those vessels less severely damaged were the British schooners the *Amoor*, 1,341 tons register, commanded by Captain Fraser and owned by Mr A. Fotheringham of London, which carried men, women and children bound for Adelaide, Australia, in addition to her 435 crew; the 78-ton *Mischief*, of Penzance, commanded by Captain Thomas Williams; the 94-ton *Victoria*, commanded by Captain Hammick, from Figuiera bound for St John's, Newfoundland; and Captain Bryant's 97-ton *Apollo* of St Ives, with coals sailing from Cardiff for Plymouth.

Throughout this gale, the lifeboat was called into action on two occasions. The *Prince Consort* was first launched on Wednesday 22 November to provide service to the Belgian brig *Espoir*, which was laden with bone ash from the Rio Grande. Following a collision with another vessel, in which her bowsprit and topsail yard had been carried away, the vessel was driven, stern first, onto rocks between Batten and Dunstone Points. It was reported that:

The lifeboat, under the command of Captain Puckford and Captain Aylen, with a sturdy crew, came out during the gale and picked off the men from two of the vessels which were upon the rocks.

The *Prince Consort's* crew saved the lives of the 11 mariners aboard the *Espoir*. When the weather moderated on Wednesday evening the *Espoir* was refloated. Of those vessels that ran ashore, she was the only vessel to have been so fortunate.

Although not recorded in the Station Service Record, the *Prince Consort's* crew also saved the lives of Captain Thomas Williams and three of his crew, from the *Mischief*. The *Mischief* was in collision with another vessel, believed to have been the Swedish brig the *Jules II*, before both vessels were driven ashore. Captain Thomas and his crewmen jumped from the *Mischief* onto the bowsprit of the brig, from where they were taken off by the lifeboat.

The second service performed by the *Prince Consort* that week was on Saturday 25 November, when she went to the assistance of the German brig, the *Commerzieweathin (Commarzianrathin) Haupt*, of Mecklenburgher. The vessel, laden with wheat, from Taganrog, had sought the shelter of the Sound earlier that day but had anchored too close to the Batten Ledges given the prevailing weather conditions. Whilst at anchor the vessel was constantly pounded by the seas until she finally dragged her anchors and ran onto the reef off Mount Batten. The local Coastguard fired rockets to summon the lifeboat crew, and the *Prince Consort* put to sea, under the command of Coxswain William Teel. The crew were to face what a local newspaper reporter described as 'the most tremendous sea known ever to veteran lifeboat men.'

As the lifeboat approached the stricken brig, the master of the tug, *Napoleon*, informed Coxswain Teel that he had been successful in taking off five of the *Commerzieweathin's* crew. The brig had, however, been driven further onshore thus preventing the tug from making further attempts at rescue. In seas, which in the words of Coxswain Teel 'rose like a wall above the lifeboat', Teel veered the *Prince Consort* down on to the brig using a hawser that he had borrowed from the *Napoleon*. Pounded by the sea, the brig

had started to break up as Teel made his rescue attempt. The lifeboat crew were successful in taking off a further five members of the crew but, in jumping for the lifeboat, the ship's captain slipped and fell, only to be immediately engulfed by the raging sea. As he raised his oar, lifeboat man William Hockaday made a grab for the seaman. The German captain seized Hockaday's arm and clung to it as only a drowning man could. After a perilous struggle Hockaday managed to pull the ship's captain into the lifeboat and to safety. Coxswain Teel again approached the tug and the remaining five members of the *Commerzieweathin's* crew were transferred to the lifeboat.

Following the transfer the lifeboat was towed by the tug back to Millbay where the German seamen were lodged and cared for at the Sailors' Home. Due to fatigue, the captain was conveyed to the lodging by cab. The gallant crew of the *Prince Consort*, who took part in this remarkable rescue, were: William Teel (First Coxswain), William Callard (Second Coxswain), and oarsmen George Blunden, George Whitelock, Samuel Stedeford, William Jobson and Michael Granville (the foregoing all being Coastguard men), together with Samuel Lawrence, William Hockaday, William Avent and James Heath (the latter four named being in the service of the harbourmaster). In recognition of the outstanding service given this day, the Royal National Lifeboat Institution awarded a gratuity of 20s.0d. to each member of the crew.

The *Western Daily Mercury*, of 27 November 1865, reported:

We should be glad to see the act of the society backed up by that of the local public. There is no man who stands before his fellows in a more honourable – we would say exalted – position than he who, at the risk of his own, saves a fellow creature's life, and such service ought to be fittingly rewarded. The boat, we have been assured by the second coxswain, behaved admirably; and it is now shown by the convincing evidence how necessary a lifeboat within Plymouth Breakwater is.

The gale-force winds and surging seas that wreaked havoc in Plymouth on the night of Tuesday 8 January 1867 culminated in the loss of two vessels and their crews. It was at about 02.00 hours that the Coastguard lookout at Batten observed a vessel off Dunstone Point drifting towards the breakers. The lookout fired signalling rockets to alert the lifeboat station at Stonehouse Point. The *Prince Consort* was immediately launched under the command of Coxswain Teel, and set off in horrendous conditions, into the darkness of the night on their quest to locate the casualty.

The rocket-apparatus team were alerted and set up their rockets on the beach, with the intention of firing lines to the distressed vessel, but the curtain of rain that fell was so dense that they could not readily make out the casualty. At this time, however, a second vessel was also seen to be drifting towards Batten Point. The rescue team transferred their equipment to a point where communication could be established with this vessel. Upon their arrival the team saw that the craft had already run aground and that the Plymouth lifeboat was making its way towards her.

As the lifeboat made her approach, the crew of the schooner were seen to be standing on the bowsprit. Coxswain Teel dropped the *Prince Consort's* anchor and veered down towards the schooner. As they neared the vessel, one of the crew, John Gooding, jumped from the bowsprit into the lifeboat. The seas were such that twice the lifeboat filled with water and had great difficulty in making further approaches to the schooner. The raging seas continued to buffet the lifeboat as her crew pulled with all their might to regain her anchor. The schooner for her part was driven in ever closer to the shore. Six rockets were successfully fired, three of which fell across the schooner, establishing communication, as the sea continued to breach over her. The crew of the lifeboat at this time were seen to be struggling in their attempts to keep the lifeboat clear of the breakers, onlookers subsequently stating that, on more than one occasion, it was thought that the lifeboat would be dashed to pieces.

Thankfully, at about 06.00 hours, the gale abated to a strong wind that continued to blow throughout the day. The vessels that had been wrecked that night proved to be the schooners *Teazer* and *Palmyra*. Captain Austin's *Teazer*, of Ipswich, was laden with coals from Sanderfoot and bound for Southwold. It was to this vessel that the sole survivor belonged. The *Palmyra* was laden with oats and was identified purely by her name-board, which was found during the course of the day. The board bore the name 'Palmyra Southampton'.

During the morning two bodies were found; one that of a man of about 40 years of age, the other a boy of about 18 years. On the body of the boy was found a letter dated 17 November; it was from his mother, E. Kellaway of 6 Crown Terrace, Bewis Valley, Southampton. On the boy's socks were the initials 'F.K.'; the boy was, it seems, a crew member of the *Palmyra*.

The sole survivor of this tragedy, the mate of the *Teazer*, John Gooding, whilst staying at the Sailors' Home, provided the following narrative, as reported in the *Western Daily Mercury*:

They arrived in the Sound on Thursday last, and yesterday morning, during the height of the gale, at about 3 a.m., their vessel dragged her anchors and drifted with great velocity towards the Batten Reef, when she soon struck. They discovered the lifeboat approaching their vessel, they all being on the bowsprit at the time. The lifeboat was brought near by a wave, and he jumped in, the others thinking that if they did they would be swamped, and thus declined to make the attempt. In about a minute a tremendous breaker caught the boat and she was carried a very great distance from the vessel. On getting near again the vessel was breaking up, and nothing could be seen of his comrades. After some time they managed to reach the Barbican, where he was landed.

Those who perished with the *Teazer* were: James Austin, Captain, of Ipswich, aged 32, who left a wife and three children, and Henry Burgess, boy, aged 19 years.

Although a lee shore in south-westerly and westerly gales, throughout the years the Mount Batten reef and Jennycliffe Bay have become the final resting place of many vessels and it was to this location that the *Prince Consort* headed on Monday 28 December 1868. That day dawned with a full south-south-westerly gale blowing and found the barque, the *Cabot* of Greenock, at anchor, about half a mile off Batten reef. At the same time the brig, the *Flying Cloud* of Bideford, was waiting in the port for orders. It was some time between 10.00 and 12.00 hours that the *Cabot*, laden with a cargo of deal (fir or pine timber boards), parted her cable and started a rapid drift towards the reef. In her drift, she ran foul of the *Flying Cloud*, which was laden with a cargo of sugar. The bowsprit of the barque became so thoroughly entangled with the rigging of the brig that she carried her away in her drift. Both vessels finally came to grief on the Batten reef.

Mercantile tugs, which were operating in the Sound, were quickly on the scene, at the same time as Coxswain Teel readied the *Prince Consort* in anticipation of her services being required. The *Secret*, the largest and most powerful of the mercantile tugs, quickly established a hawser link with the *Cabot*, one hour after low water, and, on a rising tide, took just over two hours to refloat the barque from the reef. The *Cabot* was subsequently towed into Sutton Harbour.

Approximately half an hour after the arrival of the Government tug, *Secret*, the *Carron* arrived on the scene. It was fully expected that this vessel would also render assistance but to the utter dismay of all concerned she merely stood-by. At first there appeared to be some logic in her actions for, although the *Secret* had established a hawser tow, the bowsprit and rigging of the two vessels remained entwined. When the bowsprit of the barque was finally cut away, and the two vessels separated, it was naturally expected that the *Carron* would establish a link with the ill-fated *Flying Cloud*; however, throughout the entirety of the rescue the *Carron* failed to offer assistance. Another mercantile tug, the *Wellington*, did in fact establish a hawser link with the brig but unfortunately, due to her lack of power, was unable to refloat the *Flying Cloud*.

Throughout the period of the rescue operation, the gale had blown unabated and it was in these conditions that the *Prince Consort* had been launched and her crew had made their way to the distressed vessels. A detailed account of the rescue of the crew of the *Flying Cloud* has not been found; suffice to say that at all times the master and crew remained with the brig and only abandoned the vessel when the fast-rising tide broached through the holes that had been knocked in her hull when she went aground and her destruction seemed inevitable.

It is recorded that that day Coxswain Teel and the crew of the *Prince Consort* saved the lives of the ten-man crew of the *Flying Cloud*.

There was a gap of four years before the *Prince Consort* recorded her next service which took place on Saturday 23 November 1872, when she went to the assistance of the 118-ton brigantine, the *Laurel*, bound for Bathurst, West Africa. In south-westerly gale-force winds, which were accompanied by extremely heavy rain

squalls, the vessel's captain, Captain Langdon, had sought the sanctuary of the Plymouth Sound. It was at about 18.30 hours, during a particularly heavy squall, that the brigantine's cables parted, leaving her captain with no alternative but to seek damage limitation by running his command ashore. The firing of rockets and the burning of blue signals by the crew failed, initially, to summon assistance. In consequence of the prevailing weather conditions, and the constant pitching and strains placed upon her, the *Laurel* ran aground shortly afterwards and lost her foremast over her port side. Her hull was holed and she shipped tons of water, which destroyed her general cargo.

Plymouth breakwater, c.1890.
PLYMOUTH CITY MUSEUM & ART GALLERY

Subsequently, the plight of the *Laurel* being realised, the *Prince Consort* was immediately summoned to provide assistance, although the lifeboat was not launched until 21.00 hours. Having been launched, the lifeboat was towed to the stricken vessel by the Admiralty tug, the *Carron*, and took up a position to windward of the casualty at about 23.30 hours. The *Laurel*, and now the lifeboat, continued to be pounded by the wind and seas as the *Carron* slipped the lifeboat's tow-line. Summoning all their strength, seafaring skills and courage, the Coxswain and crew of the *Prince Consort* dropped down on to the brigantine.

The *Western Daily Mercury* of 25 January reported that in making the rescue the lifeboat was 'much damaged'. The newspaper also commented upon the launch of the *Prince Consort* in the following terms:

The unfortunate delay of the lifeboat is to be attributed to the difficulty there was found in getting the crew together. Messengers were despatched to numerous public houses, and in the end the harbour master's crew had to be fetched to act as deputies.

Whether the crew of the *Prince Consort* that day were lifeboat men, or the harbour-master's crew, their bravery saved the lives of Captain Langdon, his wife and seven crewmen. Sadly, the services performed by the *Prince Consort* on Sunday 8 December 1872 proved to be her last, for the lifeboat was so severely damaged as to warrant her immediate replacement. The lifeboat was launched into winds that reached hurricane force, the like of which the port of Plymouth had not experienced for many years. An extract from a contemporary newspaper reported on the atrocious conditions under the byline:

SIX VESSELS ASHORE IN PLYMOUTH SOUND

The gale seemed to have told especially heavy upon the ships lying in Plymouth Sound, and, as far as can be ascertained up to the present, there are six ashore on different parts of the Batten Reefs. There was a very large fleet at anchor during the day, and some of these, up to the time of writing, were in not at all satisfactory positions, and, in the course of the afternoon, numbers including HMS Narcissus, *were not steadfast with their anchors.*

The first vessel to encounter the violence of the gale was the British brigantine, the *Eliza*, under the command of Captain Picknall, bound from Blythe, with a cargo of coal, for Gibraltar. At 15.00 hours that day she was lying in the Sound. Also at this time, the Italian brigantine, the *Richelieu*, was adrift in the Sound. The *Richelieu* drifted on to the *Eliza*, cutting her cables, thus causing the British brigantine to drift into Batten Bay.

A rocket was immediately sent up and, simultaneously the signal that the lifeboat was needed was raised at Mount Batten Castle. The Coastguard authorities were speedily at work, and the rocket apparatus was successfully fired. At the same time the lifeboat, manned by a crew of a dozen men, made its appearance from Millbay, and bravely it breasted the huge billows.

With the wind in their favour, towed by an Admiralty tug, the *Prince Consort* soon reached the *Eliza* and succeeded in rescuing four of her crew, but in so doing the lifeboat struck upon a reef and sustained damage. The remaining four crew members had previously been taken off the *Eliza* by the rocket apparatus team, using a 'breeches buoy'.

As the lifeboat commenced her return journey to Millbay, with the survivors from the *Eliza*, a second signal was sighted, indicating that another vessel was in distress. This vessel proved to be the 221-ton brig *Fearful*, of Portsmouth, under the command of Captain Williamson from Sunderland, with a cargo of coal bound for Devonport. The *Fearful* had arrived in Plymouth

Sound on Saturday afternoon and anchored to westward of the Cobbler Buoy. At the request of the harbour-master, Captain Williamson moved his vessel and took up an anchorage at the mouth of the Cattewater.

At 10.00 hours on Sunday morning, the *Fearful* was dragging her anchor. Her crew dropped a second bow anchor together with all the chain that they could muster. The *Fearful* had dragged to within 40 fathoms of the shore when she was hit by a tremendous gust of wind from the west-south-west and both anchors parted:

At one another "flare-up" was sent up and the steam tug Trusty, *with commendable alacrity, bore down to the scene of the accident, towing the lifeboat, with its volunteer crew. The latter soon came to the* Fearful's *assistance and took off the crew, seven in number.*

At first Captain Williamson refused to leave his vessel but, finding that no one could be induced to stay with him, he was finally persuaded to join his crew in the safety of the lifeboat. On a rising tide the *Fearful* was lifted from the rocks upon which she had settled, and slipped into deeper water where she became totally submerged.

The damage sustained by the *Prince Consort* in rescuing the crew of the *Eliza* was irreparable, for in striking the rocks she stove in her foreparts, but retained sufficient buoyancy to complete the rescue from the *Fearful*. The press reported that she was 'three parts full of water' when she arrived back at Millbay. To undertake such a rescue, knowing that the lifeboat had sustained major damage, but not knowing the severity of that damage, speaks volumes for the very commendable bravery and determination shown by the lifeboat crew.

The other four vessels that went aground that day were the Dutch schooner *Curacao Packet*, the German brig *Lorenz*, the Norwegian brig *Ornen* and the Italian brig *Fratelli Borghino*. From the vessels that foundered at Plymouth in that dreadful storm, upwards of 60 lives were saved.

The damage to the lifeboat was immediately reported to the Management Committee in London, and after nearly 11 years of service, the *Prince Consort*, the first of the RNLI's lifeboats to serve Plymouth, was withdrawn from service.

At a meeting of the Management Committee of the RNLI, held in January 1873, agreement was reached for a new lifeboat to be placed at Plymouth Lifeboat Station.

4

THE CLEMENCY

30 MAY 1873–7 MARCH 1885

Type: *Self-Righting*   **Propulsion:** *Pulling*   **Oars:** *10*   **Crew:** *13*

Length: *34' 0"*   **Beam:** *7' 9"*   **Displacement:** *2ᵀ 10ᶜʷᵗ*

Built: *1872*   **Builder:** *Forrestt, Limehouse*

Service Launches: *11*   **Lives Saved:** *38*

Coxswains: *William Teel (1873–84),*
John Lucock (1884–85)

The successor to the *Prince Consort* was a craft of similar design, a self-righter, but built with modifications to make her 'as light and fast as possible'. The public launch and dedication of the new boat, which was a gift from Mr and Mrs J.G. Hubbard of London, and cost £294, took place at Longroom, Stonehouse, on Friday 30 May 1873. Several hundred spectators watched the event, which was attended by numerous dignitaries including Sir John Hey who was accompanied by officers and crew of HMS *Indus*, aboard which Francis Edward Hubbard had served until his retirement from the service. The *Western Daily Mercury* reported that the interesting proceedings were commenced by Mr J.G. Hubbard, of Prince's Gate, London, who addressed the company as follows:

Captain Ward, my Lord Bishop, on behalf of Mrs. Hubbard and myself, let me say that we have met on the present occasion in order to offer the lifeboat which is now before us to the National Lifeboat Institution, and to the port of Plymouth. But we must explain that this boat is not our gift. The gift of this boat originates with a very dear son of ours, who many years ago left this port as one of Her Majesty's servants on board the Indus, then under the command of Captain, now Sir John Hay. During the time he was at sea he was devoted to the service which he had embraced, and when after some years of service, he was obliged from failing health to retire from it, he never lost his affection for it. During many

years his whole heart and mind were occupied in considering how he could best identify himself with the service to which he had belonged, with the hope that he might leave behind some memorial of his connection with it. This idea was in his daily thoughts, and in his nightly dreams and prayers, and such was the impression upon his mind, that constantly in his prayers his object was to intercede for those who were imperilled by water, and to mourn for those who had been lost at sea. For many years he tried to collect a fund to form the foundation of a lifeboat, and he carried on that labour of love to such an extent, that we have had nothing to do but to supplement his efforts. We are, therefore, here now to present this lifeboat to the National Lifeboat Institution, and to the port of Plymouth; and it is a great gratification to us to know that there was a vacancy for it at Plymouth, because the place is endeared to us by the recollection of its being the port from which our son sailed, and if anything more were required to make us feel a pleasure in the selection which has been made, it is the extreme cordiality and kindness with which our efforts have been received and welcomed by the gentlemen connected with the port itself. It must be a great gratification to those who enter upon an undertaking of this kind to know that they are committing it to the hands of a body of men than whom none can equal for their devotion to the service in which they are engaged. If there is one occupation in the world to be looked upon with proud satisfaction it is the occupation of a lifeboat crew. I may now explain why it is that this boat has received the name of the "Clemency." It had been the desire of my son to have a yacht of his own, and to call it after his youngest sister "Clemency," but in relation to this boat his thoughts took a wider and higher range, and in his last illness his desire was that the lifeboat should be so called, not merely in connection with any earthly relative, but in recognition for the clemency of God. We all know that the clemency and mercy of God are especially evidenced in these great efforts of human skill and industry which have resulted in the saving of so many lives from a watery grave, and I can conceive nothing more glorious than the avocation of these men who peril their healths and their lives, and devote themselves day after day and year after year to carry out this great and god-like mission.

Mr Hubbard then presented the boat to Captain Ward on behalf of the Royal National Lifeboat Institution, with the fervent prayer that it might be as successful in its work of saving life as the one which was presented some years ago since by Lady Burdett Coutts, a name which was highly honoured by those who entertained a respect for philanthropic efforts.

In accepting the lifeboat, Captain Ward, RN, expressed the gratitude of the RNLI for the gift. He told those gathered that:

Through the philanthropy and charity of the wealthy and others in this country, including the Freemasons, the Odd fellows, the Foresters, the pence of the poor, and from other sources, the institution now possessed the most magnificent fleet of lifeboats that ever existed, being 333 in number, but amongst all of these there were none in which they took a greater interest than in the few which they had as memorial lifeboats.

Captain Ward added that a more perfect specimen of a lifeboat than the one which stood before them could not be built, and he was sure that the crew would be well satisfied with her.

Captain Puckford, RN, bore testimony to the bravery and courage of the lifeboat crew and further mentioned, in respect of the *Clemency*, that the boat's construction was such 'that even if she met with a similar disaster to that which befell the last one, and had half-a-dozen holes in her, she would still retain her floatation power.'

Prayers were offered by the Bishop, following which the Choir of St Peter's chanted several Psalms, and a portion of the sixth chapter of St Mark's Gospel was read. Miss Clemency Hubbard then duly named the boat with the customary bottle of wine. The 222nd hymn was sung. This same hymn had been sung at St Andrew's Church on that Sunday evening when the *Prince Consort* lifeboat went onto the rocks at Batten. The report of the disaster had been conveyed to Captain Puckford, in the church during the service, the news causing the deepest emotion amongst the congregation. The new lifeboat was to occupy the existing boat-house.

In common with her predecessor, nine months passed before the *Clemency* was launched on active service. Her first service launch took place on Thursday 26 February 1874, when she went to the assistance of the *John Barbour* of St John, New Brunswick. Together with an Italian brig, the *John Barbour* had sought the comparatively calm waters of the Sound, to ride out a southwesterly gale. In the strong winds and heavy seas, the *John Barbour* parted her cables and ran foul of the Italian brig. Having collided, their shrouds and bowsprits became entangled and both vessels drifted helplessly towards the shore. The *Clemency* was launched, under the command of Coxswain Teel, and towed to the scene by an Admiralty tug. At great risk to his boat and crew, Teel skilfully manoeuvred the lifeboat around the interlocked vessels and succeeded in taking a hawser from the *John Barbour* to the tug. The lifeboat cleared the stricken vessels and, by using the hawser, the tug succeeded in separating and saving both vessels and their crews. In acknowledging the role that the crew of the *Clemency* played in this rescue, the service was assigned the classification 'assisted to save vessel'.

In 1877, the Great Western Railway purchased the land upon which the lifeboat house stood; this in turn required the relocation of the boat-house. An alternative site was found, at the Camber, and in 1879 a new boat-house was built. The Camber lifeboat station was a magnificent stone building with a slipway, down which the lifeboat slid, on rails, into the small harbour. The

The former lifeboat station at the Camber.

building and slipway were constructed at a cost of £350, of which the Great Northern Railway Company paid the sum of £250. Directly behind the station was the watchman's cottage, and near-by another cottage where the lifeboat's crew was expected to muster. Still to be seen in the cottage are the hooks from which the lifeboat men slung their hammocks during periods of inclement weather, when they lived on the premises, the faster to respond to any requirement to launch. The former boat-house now serves as the sailing school for the Royal Marines Barracks, Stonehouse. The lifeboat men of the Camber were often to be seen accompanied by a faithful spaniel dog, and a small headstone can be found, at the Camber, to mark its grave. The headstone reads: 'Here rests Dear old JOE. For many years the faithful spaniel and companion of C.W.S and L.C.S. Died 27 March 1912.'

On Tuesday 19 August 1879, the *Clemency*, together with the Looe lifeboat, the *Oxfordshire*, was present at the laying of the foundation-stone of the new Eddystone Lighthouse. Due to bad weather, the ceremony had been postponed from 21 June. His Royal Highness the Prince of Wales and the Duke of Edinburgh laid the stone.

The next service of note to be provided by the *Clemency* took place on Monday 9 February 1880. Large crowds of people gathered on The Hoe and other vantage points around Plymouth, following reports that a fine vessel lay outside the breakwater, helplessly straining at her cables. Throughout the night Plymouth had been lashed by a full southerly gale and towards morning distress guns had been heard summoning assistance, when for the time no help was possible. With daybreak came the realisation that the vessel summoning assistance was the SS *Hankow*, returning from Sydney to London and carrying a valuable cargo, which included specie, mail and a number of passengers. The vessel had experienced engine trouble off the Lizard and had been taken in tow by two Falmouth steam tugs. During the tow the wind and seas continued to increase in ferocity until, at a point off Plymouth, when the wind force had reached severe storm, the tugs were forced to slip their lines, leaving the *Hankow* to make for Plymouth in the best way she could.

A map of the Camber, c.1879.

The vessel had been driven perilously close to the breakwater and her captain, upon finding that she lacked power and manoeuvrability, let go the anchors. At first her anchors failed to hold and she drifted to within three boat lengths of the breakwater before the anchors found purchase, but even then she remained in imminent danger.

The *Clemency* was launched and given the weather conditions was in all probability towed out to the stricken vessel by the Admiralty steam tug, the *Trusty*. The Great Western Railway steamer, the *Sir Walter Raleigh*, had previously made an attempt to reach the *Hankow*, but found she was unable to make headway in the atrocious conditions which, outside the breakwater, proved too hazardous for the *Trusty* to approach the *Hankow*, so it was left to Coxswain William Teal and the crew of the *Clemency* to effect the rescue.

Battling against the mountainous seas and near hurricane-force wind, time after time the crew of the *Clemency* carried and secured a hawser from the *Trusty* to the *Hankow*, and time after time the hawser parted. Finally, however, with the crew nearing exhaustion, a link was established which held. The *Trusty*, with the help of two other tugs, succeeded in pulling the *Hankow* out of danger and took her to a safe anchorage. The service provided by the crew of the *Clemency* that day is recorded within the annals of the RNLI as 'assisted to save vessel'.

Throughout Wednesday 27 October 1880, the skies over the port of Plymouth gave every indication that a gale of some ferocity was brewing. Conditions deteriorated, preventing the sailing of two mail steamers and a man-o'-war. Captain Bruce, of the Royal Mail Company's steamship, *Para*, on his first arrival in the Sound that afternoon, likewise made the decision not to put back to sea. The commander of HMS *Tourmaline*, commanded by Captain Dennistoun, had put to sea that morning to join the flying squadron at Madiera, but on viewing the weather conditions in the English Channel returned to the safe anchorage of Plymouth Sound.

The full ferocity of the storm broke at 04.00 hours on Thursday 28 October, when numerous vessels that had been at anchor in the Sound began to drag their anchors. In all, four vessels were driven on to the rocky shore, three being sufficiently close to land for their crews to be rescued by Mr Philip Mann and his rocket-apparatus team. A less fortunate vessel was the schooner, the *Fortuna*, bound from Wales to London with a cargo of paving stones. Having dragged her anchors, the schooner went aground, just outside Dunstone Point, rapidly filled with water and sank. The *Fortuna's* crew, who were three in number, took to the comparative safety of her rigging, from where, it is reported, 'they were rescued by the Millbay lifeboat'.

The *Western Morning News*, of Friday 29 October 1880, reported:

Anticipating a gale, Captain Sadler, the Hon. Secretary, on the previous night directed the coxswain to have the lifeboat ready, and at half-past five, when rockets were sent up by the coastguard at Batten, the boat was promptly manned and proceeded to the spot. The first vessel reached was the John May, *the crew of which, with the exception of the captain, who was drowned, had landed. The two schooners... were then visited, but in those cases also the coastguard had already rendered noble service by saving the crews with the aid of the rocket apparatus. The lifeboat reached the* Fortuna, *and, at 7a.m., took off the crew, who, as might be supposed, were very grateful for their timely rescue.*

The storm-force winds, heavy seas and driving rain that lashed Plymouth on Sunday 27 November 1881 were comparable, in the eyes of local people, only to those of December 1872 when seven vessels, including the ill-fated *Eliza* and *Fearful*, were driven ashore. The first indications that a gale was brewing were noticed at about noon the previous day. By 14.00 hours the skies had darkened, the wind had risen in ferocity and the cold grey seas had become boisterous and confused. By late afternoon the wind was blowing from the south, having backed from the south-west. The trawler fleet hastily returned to port and those who were prevented from entering Sutton Harbour by the sea and tide were forced to seek refuge in the Cattewater. Larger ships sought the sanctuary of the Sound.

The Union Steamship Company's steamer, the *Arab*, had entered harbour at 08.00 hours, bound for Madeira and the Cape. Having embarked 14 passengers and 12 sacks of mail, given the prevailing weather conditions, her captain, Captain S.R.P. Caines, RNR, resolved to remain in port. Later in the day the Orient Line steamship, the *Lusitania*, arrived in Plymouth from London. She embarked 54 passengers and 33 sacks of

mail. The captain of the *Lusitania*, Captain A. Charlton, likewise chose to remain in port and wait for the storm to abate. However, the storm continued throughout that day, the ensuing night and into the following day. The winds raged with terrifying force and the rain fell in torrents.

As dawn broke at just after 07.00 hours on that Sunday morning, the Coastguard at Batten sighted a barque drifting rapidly towards the shore. Two rockets were immediately fired to summon the lifeboat and the Coastguard men set out for Jennycliffe Bay, that being the area in which, it was anticipated, the vessel would founder. Not having access to horses, the Coastguards, under the command of Chief Officer Mills, set out on foot having recourse only to the equipment that they could carry. Mr W. Hooper, who was on lookout for the mail steamer, the *Asiatic*, from Cape Town, observed the distress rockets and summoned John Lucock, the Second Coxswain of the Plymouth lifeboat. Lucock made his way to the lifeboat station and fired two rockets, firstly to summon the lifeboat crew, and secondly to convey to the Coastguard team that assistance would be at hand. At 08.45 hours the *Clemency*, with Coxswain William Teel in command, was launched into the teeth of the gale in conditions from which most other vessels shied. One can only imagine the truly terrifying conditions faced by the lifeboat crew as they pulled their small craft out from Millbay, across the Sound under The Hoe, around Mount Batten and on to Jennycliffe Bay. As the *Clemency* made this torturous journey, the barque ran aground at a point between Withy Hedge and Dunstone Point. The Coastguard team – ten from Batten and eight from Bovisand – established their rocket apparatus on the cliff above the vessel but the dense furze that grew in that area proved detrimental to the successful firing of the apparatus. With the imminent approach of the lifeboat further use of the rocket apparatus was suspended.

Ashore, it became known immediately that a vessel had foundered and a quick examination of the vessels remaining in the Sound identified the casualty as the Dutch barque, the *Baron Van Pallandt* of Rotterdam. Built in 1859 and owned by Mr Ivan Renswoud, she was under the command of Captain O.D. Duintyer, bound from Moulmein, East Indies, with a cargo of jute. The barque, having been on passage for 139 days, had been at anchor in the Sound awaiting orders. In the turbulent seas she had lost one anchor, and dragged a second before stranding. Upon arriving at the scene, Coxswain Teel placed the *Clemency* in the lee of the *Baron Van Pallandt* in order to effect a rescue but, it being low water, Captain Duintyer declined the offer to have his crew taken off the ship. The lifeboat withdrew and was placed at anchor. Some time later that morning the harbour-master, Captain Moore, was taken out to the stranded vessel by the Admiralty tug, the *Carron*. Having been acquainted with the situation by Coxswain Teel, Captain Moore instructed the lifeboat to carry a rope to the barque and make fast. The *Carron* then paid out and secured a steel hawser; she then steamed slowly ahead, hoping to refloat the Dutchman. The hawser parted. At the same time a small boat was seen to put out from the barque and it was evident that the crew of the *Baron Van Pallandt* were contemplating a landing. The lifeboat moved in and Coxswain Teel successfully dissuaded the crew from making any such attempt; he took the seven crewmen into the lifeboat and then transferred them to the safety of the *Carron*. The *Clemency* returned and took off a further five crewmen, who joined their shipmates.

During the course of the morning the ferocity of both the wind and sea decreased and the lifeboat made two further runs to the barque, recovering the personal effects of the crew. Captain Duintyer, the chief officer and the steward continued to decline offers of rescue, even though the ship's rudder had broken away and, being broadside-on to the waves, the vessel was full of water with little or no freeboard. At 13.00 hours the *Carron* steamed away from the scene with the *Clemency* in tow. The lifeboat was cast off at Millbay, the *Carron* proceeding to Devonport Dockyard where she landed the Dutchmen. They were then placed in the care of the Sailors' Home. Captain Duintyer, the chief officer and the steward finally left the *Baron Van Pallandt* and reached the safety of the shore in the ship's boat.

The next effective service rendered by the crew of the *Clemency* took place on Sunday 2 September 1883. At about 06.00 hours on Saturday 1 September, the 430-ton Norwegian barque, the *Elise*, of Porsgrund, was making her way up the English Channel when a strong breeze sprang up from the south-west. The vessel, bound for London with a cargo of deal, from Philbas on the coast of West Africa, was under the command of Captain Wright. The intensity of the wind rapidly increased and Captain Wright found it necessary to take in all sail, with the exception of the main lower topsail. The *Elise* passed the Lizard at about 12.00 hours and, as the wind backed to the south, the vessel was kept close-hauled. The Eddystone Light was sighted at about 23.00 hours and soon after midnight the breakwater light was sighted. Knowing Plymouth Harbour well, Captain Wright set his sail for the breakwater, getting inside just after 03.00 hours on Sunday morning. The first anchor, with approximately 35 fathoms of chain,

was let go but it parted at once. The second anchor, with 40 fathoms of chain, was dropped but did not hold. A mist had descended and, realising at once that the *Elise* was dragging her single anchor, the crew hoisted signals of distress. The barque continued her shoreward drift and eventually ran aground, stern first, on the 'Needles', a ridge of sharp, pointed rocks, just outside the Ladies Bathing Place and directly below Smeaton Tower. An eyewitness reported:

Having grounded, the tide swung her round and she was driven broadside-on the rocks, and with the heavy tide that was running, gave two lurches and then broke in two.

The stern section of the vessel sank immediately, although the bow section remained stranded on the rocks, with the waves breaking clear over it. The crew of nine were seen to be standing in the bows, clinging to the forward rigging.

Thomas Penny, who had been on The Hoe, keeping a lookout for the vessel to which he belonged, witnessed the signal made by the *Elise*. He hurried to the home of the Coxswain of the Plymouth lifeboat, William Teel, at Bishops Place, Millbay, and raised an alarm. Teel summoned his crew and by 05.00 hours they had mustered and launched the lifeboat; the crew comprised: William Teel, Coxswain, John Lucock, Second Coxswain, Thomas Penny, H. Mumford, W. Dee, T. Crocker, S. Little, J. Amery, C. Rhodes, W. Hockaday, J. Hosking and a marine. By 05.20 hours the *Clemency* had reached the wreck. Just prior to the lifeboat reaching the barque, the *Elise's* foremast fell over the side.

It proved impossible for the lifeboat to get alongside the wreck, for the wind, which continued to blow from the south-west, had intensified and threatened to drive the *Clemency* onto the Needles. Coxswain Teel anchored the lifeboat and, with great skill, negotiated the Needles and veered down on to the *Elise*. A rope was thrown from the lifeboat to the barque and, one by one, her crew of nine were drawn through the breaking seas to the safety of the *Clemency*. Thanks to the titanic efforts of the lifeboat crew, the Norwegian sailors escaped injury and were taken to the Sailors' Home, where they received every attention.

The *Clemency* did not escape this rescue unscathed for, in approaching the *Elise*, on three or four occasions she struck heavily upon the rocks. The rudder of the lifeboat was broken off and one of her oars was broken; but luckily she shipped little, if any, water.

In 1884, after many years of loyal and dedicated service to the RNLI, William Teel retired as Coxswain of the Plymouth lifeboat. In recognition of

Gravestone of William Teel, Plymouth's first RNLI Coxswain.

his service, the Committee of Management awarded him the Institution's Silver Medal. William Teel died on 27 November 1896, at his home at 22 Bishops Place, West Hoe, Plymouth. A gravestone, commemorating William's service as Coxswain of the Plymouth lifeboat, was erected at Ford Park Cemetery, Plymouth. William Teel was succeeded as Coxswain by the former Second Coxswain, John Lucock.

The final service launch of the *Clemency* took place on Wednesday 28 January 1885 when, under the command of Coxswain John Lucock, she rendered assistance to the barque, the *Wellington* of Nova Scotia. The 1,000-ton vessel had been bound for New York, from Havre, with a cargo of copper ore, but had returned to Plymouth, from the Atlantic, following an alleged mutiny during which her Captain had been killed.

The ship arrived off the Eddystone during Wednesday night in a heavy gale, which was blowing from the south-west. In spite of the wind, a thick fog prevailed, preventing the lookout from distinguishing the Eddystone Light. It was the ship's mate who realised the error and the fact that the heavy seas were driving the vessel on to the rocks off the Mew Stone. Distress signals were made and the Plymouth lifeboat, the *Clemency*, was launched. At the same time, at the neighbouring River Yealm station, the 35-foot lifeboat, the *Bowman*, was also launched. This was, in fact, the only service launch performed by this lifeboat.

The *Clemency* was towed out into the teeth of the gale, and to the distressed vessel, by the government's tug, the *Scotia*, the latter having the harbour-master, Staff Captain Sutton, on board. The *Wellington* was located, lying to two anchors, close to the reef between the Mew Stone and the mainland. The *Clemency* was instrumental in passing a tow-rope between the tug and the barque, but in the heavy, confused seas, the *Scotia* was unable to make headway with the ship in tow. The *Western Daily Mercury*, of 30 January 1885, reported the following in respect of this rescue:

The Yealm lifeboat went out and the crew

had a miraculous escape from drowning. The heavy sea carried the lifeboat under the paddle-box of the tug boat, and the lifeboat, which was seriously damaged, was put under water twice. The majority of the crew jumped onboard the Scotia. *The lifeboat was carried to sea with three men in her, but meeting outside with a fair wind the three men were able to make for the river.*

The master of the *Scotia* made every effort to tow the barque to safety but, with every minute, the *Wellington* was being driven closer to the shore. At this point it was deemed advisable to tow the *Wellington* into the River Yealm. Having safely crossed the bar, into the river, the *Wellington* attempted to set her anchors; they failed to hold, the cables parted and she began to drift up the river, pulling the *Scotia* with her. The barque grounded twice and finally ran aground approximately one mile upriver; her crew were successfully taken off. On this occasion the Plymouth lifeboat was credited with having 'assisted to save the vessel and 15 lives'.

On 30 January the *Wellington* was taken into the Sound where, in the early hours of the following day, she parted from her mooring and was driven ashore near Millbay Pier. The *Clemency* was launched and once again assisted in establishing a tow-line between the barque and a tug. Having lost her anchors, the *Wellington* was moored to a buoy. The *Clemency* remained in attendance until 10.30 hours, when the weather moderated.

The crew of the *Wellington* underwent trial, at Exeter Assizes, in answer to the death of their Captain. It was established by the Court that Captain Charles Armstrong had been drunk and had 'run amuck' with a firearm, shooting the ship's carpenter in the throat, the ball lodging close to his windpipe. He also seriously injured a seaman, Martin Nest, whom he shot in the eye. Captain Armstrong was overpowered by being struck a heavy blow from behind with a belaying pin. The crew put Armstrong in irons and after three hours of struggling to free his bonds he dropped exhausted and died from his exertions. The crew of the *Wellington* were acquitted of all charges.

The headstone at the grave of 'Joe', faithful spaniel of the Camber lifeboat men.

5

THE *ESCAPE*

27 MARCH 1885–24 MARCH 1898

Type: Self-Righting   *Propulsion: Pulling*   *Oars: 10*   *Crew: 13*
Length: 34' 0"   *Beam: 7' 6"*   *Displacement: 3ᵀ 10ᶜʷᵗ*
Official number: 44   *Builder: Forrestt, Limehouse*
Service Launches: 15   *Lives Saved: 7*
Coxswain: John Lucock

Following the removal of her outer skin during a refit, Captain Nepean, the visiting Inspector for the Royal National Lifeboat Institution, discovered that the inner planking of the *Clemency* was defective. Plymouth Lifeboat Station's Hon. Secretary, Mr J. Rooney, ordered that the repairs should cease immediately and telegraphed the Secretary of the Royal National Lifeboat Institution for instructions. The Secretary instantly recognised the inexpediency of a large port such as Plymouth being without a serviceable lifeboat and the Institution, at about 14.30 hours, telegraphed Mr Rooney to the effect that a replacement lifeboat would be dispatched to Plymouth immediately. By 18.00 hours that same evening, a new boat was placed on the Great Western Railway, at Poplar, for transportation to Plymouth. The new boat arrived at its destination on Saturday 7 March 1885. On the morning of Monday 9 March, the truck was run into the dock of the floating basin and the lifeboat was launched into the water by a 10-ton crane. The lifeboat was then pulled into the boat-house, where it was safely stored.

The new lifeboat was of similar specification to her predecessor, albeit a ton heavier. She was built of mahogany with both her inner and outer skins being diagonally laid. The vessel had air cases fitted to her bottom and sides, 'so that in the event of a hole being knocked in her bottom,

The Escape *and her crew* (see also p.6) *on the launch slipway rails of the Camber lifeboat station, 1 April 1887.* WESTERN MORNING NEWS

her buoyancy will not be affected.' The fore and aft tanks were larger than those fitted to her predecessor, and had handrails fitted to them. Being self-righting the boat could, reportedly, 'clear herself of water in a minute and a half in the event of a heavy sea filling her.' A new feature, which stimulated great interest and speculation, was the introduction of two water tanks, which were under the charge of the coxswain, and into which he could admit water in order to increase the stability of the vessel. These tanks were fitted with 'two ingenious hand pumps' by which means two men could pump the ballast water out in one minute. The lifeboat would carry a crew of 13 but in time of emergency could carry 50–60 persons.

The lifeboat was a gift of Miss Lucy Harris of London and was built at a cost of £327. The *Western Morning News* initially speculated that the new boat would take on the name of her predecessor; however, this was not the case as the new lifeboat was named the *Escape*.

The *Escape* remained on station at Plymouth for just four days short of two years before she was launched on her first active service. The call came in the early hours of Wednesday 23 March 1887. Since the previous evening Plymouth had been lashed by a severe gale, continuous rain and extremely heavy squalls. In the exceptionally nasty seas that were running, damage was caused to HMS *Acorn* as she played out cable. Steam launches belonging to the Admiral Superintendent and the Captain of the Steam Reserve, whilst lying in the Camber, were struck by heavy seas which smashed bulwarks and cabin windows. Ashore, severe structural damage to buildings was experienced.

Some days earlier the 192-ton barquentine, *Kate*, owned by J. Denholm of Greenock, and under the command of Captain Oates, had put into Plymouth, from Laguna de Terminos in the Gulf of Mexico, with a cargo of logwood. Due to the continuous pounding by the seas, at about 03.00 hours the port anchor cable parted and, before the starboard anchor could find sufficient purchase to bring the vessel up, the *Kate* struck a reef, broadside-on, about 200 yards off the Coastguard station at Batten. As Captain Oates was not on board the vessel at this time, the mate sent up distress signals as the vessel continued to be bumped unmercifully on the reef. The Coastguard had observed the drift of the *Kate* and, in anticipation of her running aground, had prepared the rocket-line apparatus. As the vessel

grounded, the first rocket was fired, but the line broke. Mr P. Mann, the Chief Officer of Coastguards, fired a second line over the vessel. Finding that the crew of the stricken vessel did not recover the line, Mr Mann made the signal requesting the assistance of the Plymouth lifeboat. This signal was answered from Millbay, and the *Escape*, under the command of Coxswain John Lucock, was launched at 04.30 hours. The lifeboat was followed to the scene by an Admiralty tug with Staff-Captain Burniston, Master Attendant at the dockyard, and Staff-Captain Sutton, harbour-master, on board.

The lifeboat crew battled their way across the Sound in a heavy, confused sea and a full westerly gale. Upon reaching the casualty, John Lucock placed the lifeboat directly under the weather bow of the stranded vessel. The lifeboat's crew battled to maintain this position as the *Kate's* crew of seven were taken off from the bowsprit of their vessel. The *Kate* succumbed to the ravages of the sea, her timbers were badly strained and her deck burst upwards. Finding that her services were not required, the Admiralty tug returned to the Dockyard. The *Escape* landed the crew of the *Kate* at Sutton Harbour, where they were placed in the care of Mr T. Hopkins of the Shipwrecked Mariners Society. Later that day, when the weather had abated, the crew returned to the *Kate* and took off their personal belongings. The *Kate* had been driven high onto the reef and ultimately became a total wreck. Miss Harris apparently recognised the rescue:

April 1st 1887

Dear Madam,

We the undersigned Coxswains and crew of the Plymouth Life Boat Escape request the favour of your acceptance of the accompanying photograph of our Life Boat and crew as a small mark of our appreciation of your kindness in so generously recognising the services we had the opportunity of rendering to the crew of the barquentine Kate wrecked in Plymouth Sound during the storm of 23rd ult. We are Madam Yours very respectively

John Lucock 1st Coxswain
C. Mumble Coxswain
C. Rhodes   *W. Dee*
W. Hooper   *W. Cowles*
John Mumford   *J. Penny*
James Bennett   *D. Mumford*
Joe Mumford   *J. Crocker*
J. Amery.

Walter Crowther and Fred Fowler with the Service Board for the Escape, *Plymouth's lifeboat 1885–98.* PETER CROWTHER

Another year was to pass before the services of Coxswain Lucock and the *Escape* were once again called upon. As in the previous year, it was the notorious March gales that wrought havoc in the port of Plymouth and the vessels that sought the comparative shelter of the Sound. A fresh wind had prevailed for most of Saturday and from 02.00 hours on the morning of Sunday 11 March 1888, the weather deteriorated into a violent south-westerly gale, accompanied by squalls. Wind speeds reaching hurricane force 12, 64–71 knots, raged over Plymouth and the surrounding coastlines. As the seas increased in ferocity Plymouth's harbours filled with shipping, all of which safely rode out the gale until 07.00 hours, when a particularly heavy squall passed over the Sound. The previous Thursday had seen the arrival in Plymouth Sound of the 400-ton Norwegian barque, the *Souvenir* of Arendal. The vessel, which was under the command of Captain Thorstensen, had arrived from Buenos Aires with a cargo of maize. Upon reaching Plymouth she had received further orders, on Saturday, to proceed to Dunkirk. The adverse weather conditions had forced the *Souvenir* to remain in Plymouth Sound but, unable to withstand the full force of the gale, her anchors began to drag. Realising that his vessel was being driven towards the shore

of Batten Bay, Captain Thorstensen hoisted signals of distress. The crew of the Plymouth lifeboat was summoned and within half an hour, at 08.15 hours, the *Escape* was launched with Coxswain Lucock at the helm. Having fought their way through turbulent seas, the lifeboat came within hailing distance of the barque only to discover that she had grounded on the beach and that, in an attempt to lighten the vessel, the crew were in the process of cutting away her mainmast. In a few minutes the mainmast fell by the board, but in falling it carried away the majority of the mizzenmast, narrowly missing the lifeboat. The ship's captain, who requested the attendance of a tug, declined an offer made by Coxswain Lucock to take off the *Souvenir's* crew. John Lucock hoisted a signal requesting a tug, but although the Great Western Railway Company's steam tender, *Sir Walter Raleigh*, and the tugs *Vixen, Belle* and *Deerhound* were in the vicinity, they did not render assistance. The *Escape* then went alongside the *Souvenir* and took off the chief mate, in order to land him ashore where he could make arrangements for a tug. The lifeboat was towed back to Millbay by the tug *Deerhound*.

After the lifeboat had left the scene, three men from the *Belle* used the tug's boat to carry a line to the *Souvenir*. The crew of the *Sir Walter Raleigh* followed suit. By this time the barque, which had been under the relentless pounding of the waves, had lost her rudder. With a view to assisting the other tugs, the *Vixen* threw a line to the *Sir Walter Raleigh*, but in so doing she was caught by the wind and tide and, before she could feel the effect of steaming ahead, was carried down onto the bows of the *Sir Walter Raleigh*, smashing her stem and causing other damage to her bulwarks, rails, bridge and stanchions.

Although the tide had been on the ebb for four hours, the *Sir Walter Raleigh* and the *Belle* succeeded in towing the badly damaged *Souvenir* off and, with the aid of the *Vixen,* took her into Sutton Harbour.

The townsfolk of Plymouth woke up, on Thursday 11 December 1890, to find startling headlines in the *Western Daily Mercury*: 'DENSE FOG IN THE CHANNEL', 'THE P. AND O. *NEPAUL* ASHORE OFF PLYMOUTH', 'PERILOUS POSITION', 'THE SHIP DESERTED BY CREW AND PASSENGERS'. On the evening of Wednesday 10 December 1890, the Orient Company's mail steamer, *Orizaba*, commanded by Captain Dixon, put into Plymouth Sound.

She immediately raised the alarm that, in dense fog, the Peninsular and Oriental Line's Royal Mail steamer, *Nepaul*, had run onto rocks near the Shag Stone. The steamer, under the command of Captain E.W. Brady, was bound for London from Calcutta, via Marseilles. The *Nepaul* sent up distress rockets, which were immediately answered by the mail tender, *Sir Francis Drake*, and a pilot boat that was nearby. The steam tender *Sir Walter Raleigh* and the Plymouth lifeboat, the *Escape*, also answered the call for assistance.

It was low water at the time of the incident, and there was very little sea running, but the *Nepaul* had taken some 5 feet of water into her fore-compartments. Most of the ship's passengers had disembarked at Marseilles, but those who remained, including two first-class, six second-class and three child travellers, were taken off by a pilot boat at about 23.00 hours, and landed at Millbay. The passengers were taken to the Duke of Cornwall Hotel where they spent the night.

At 00.20 hours, John Cumming, a representative of the Peninsular and Oriental Line, put out to the casualty in an Admiralty tug, accompanied by the harbour-master, Staff-Captain Tomlin, RN. Enquiries subsequently revealed that the *Nepaul* had passed the Lizard at 16.30 hours and met with a slight fog coming up the channel. She sighted the Eddystone Light at 19.00 hours and her captain had then steered a course which he thought would bring the vessel into Plymouth Sound. All too late, the second mate sighted breakers off the vessel's bow, she grounded by the bow, pivoted and swung towards the shore, stern first.

Following the disembarkation of the passengers, Captain Brady of the *Nepaul* requested Coxswain John Lucock to stand-by with the lifeboat until the next high tide, when attempts would be made to refloat her. However, these attempts failed due to the amount of water taken into the engine-room of the steamer. The *Escape* left the scene, Coxswain Lucock promising to return, with the lifeboat, when the next attempt to refloat might be made. The *Escape* returned to the *Nepaul* on the afternoon of 11 December, but once again attempts to refloat the vessel were unsuccessful. The crew of the stricken vessel were taken off by tug and the lifeboat returned to her station without rendering service.

The last launch during which the *Escape* provided active service took place on Tuesday 8 December 1896. In a severe southerly gale, the schooner, the *Elizabeth Ann* of Teignmouth, had laid her anchors on the western side of the Sound in the vicinity of Picklecombe Fort. At 20.30 hours, the lookout at the harbour-master's office saw a distress signal coming from the vessel. The alarm was raised and with considerable promptitude the *Escape* was launched, under the supervision of Coxswain Lucock. The lifeboat was immediately taken in tow by the tug *Deerhound*. The tug and lifeboat were seriously hampered in their progress towards the casualty by the heavy seas and gale-force wind but, at about 22.30 hours, the lookout men sighted the two craft approaching the disabled vessel. By now the *Elizabeth Ann* had dragged her anchors and was dangerously near a reef, known locally as 'The Bridge', under Mount Edgcumbe. At first considerable difficulty was experienced by the crews of both the *Deerhound* and the *Escape* as they struggled against the elements to bring their craft alongside the schooner.

After several attempts, Coxswain Lucock and his crew succeeded in attaching hawsers between the *Elizabeth Ann* and the *Deerhound* and by 23.00 hours, with the lifeboat also in tow, the tug had the schooner under tow for the Hamoaze.

The *Escape* returned to Millbay Docks where Coxswain John Lucock received orders to proceed and render assistance to a vessel that had been wrecked underneath The Hoe. It fortunately transpired that the services of the lifeboat were not required and the *Escape* speedily returned to the boat-house.

'I have been in this job now for over 25 years, been around the world a few times, been to the Antarctic three times, been in three hurricanes in one week, given assistance to other mariners at sea in distress. But since leaving the RNLI, I have never experienced the rush of adrenaline that the lifeboat maroons used to give me. Those days of wearing the RNLI jumper, and being with likeminded people, I hold dear to me.'

Glenn Pook
CPO Deck (Bosun)
Former Plymouth lifeboat man

6

THE *ELIZA AVINS*

24 MARCH 1898–6 SEPTEMBER 1922

Type: Self-Righting   *Propulsion:* Pulling-Sailing   *Oars:* 10   *Crew:* 13

Length: 37' 0"   *Beam:* 9' 3"   *Displacement:* 4^T 10^{Cwt}

Official number: 412   *Builder:* Simpson, Strickland & Co., Dartmouth

Service Launches: 27   *Lives Saved:* 27

Coxswains: R.H. Lucock (1898–1901), David Mumford (1901–20), Frederick Eagles (1920–22)

The lifeboat that was to replace the *Escape* was built from the legacy of John Avins of Moseley, Worcester, at a cost of £699. The boat-yard of Simpson, Strickland & Co. of Dartmouth built the boat at their premises on the River Dart. The boat was of a self-righting design, pulled ten oars and had a crew of 13. She was larger than her predecessor, being 37 feet in length. She was named the *Eliza Avins*.

The *Eliza Avins* was launched, in horrendous weather conditions, on Friday 3 November 1899, but returned to shore without providing a service. The casualty on this occasion was the 363-ton *Shamrock*, a former brigantine, which had been converted into a float-ing factory ship. The vessel belonged to the Fish Oil and Guano Company of London and Dublin.

Throughout Thursday and Friday, widespread south-south-westerly gales swept across the United Kingdom. The gales caused major disrup-tion, reaching their peak between 12.00 and 15.00 hours on Friday 3 November. At that time the *Shamrock* was anchored about half a mile from the shore, in Jennycliffe Bay. Two of the ship's crew were ashore, leaving the master of the Shamrock, Captain J.B. Tackaberry, Owen Bulger (the mate), John Mahony and Michael Foley (engineers), and a boy, James Oates of Plymouth, aboard. The ship's tender had been washed away in the storm, leaving the crew with-out means of escape. At 14.00 hours, the *Shamrock* was seen by people at the Barbican to drift from her mooring towards Mount Batten.

The vessel was flying a recognised distress signal – her ensign hoisted upside-down.

At 14.30 hours the tug *Sleuthhound* set out to render assistance but before she could come up to the vessel the factory ship was driven onto the rocks below the Mount Batten Coastguard Station. The *Shamrock* was holed and severely damaged; she quickly began to take in water and finally settled on her starboard side.

The *Eliza Avins* had been launched but was unable to make headway in the heavy seas and strong onshore winds. The Coastguard had successfully fired the rocket apparatus, passing a line over the stricken vessel, but this could not be secured and was lost.

The No.1 pilot cutter, *Drift*, was manned by the Trinity Pilots, from Turnchapel, but likewise was unable to make headway. Three of their number, John Pascho, George Skilton and Thomas Staddon, accompanied by two experi-enced crewmen – 'strappers' William Skilton and Robert Frood – then set out in a 16-foot tender. The small rescue party rowed the tender to Batten, where the boat was pulled from the water and beached. Aided by the numerous spec-tators, the boat was manhandled up the cliffs, across fields and down the cliffs, to a point where it was once more launched into the heaving and confused seas. Placing themselves at great personal risk, and displaying outstanding sea-manship, the small group reached the *Shamrock*, took off the crew of five and rowed back through the raging sea to regain the shore.

Below: *The Lloyds Bronze Medal awarded to Robert Frood for his part in the rescue of the crew of the Shamrock, 3 November 1899.*

Crew of the No.1 Pilot Cutter, Drift, *and the boat in which they rescued the crew of the* Shamrock. *Left to right: R. Frood, G.H. Skilton, J. Pascho, W. Skilton, T. Staddon.*

Right: *Robert Frood, a crew member of the No.1 Pilot Cutter,* Drift.

Crew of the No.1 Pilot Cutter, Drift, *and the shipwrecked crew of the* Shamrock, *wrecked at Mount Batten, 3 November 1899. Left to right: the saved (wearing hats): O. Bulger, Captain J.B. Tackaberry, M. Foley, J. Oates and J. Mahoney; the salvagers: T. Staddon, W. Skilton, J. Pascho, G.H. Skilton, R. Frood.*

To acknowledge this outstanding act of bravery and seamanship, a civic reception was held in the Balfour Hall, Notte Street, Plymouth, on Thursday 18 January 1890. Each pilot and seaman who took part in the rescue was awarded a gold watch, the Lloyds Bronze Medal and Vellum for Saving Life at Sea, the Board of Trade Silver Gallantry Medal and the Royal National Lifeboat Institution's Vellum Certificate, signed personally by the Prince of Wales, and a sovereign.

In 1901, on the retirement of Coxswain John Lucock, David Mumford was appointed Coxswain of the Plymouth lifeboat.

Although the *Eliza Avins* took up station in Plymouth on 24 March 1898, the first occasion on which she rendered active service did not occur until Tuesday 25 November 1902. It was at 03.30 hours on the previous morning that a violent storm broke over Plymouth. The storm, accompanied by a deluge of rain, raged for several hours. By late morning, the storm had decreased in its intensity and the remainder of the day was comparatively fine; however, there was every indication of an early return to stormy conditions.

As the evening closed in, the wind once again increased in strength, carrying with it very heavy showers. By midnight a full south-south-westerly gale was blowing, with winds gusting to almost hurricane force. At intervals powerful rain squalls broke out, with what was described as 'tremendous violence.' The weather continued to worsen and the seas in the Sound rose in ferocity. As a precautionary measure a watch was placed on The Hoe in order that an early alarm could be raised should the services of the Plymouth lifeboat be required. Indeed, at 01.30 hours on Tuesday, a sailing vessel which had been moored in the vicinity of the Batten breakwater was reported to be in difficulty. The brigantine was dragging her anchors and as those on board were in fear of the vessel being driven ashore, near the Ladies Bathing Place, they continually burnt flares and used the vessel's foghorn to attract attention. The lookout on The Hoe acknowledged the distress signals by burning a blue flare, and, at 02.35 hours, fired rockets to summon the lifeboat crew. The latter signal was repeated at Millbay.

The *Eliza Avins* was launched, under the command of Coxswain David Mumford, into the full force of the gale, which was now blowing from the south, accompanied by exceedingly heavy seas and torrential rain. Having worked clear of the pier heads at Millbay, the lifeboat entered the Sound at about 03.25 hours. A contemporary newspaper report stated:

The storm was now at its worst, and in nothing more or less than a howling tempest the lifeboat sailed down across the Sound, in the direction of the Mallard Buoy, which is not far from Batten Breakwater.

After an exhausting battle against the sea, the lifeboat reached the brigantine, the 125-ton *Snowdrop*, at 03.45 hours. The vessel, belonging to the Plymouth Mercantile Shipping Company and laden with 240 tons of coal, had moored in the Sound on Sunday and was awaiting suitable tides to take her to her berth at Calstock. Coxswain Mumford ascertained there to be only two crew members on board, the cook and an ordinary seaman, neither of whom he estimated to be more than 18 years of age; the ship's master, Captain Taylor of Plymouth, the mate and an able seaman had gone ashore. Upon the arrival of the lifeboat, the two young crewmen were anxious to leave their vessel, which, at that time, was only three or four cable lengths from the rocks. Having assessed the situation, David Mumford, together with seven members of the lifeboat's crew, boarded the *Snowdrop* and, after convincing the youths that their lives were no longer in danger, set about hauling in the slack chain.

Realising the close proximity of the vessel to the shore, Coxswain Mumford ordered the burning of a series of red flares to summon the assistance of a tug. At about 04.30 hours, the *Snowdrop* brought up for a while, but her anchors did not hold and slowly but surely she recommenced her drift towards the rocky shore. Not long after this, at just after 05.00 hours, the tug *Reynard*, owned by Mr George Andrews and chartered by Sir John Jackson, arrived on the scene. In the heavy seas, with the assistance of the crew who had remained in the *Eliza Avins*, a hawser was passed from the tug to the brigantine, and a tow established. By this time the *Snowdrop* was about two cable lengths from the shore and, according to Coxswain Mumford, she would surely have been driven ashore had it not been for the timely arrival of the *Reynard*.

The wind, which had blown from the south-south-west for the majority of the night, backed to the south-east shortly before daybreak, but neither the force of the wind nor the turmoil of the sea reduced in ferocity.

The Eliza Avins *beached near the boatyard at Cremyll (looking across the Tamar towards Devonport at HMS* Impregnable*).* PLYMOUTHIANS: MORE PHOTOGRAPHS AND MEMORIES *BY ANDREW CLUER*

After the tug had been taking the strain of the *Snowdrop* for about an hour, it was found that one of the brigantine's anchors had fouled the chain of the Mallard Buoy; consequently the shackle was knocked out and the chain was slipped, after it had been marked with a buoy in order that the anchor could be recovered when the weather moderated. By 20.00 hours the *Reynard* had the tow well under way, taking the *Snowdrop* into the safety of the Cattewater. Coxswain Mumford and his crew returned the *Eliza Avins* to the boat-house at Millbay, arriving at 21.00 hours.

The newspaper headlines carried by the *Western Morning News* of Friday 27 December 1912 bore witness to the ferocity of the gale that wreaked havoc on Plymouth on the morning of Boxing Day, Thursday 26 December 1912: 'FOUR VESSELS ASHORE IN PLYMOUTH SOUND', 'STEAMER HIGH AND DRY ON THE ROCKS', 'SCHOONER'S PERIL', 'BATTLE-CRUISER'S FITTINGS CARRIED AWAY'.

The gale, which raged for several hours over Devon on that Thursday morning, resulted in considerable damage being caused to property and shipping alike. The full force of the gale was experienced in Plymouth where the *Eliza Avins* and the port's tugs were called upon to render assistance to no less than six vessels, three of which were driven onto rocks on the eastern side of the port. The townsfolk of Plymouth, who were returning home in the early hours of that Boxing Day morning, having enjoyed the Christmas Day festivities, did so on a clear, still, moonlit night, but by 02.00 hours the storm had broken over the port. The severity of the wind was such that, in the huge seas outside the harbour, mountainous waves crashed and pounded against the breakwater, whilst within the Sound vessels with even two anchors down were driven slowly but surely towards the rocks. High water was at 07.00 hours and coincided with the height of the storm. At 09.30 hours the maroons were fired to summon the lifeboat crew and many people made their way to the various vantage points to watch the spectacle of the launch of the lifeboat. The *Eliza Avins*, under the command of Coxswain David Mumford, was launched at 09.50 hours. In Batten Bay a two-funnelled steamer lay in a perilous position, whilst at the same time two schooners were in imminent danger of becoming stranded. Onlookers watched helplessly as all three vessels were driven ashore, at the same time receiving news that a ketch had struck rocks and become a wreck off Queen Anne's Battery Point. The vessels that foundered were the river steamer *Goyaz*, from Portreeth, the *Ottawa*, a schooner from London bound for Waterford, the schooner *Guild Mayor* from Poole headed for Runcorn, and the ketch *Johnny Toole*, from Cowes bound for Salcombe with a cargo of cement.

The first of the vessels to encounter problems was the steamer, which had recently been built at a cost of £50,000. The vessel, manned by a Dutch crew, was destined for service on the rivers of South America and, in common with all vessels of her type, had an exceedingly shallow draft with what appeared to be a disproportionate super-structure. This construction made the *Goyaz* particularly susceptible to bad weather conditions and placed her at the mercy of the high winds when her anchors failed to hold. The steamer fouled the schooner *Guild Mayor*, the latter loos-ing her bowsprit, foremast and main topmast. Clearing the schooner the steamer drove rapidly towards the rocks and ran aground. The crew of the *Goyaz* were able to get safely ashore.

The 230-ton schooner, *Ottawa*, was under the command of Captain J.H. Roberts. The crew comprised mate and brother of the captain W. Roberts, able seaman W. Tyrrell, ordinary sea-man W. Sweeting and the cook, T. Malledant. The *Ottawa* was on a voyage from London to Waterford with a cargo of manure, when she was forced to shelter in Portland in the company of the *Guild Mayor* and the *Johnny Toole*. The three vessels had left Portsmouth on the previous Saturday, the weather later forcing all three craft to seek the shelter of Plymouth, which they made on Monday evening. Mr W. Roberts, mate, picks up the story:

Early yesterday morning it came on dirty and we had two anchors down. The wind veered to the westward, but at about 9 a.m. the starboard anchor chain parted, and the port anchor proved insufficient to hold the schooner. We drifted into Batten bay, and the vessel was very soon on the rocks, although we did everything to save her. The lifeboat came to our assistance, and remained along-side about an hour. Seeing that there was no possibility of saving the schooner at that time, we all boarded the lifeboat, but not without great difficulty. As soon as we were all safely aboard, the lifeboat, which was still moored to

the schooner, grounded, and there we were for another hour. In the end we found the shore more inviting, and we managed all of us to wade through the boiling surf on to the greasy slopes of Mount Batten.

Mr Roberts added that whilst he was in the *Eliza Avins* she bumped heavily, but the crew said that the only thing that they could do was to await the rising tide.

Mr W. Demilwick, who was in charge of the Mount Batten Lifesaving Apparatus Brigade, described the service to the *Ottawa*:

The tug Boarhound *and the lifeboat were there, but the seas were so mountainous that they had to get in a very perilous position to do any good. Having failed to make fast a line, the* Ottawa *slowly drifted on to the rocks. When she had stranded the lifeboat attempted to take the schooner's crew off, but the weather was terrible. The men on the lifeboat worked hard and got to the schooner. The work of rescuing was very difficult, but it was safely accomplished. After this the velocity of the wind seemed to increase, and the lifeboat, in the midst of a raging sea and surrounded by treacherous rocks, looked to be in a bad way. Then it was that my men, Tucker, Colan and Ford, swam off to the rock that lay between the* Goyaz *and the* Ottawa. *Once they were there, they could take with the lifeboat. It was a plucky thing to do and they did it well. Burdened with lifebelts and lifelines they swam to the rock in the cold sea. True, it was only a few feet to swim, and some distance to walk, but it required courage. Arriving at the rock, the lifeboat crew told them that all was well, but my men could see that was not so, and they remained for one solid hour on that rock, running the risk of being washed off and drowned. In that hour we could see the lifeboatmen struggling unsuccessfully against the furious sea. They kept their craft beauti-fully head to wind, but pulling with all their might they could make no progress. On the contrary she drifted back and struck. Then my men rushed into the sea again, reached the rock, dived off, and got near the lifeboat. The sea that ran in there was enormous. I cannot remember seeing anything like it.*

The *Eliza Avin* grounded at about midday and within half an hour was left high and dry. Some of the lifeboat's crew managed to get ashore; one of their number reporting the position of the lifeboat, from the outset, as a bad one. 'We were in seas', he said, 'the like of which I have never seen in Plymouth Sound before.'

It was a fine, cloudy night on Saturday 13 September 1913, with a strong south-westerly breeze and moderate sea prevailing, when *Hopper No.42*, of London, which was heading for Plymouth from Corunna, Spain, struck on the south side of the Plymouth breakwater. The first warning of the disaster was raised at 23.45 hours, and the *Eliza Avins* was launched at 00.30 hours. Under sail and oars, the lifeboat reached the wreck at 01.30 hours. Upon nearing the break-water, the lifeboat was met by the harbour-master's launch that had attended the stranded vessel and taken off the crew of eight. The crew were transferred to the lifeboat and landed at Sutton Harbour. The Hopper's captain had simply misjudged his approach to Plymouth, and the proximity of the breakwater. The crew of the lifeboat on this occasion were: D. Mumford (Coxswain), E. Mumford, J. Wakeham, J. Sture, E. Davey, F. Foot, J. Watson, A. Tribble, W. Angel, J. Angel, ? Reid, W. Weaver and F. Eagles.

At the height of a south-south-easterly gale, which was accompanied by exceedingly heavy rain squalls, on the evening of Saturday 21 February 1914, rumours spread throughout the port that a vessel was drifting across Plymouth Sound. However, due to the weather conditions, no craft could be seen from the shore. Following a report that a distress signal had been sighted at 23.00 hours, telephone communication was established between the boat-house and the Coastguard at both Batten and Stonehouse, but no useful information could be obtained. On the advice of the harbour-master, the lifeboat was launched at 23.30 hours under the command of Second Coxswain F. Eagles. Under sail, the *Eliza Avins* made her way into the Sound and, after a search undertaken in a heavy sea and swell, a vessel was located on the rocks at the back of Drake's Island. The stranded vessel was identified as the German iron schooner, *Erna* of Bremen, which had rolled over and was on her beam-ends.

The lifeboat crew now had to contend with 64–71 knots of wind (hurricane force 12) and a sea that was breaking clean over the schooner. Showing exceptional skills of seamanship, Second Coxswain Eagle, manoeuvred the lifeboat through the breaking seas that covered the reefs

surrounding the island, until he was in a position where he could anchor the lifeboat and veer down on to the *Erna*. Using the boat's oars, the crew veered the lifeboat down until she was directly under the bowsprit of the schooner, from which the crew of five were able to drop to the safety of the *Eliza Avins*. During this operation, the lifeboat lost one 'blue' oar. (Port oars were coloured white and starboard blue, a tradition continued to this day in the colour coding of boat hooks.) Following the rescue, which was performed in a skilful manner under difficult and trying circumstances, Second Coxswain Eagles landed the *Erna's* crew safely at the Great Western Docks, at 02.30 hours. The *Erna* was to become a total wreck. The lifeboat crew included: F. Eagles (Second Coxswain), J. Wakeham, E. Davey, J. Watson, A. Tribble, N. Cuddeford, J. Southwood, F. Hearn, J. Reed, W. Angel, C. Butters, J. Stoneman and J. Toddard

In a newspaper interview some years later, Coxswain Fred Eagles' son, Reg, who like his brother Stan was also a member of the Plymouth lifeboat crew, recalled the fact that his father received a Vellum Certificate from Kaiser Wilhelm for saving the lives of the German crewmen of the *Erna*.

At 22.40 hours on Saturday 21 November 1914, Coxswain Dave Mumford received a message from Longroom that a steamer was aground on the rocks outside Plymouth Harbour. The crew were summoned immediately and the *Eliza Avins* launched at 23.15 hours. At that time, the tide was on the ebb, the sea was moderate and a strong breeze was blowing from the north-east. The night was exceptionally cold. Under sails and oars, the lifeboat reached the casualty, the *Veghstoom* of Amsterdam, at 00.15 hours. The steamer, bound from Fowey to Amsterdam with a cargo of china clay, was stranded between the Mew Stones. The Yealm River lifeboat, the self-righter, *Michael Smart*, was also launched and attended the scene of the stranding.

Coxswain Mumford boarded the steamer at the request of the ship's master, who asked that both lifeboats stand-by for the duration of the night. At 05.30 hours, Coxswain Mumford advised that a tug should be summoned in order to tow the vessel off; he did not, however, receive a response to his signal. At 07.30 hours, the *Veghstroom* refloated, unaided, and Coxswain Mumford remained on the bridge of the steamer with her master, with a view to taking the vessel into the Cattewater. It was found, however, that the ship's pumps were keeping pace with the intake of water and the master decided to continue with his voyage. It is interesting to note that he attributed the stranding of the *Veghstroom* to the glare of the searchlights on the lookout post. The lifeboat crew on this occasion were D. Mumford (Coxswain), F. Eagles, E. Davey, A. Tribble, F. Hearn, W. Angel, F. Foal, W. Weaver, A. Hockings, R. Eagles, C. Sprague and F. Blight.

The crew of the Plymouth lifeboat were, somewhat surprisingly, mustered for duty on only two occasions during the years of the First World War, but were not required to provide service on either occasion. The first of these was on the morning of Wednesday 17 February 1915 when, at 08.10 hours, a message was received from Looe that a steamer was in distress in Whitsand Bay. During the short time it took to muster the crew, a further communication was received, this time from the Rame Head Signal Station, stating that the steamer was at anchor, which was holding firm, near to the shore, and flying the signal NC – 'not under command'. Under these circumstances, together with the fact that she was not too far from the Looe Station, the harbour-master did not deem it necessary to launch the Plymouth lifeboat but dispatched the Admiralty tug, *Illustrious*, to her assistance.

It was subsequently established that the steamer, the *Panama*, had been steaming in convoy, down the channel, when she lost blades from her propeller and, in a heavy gale, drifted towards the shore. The lifeboat crew were stood down at 10.00 hours.

The second wartime muster took place on Friday 27 October 1916. During that day a severe south-westerly gale had set in which, with the approach of nightfall, showed every likelihood of increasing in intensity. With this forecast in mind, it was considered prudent, at 18.00 hours, to assemble the lifeboat crew in readiness for any emergency. Fortunately, the night passed without incident and the six men on watch were dismissed at 07.00 hours.

David Mumford retired as Coxswain of the Plymouth lifeboat in 1920, and was succeeded by Coxswain Frederick Eagles.

The *Eliza Avins* rendered service on Sunday 3 October 1920, when the 1,800-ton, four-masted barquentine, the *Yvonne* of Marseilles, bound from Jamaica to Havre with a cargo of logwood, fell victim to the tempestuous seas, severe gale-force winds and torrential rain which relentlessly pounded the shoreline of Plymouth. Mountainous waves crashed ashore beneath the

The Hoe and clouds of spray were driven across Grand Parade. Such were the conditions in which the *Yvonne* was driven ashore on the east side of the breakwater.

The first indication of this disaster came at 20.45 hours when distress signals from the barquentine were first sighted by a lookout at Plymouth Breakwater Fort. The lifeboat's crew were summoned and by 21.45 hours, having waited for a tug, the *Eliza Avins*, had set out on her rescue mission under the command of Coxswain Frederick Eagles. As the lifeboat battled into the teeth of the raging southerly gale, she was initially taken in tow by the harbour-master's launch. The launch itself had been damaged earlier in the storm when she had been driven against a pier head. The damage was of such severity that water had flooded her engine-room. Leading stoker Harvey did his utmost to maintain engine speed but when the opportunity arose the tow of the lifeboat was transferred to the duty tug, the *Rover*, which was under the command of the harbour-master, Commander Geoffrey Freyberg, RN.

Upon reaching the breakwater and the casualty at 22.45 hours, Coxswain Eagles and his crew were confronted by waves which were estimated to have been 30 feet in height crashing over the barquentine. By this time the vessel had been driven right onto the top of the breakwater. She was lying about 50 yards off the eastern beacon, bow to the east, but on a perfectly even keel. The gradient of the breakwater made any approach to the windward side of the vessel impossible. As the heavy sea made it impracticable for the tug to go outside the breakwater, the lifeboat proceeded under canvas. At this time the harbour-master, Commander Freyberg, transferred to the lifeboat. Conditions outside the breakwater proved atrocious so, in order to attempt a rescue, the *Eliza Avins* returned inside the structure where flares were burned to indicate to the ship's crew the proximity of the lifeboat. After careful consideration it was decided that the only possible avenue of escape for the crew of the *Yvonne* was for every man to jump into the cold, treacherous, uninviting sea and swim to the lifeboat. Thus 19 members of the crew of the Frenchman took that option, jumping first onto the breakwater and then into the sea. The crew of the *Eliza Avins* pulled, dragged and manhandled 17 of the crew into the safety of the lifeboat, whilst one man was rescued by the tug. The nineteenth crew member, a 60-year-old cook, was lost. Quite surprisingly, whilst the *Yvonne's* sails were torn to shreds the vessel escaped serious damage.

The *Eliza Avins*, in tow by the *Rover*, eventually reached Millbay at 02.15 hours, where K.H.M. Commander Freyberg gave the following account of the rescue to a representative of the *Western Morning News*:

I think the lifeboat was manned very quickly with the duty tug Rover. *We anchored the tug under the Breakwater, and then we got the lifeboat under sail and we sailed her out to the eastern entrance. There was a heavy sea running, however, and it was impossible to get alongside, so we came back again, and tacked in close to the leeside of the Breakwater, where we burnt fires. The crew of the stranded vessel saw us and clambered down the port side of their ship and they ran across the Breakwater, over which very heavy seas were breaking, finally plunging into the sea and swimming out to us in their lifebelts. We picked up 17 of the crew, and I think one was picked up by the* Rover. *One man is missing. He is the cook, 60 years of age, and I think he drifted out through the eastern entrance on the ebb tide. I have instructed the tug,* Rover, *to go out and search for him.*

At this stage Coxswain Frederick Eagles interjected, exclaiming: 'Now, you (pointing to Commander Freyberg) actually walked across the breakwater yourself.' Turning to the gathered reporters he said, in a manner that was reported to have revealed his strong admiration for the harbour-master's coolness, 'Yes he got onto the breakwater.' 'We found no one there', responded the modest Commander. It subsequently transpired that, at great personal risk, Freyberg had scrambled from the lifeboat onto the breakwater in an attempt to locate the missing ship's cook. This brave effort had been made in vain. Commander Freyberg reportedly spoke in 'glowing terms' of Coxswain Eagles and the crew of the Plymouth lifeboat.

The master of the *Yvonne*, Captain Gerhard Tannessan, expressed himself as being entirely satisfied with the way the lifeboat crew did its work, stating that 'Nothing could have been done better.' The crew were: F. Eagles, ?, Mumford, Wakeham, F. Foot, J. Watson, A. Tribble, N. Cuddeford, C. Sprague, R. Eagles, ? Goddard, ? Woodman, N. Richards and A. Hamebey.

On Tuesday 5 October 1920, Captain Robins, the Hon. Secretary of the Plymouth Lifeboat Station, received the following signal, via the harbour-master, Longroom, Stonehouse:

> *Plymouth*
> *5th October 1920*
>
> *From the First Sea Lord*
> *to the Life-Boat's Crew, Plymouth*
>
> *Accept my sincere congratulations on your conduct and the splendid services you rendered in saving the crew of the French vessel "Yvonne."*

Captain Robins replied:

> *From Hon. Secretary,*
> *Plymouth Lifeboat*
> *to The First Sea Lord*
>
> *Please accept my heartiest thanks on behalf of the crew of the Life-boat "Eliza Avins" for your appreciation of services rendered and for the kind congratulations sent.*

On Thursday 7 October 1920, the following letter appeared in the *Western Daily Mercury*:

THE WRECK OF THE YVONNE

Sir, - Will you kindly allow me, through the medium of you journal, to tender heartfelt thanks, on behalf of myself and the other survivors of the French vessel Yvonne, *for the gallant services rendered by the crews of the Plymouth Life-boat and the two tugs on Sunday night during a heavy southerly gale, whose courageous efforts resulted happily in the whole of us being safely brought ashore with the exception of our cook.*

On such an occasion, when every man gave of his best, it would be unfair to refer to individuals, and I will content myself with expressing my gratitude to all concerned.

I also wish to thank all those who so kindly came forward and gave food, clothing and hospitality when we landed.

> *Gul Tannessan.*
> *Master, French vessel* Yvonne.
> *Plymouth. October 6, 1920.*

In recognition of this outstanding service, the

Royal National Lifeboat Institution made the following awards: Thanks on Vellum to the King's Harbour-Master Commander Geoffrey H. Freyberg, OBE, RN; to Coxswain W. Williams and Leading Stoker J. Harvey, of the King's Harbour-Master's steam-launch, Thanks on Vellum, plus a 20s.0d.; Mr D. St Croix, Master of the Tug *Rover*, was awarded a Letter of Appreciation and the sum of £2; to the remainder of the crew of the steam launch and the remainder of the crew of His Majesty's tug *Rover*, a monetary award of 20s.0d. each.

His Worship, the Mayor of Plymouth, W.S. Knight, Esq., in the presence of members of the Local Board, presented the thanks of the Institution to the recipients, at the Council Chambers on Thursday 10 February 1921. For their part in this outstanding service, Coxswain Eagles and his crew received the congratulations of the Chairman of the Local Board.

The lifeboat was launched on Friday 3 March 1922 in response to a report of a vessel being ashore on the Eddystone. As the *Eliza Avins* put to sea the weather was thick and the Sound was totally enveloped in a haze.

It was at about 06.20 hours that the Rame Head Wireless Station picked up the SOS message from a vessel stating that she was ashore on the Eddystone. The stranded vessel requested the assistance of a tug. At this time the casualty had not disclosed her name. The request for assistance was telephoned to Plymouth, and the Naval authorities arranged to dispatch a tug to the scene; it was also considered advisable to launch the Plymouth lifeboat. The assembly rockets were fired at 07.05 hours and 16 minutes later the lifeboat was readied. By 07.30 hours she was away, in tow of the dockyard tug, the *Pert*.

Upon reaching the Eddystone, the tug and the lifeboat searched the area but found no trace of the stricken vessel. They then searched to the eastward, as far as Stoke Point, before returning back along the foreshore to Plymouth. Neither vessel, nor any wreckage was found.

At 09.42 hours, the Hon. Secretary of the Local Committee, Mr David Crowther, received a message from the Looe lifeboat, stating that she had returned to station with the crew of the French fishing trawler, the *Marguerite* of Boulogne. The vessel, which was stranded in Talland Bay, three miles west of Looe, was hung up amidships by rocks but was in such a position that she was expected to refloat on the evening tide. Mr Crowther commented to the *Western*

Evening Herald:

How the accident happened, of course, I don't know, but in all probability it was due to the thick weather. Apparently the skipper must have been out on his reckoning in the thick weather, as his message gave his position as being east of the Eddystone.

There were no other calls for help received, and we know that the Looe boat was first sent in the direction of the Eddystone, so that no blame can be attached to anyone but those who despatched the first message.

At 02.05 hours, on Friday 21 July 1922, the following message was received from the GPO, Plymouth:

From Lands End Wireless Station S/S Remuera Lat 50.02 North Long 3.54 West 12 miles south of Bolt Tail in collision with vessel unknown. Plymouth Life Boat assistance.

The lifeboat crew was summoned and the *Eliza Avins* was despatched. Telephone messages were also sent to the Looe and Yealm lifeboats, no reply being received from the latter. Telephone calls were also made to the Shallowborough (Challaborough?) Coastguard Station. The Hope Cove Lifeboat Station reported that their boat, the *Alexandra*, was out of service, but that the Salcombe boat, the 35-foot *Sarah Ann Holden*, had been launched. In thick fog the *Eliza Avins* made her way to the given location but the search failed to turn up any trace of the steamship. At 09.00 hours the lifeboat returned to her station.

It was ascertained later in the day that the unknown vessel, with which the *Remuera* had collided, was in fact the SS *Marengo*, bound from New York to Hull, and that the *Remuera* was outward bound from Southampton to New Zealand. Following the collision, the *Remuera* made for Portsmouth whilst the *Marengo* completed her passage.

This uneventful service was the last provided by the *Eliza Avins* in her capacity as the Plymouth lifeboat for, when inspected by the Institution's Surveyor, it was found that 'she would require some heavy repairs' to continue in service. At the committee meeting of 19 October 1922 it was reported that the *Eliza Avins* had been sent to London for the repairs to be carried out and that a temporary boat had been sent to Plymouth in her place.

The Brothers Freeman, *Plymouth's last sailing lifeboat, 1922–26.* RNLI

A lifeboat is hauled towards the Stonehouse Bridge during a fund-raising event, c.1910.
PLYMOUTH CITY MUSEUM & ART GALLERY

7

THE *BROTHERS FREEMAN*

6 SEPTEMBER 1922–1 JUNE 1926

Type: Self-Righting   *Propulsion:* Pulling-Sailing   *Oars:* 10   *Crew:* 13
Length: 35' 0"   *Beam:* 8' 6"   *Displacement:* $3^T 16^{Cwt}$
Official number: 531   *Builder:* Thames Ironworks
Launches: 2   *Lives Saved:* 2
Coxswain: Frederick Eagles

The *Eliza Avins* was succeeded by the *Brothers Freeman*, built in 1904, the cost of £800 being met from the legacy of Mr F.J. Freeman of London. The boat was re-allocated to Plymouth from the recently closed station at Littlehampton.

The first recorded launch of the *Brothers Freeman* was on Wednesday 18 October 1922, following a report, at 09.23 hours, from Land's End Wireless Station, that the SS *Royal City* was on fire, three miles south of the Eddystone. Coxswain Eagles was requested to stand-by with the lifeboat and crew. The 3,480-ton-registered SS *Royal City*, of London, which was carrying 37 persons, including four passengers, reported a fire in her No.2 hold. The lifeboat was launched at 09.50 hours into an easterly gale and heavy seas, and proceeded under sail to the casualty, meeting the steamer off Penlee Point at the entrance to the harbour. It was quickly ascertained that the fire aboard the *Royal City* was being brought under control and that the services of the lifeboat were not required. The *Brothers Freeman* returned to the boat-house at 11.00 hours.

The weather on Sunday 8 April 1923 was hazy and overcast with a strong, cold breeze blowing from the east-south-east, when the SS *Unicorn*, of Milford Haven, foundered three miles south-west of Rame Head. At 16.10 hours the policeman on duty at the main entrance to Plymouth Docks received the following message from Rame Head Wireless Station: 'Two men walking on the cliffs near the Rame Head had seen a small steamer turn over and sink, three miles S.W. of the Rame

Head.' It was added that 'a boat from the vessel with two men in her was drifting before the wind.'

The 124-ton former trawler, *Unicorn*, owned by the Hare Steamship Company of Plymouth and carrying a crew of five, was on passage from Bridgwater to Jersey with a cargo of bricks when, with a rising sea, her master, A.G. Bisson, decided to seek the safety of Plymouth Sound. However, three miles from Rame Head she was 'pooped' (overwhelmed by waves from astern) and foundered. On the authority of the station's Hon. Secretary, Mr D.J. Crowther, the *Brothers Freeman* was launched at 16.40 hours. Under sail and oars, she reached the breakwater before being taken in tow by the tug *Atlas*. The steam pilot cutter, *W. Woolven*, also made her way to the scene. Upon reaching the given location of the ship, the hopes of the lifeboat men were initially dashed as they found only wreckage and a lifebuoy bearing the name *Unicorn*. Mr Crowther, who had sailed with the lifeboat, communicated with the pilot cutter and agreed that the lifeboat would search to the westward, with a view to locating the ship's boat. At 18.00 hours spirits were lifted when, at a position six miles 'west-^{1}/$_2$-south' of Rame Head, the lifeboat came across a boat belonging to the *Unicorn* containing two members of her crew, the mate, C.S. Bisson (aged 22), and the cook, L.G. Barnes (18). Bisson was at the oars whilst Barnes was totally exhausted and had to be physically lifted into the lifeboat. The search failed to locate the remaining three members of the *Unicorn*'s crew.

The *Brothers Freeman* was again taken in tow by the *Atlas*, and returned to port at 17.45 hours, with the survivors. Those who lost their lives were: A.G. Bisson, master; J. Prettyman, chief engineer, and W. Herbert, second engineer. The lifeboat crew were: F. Eagles, F. Foot, A. Foot, R. Eagles, T. Cross, W. Richards, T. Goddard, A. Woodman, J. Cowell, F. Gosling, D.J. Crowther (Hon. Sec), A. Roberts and B. Hewsham. A local newspaper was full of praise for the prompt action of Coxswain Eagles and his crew, at the same time reporting: 'We believe that the official report, already sent to the Institution, states that she (the lifeboat) proved a sluggard in the water.' 'But for the help of the tug,' it was claimed 'she would have been too late.' The newspaper was quite correct for in the Return of Service, the report of the Hon. Secretary and the Coxswain, it was reported that the *Brothers Freeman* handled 'very well', but that it was a 'slow sailer'. Reporters also stated:

The conditions of sea and wind were favourable. Had they been unfavourable it is very probable that quite another half hour would have been lost. On the other hand, the crew are certain that with a fast motor lifeboat they would have reached their quest half an hour sooner than they did. They might, in that case, have had the chance to pick up other survivors. It is just possible that life was lost on Sunday for the lack of the motor lifeboat for which Plymouth had agitated for so long, and without which the lifesaving equipment of the port is virtually obsolete.

Following a local committee meeting, held at the Great Western Dock Offices on 12 April 1923, other local newspapers also took up the case:

Plymouth ought unquestionably to have a motor lifeboat. The very fact that the boat has to go a considerable distance to sea before, in the majority of cases, she can render any service to ships approaching the coast is in itself justification enough for the demand. The motor boats cost a great deal more than the old rowing and sailing boats, but the latter can only be now described as obsolete and cannot be regarded as an efficient protection for shipping at any port with a considerable maritime trade.

The Chairman of the Local Committee, Admiral John de M. Hutchison, commented that, 'the day of the sailing boat has passed.'

On the instructions of the station's Hon. Secretary, the Coxswain and crew were mustered at 16.00 hours on Saturday 27 October 1923, in anticipation of service requests, as a heavy south-westerly gale and high seas swept the coast. There were several vessels in the Sound, four of them 'in risky berths'. However, the services of the lifeboat were not required.

The Coxswain and crew carried out a rescue on Friday 6 November 1925 without the use of a lifeboat. It was at about 23.00 hours that the three-masted schooner yacht, the *St George* of Cowes, with David Blair as master and seven persons on board (on passage from Dartmouth–Plymouth) stranded abreast of the Plymouth lifeboat house. At the time of the incident, a strong south-south-westerly gale was blowing, accompanied by torrential rain. The lifeboat crew were assembled and a line was passed and secured to the schooner. Due to the heavy sea, and the position of rocks on the weather side of the schooner, the lifeboat crew manned a 35-foot Naval cutter in order to take a woman passenger off the *St George*. Likewise, on the lee side of the schooner, there was insufficient room in which to manoeuvre the *Brothers Freeman* without probable damage being caused. Using the cutter, the lifeboat crew refloated the schooner and re-berthed her at Plymouth.

During the time that the *Brothers Freeman* was in service at Plymouth, many were the comments regarding her lack of speed. Despite the constant appeals and protestations, the first motor lifeboat to be placed on the coast of Devon was stationed at Brixham on Saturday 18 March 1922.

Commander Hayes, the RNLI's District Inspector, attended the Local Board's Committee Meeting on 14 November 1924. In his report, the Inspector stated that he was pleased to announce that the order for a new motor lifeboat for Plymouth had been placed with Messrs White of Cowes, Isle of Wight. The Local Committee were informed at their meeting on 29 October 1925 that facilities for mooring the new motor lifeboat had been approved by the Great Western Railway Dockmaster and the Superintendent. They were also informed that, with the new boat nearing completion, a tender by Messrs Rogers of Cremyll, in the sum of £39.10s.0d., had been accepted for the provision of a 16' 0" by 5'6" boarding boat. Seven months later, the Plymouth lifeboat station was to receive its first motor lifeboat.

8

THE *ROBERT AND MARCELLA BECK*

1 JUNE 1926–21 MARCH 1943

Class: *Barnett* **Propulsion:** *2 x 76hp petrol engines* **Crew:** *8*
Speed: *9.5 knots* **Length:** *60' 0"* **Beam:** *15' 0"* **Displacement:** *44^T 4^{Cwt}*
Official number: *696* **Builder:** *J.S. White, Cowes*
Service Launches: *36* **Lives Saved:** *70*
Coxswains: *Frederick Eagles (1926–29), James Roach (1929–39), Walter Crowther (1939–43)*
Mechanics: *Charles Mallalieu (1926–35), Arthur Banham (1935–43)*

On Thursday 1 June 1926 the Plymouth Lifeboat Station received its first motorised lifeboat. The vessel had been 'laid down' in October 1924 at the shipyard of J.S. White, of Cowes, Isle of Wight. She was a 60-foot Barnett Class lifeboat, the second of four to be built for stations with a wide operating radius. Plymouth was identified as such a station as it was about to take on additional responsibilities with the impending closure of both its adjacent stations, namely Yealm River in 1927, and Looe, Cornwall, in 1930.

Funded through the legacy of Mr Robert A. Beck of Worthing, the lifeboat, which cost £14,536, was powered by two 76hp DE6 petrol engines and was capable of speeds of up to 9.5 knots. Cruising at a speed of 8 knots the Barnett could travel up to 500 miles without refuelling. The lifeboat had two cabins that could accommodate 50–60 persons. In calm conditions, she could carry up to 300 people, or up to 150 in adverse weather conditions. The new lifeboat was fitted out with several modern items of equipment, which included a searchlight, an electrical capstan, a line-throwing gun, built-in fire extinguishers and an oil spray for quelling waves around a casualty. She was additionally fitted, amidships, with a jumping net, an idea copied from the Dutch life-saving service. Being larger than her predecessors, the new boat was kept afloat on a deep-water mooring. Frederick Eagles was her first Coxswain and Charles

Mallalieu was appointed as the Plymouth Lifeboat Station's first mechanic.

The AGM of the Local Committee, over which the Mayor, James Moses, presided, was held at the Mayor's Parlour, Guildhall, on Thursday 28 October 1926. The report of the Committee included the following comments on the new lifeboat:

The old boat was taken out for her quarterly exercises up to June 1st when she was replaced by the arrival of the new motor Life Boat. This up to date and magnificent Boat is a marked improvement on the old one, for in addition to the radius she can cover, she is provided with all the latest devices for saving life and has large cabin accommodation for the comfort of crews who may be rescued.

The new Boat has been highly praised by those who have seen her and is a valuable acquisition to such an important port as Plymouth.

Although the Boat has been officially received by the Local Committee, the actual naming ceremony has been postponed until such time as the Institution can make formal arrangements.

The first recorded launch of the 'motor lifeboat' – for at that time she was unnamed – took place on Wednesday 12 January 1927. In a severe south-westerly gale, heavy seas and heavy rain, the lifeboat left her mooring at 14.18 hours following

Left: *Fund-raising in Plymouth, 1939.*

Below left: *James Roach, Coxswain of the Plymouth lifeboat 1929–39.*

Below: *The lifeboat crew on the steps of the Plymouth Guildhall following an award ceremony. Left to right, back: ?, ?, ?, Walter Crowther, ?; front: ?, James Roach, Sid Harris.* PETER CROWTHER

The Robert and Marcella Beck

The naming ceremony of the Robert and Marcella Beck, Plymouth Hoe Pier, 12 July 1927.

the receipt of a report from the Hope Cove Coastguard that distress signals had been sighted in the vicinity of the Eddystone. The lifeboat reached the Eddystone at 16.15 hours and began a thorough search. Failing to find any vessel in need of assistance, Coxswain Eagles returned the lifeboat to her mooring at 18.00 hours. The crew were: F. Eagles (Coxswain), R. Eagles, A. Foot, S. Eagles, J. Cowell, O. Kerslake and J. Shutton.

The inauguration of the lifeboat took place on Tuesday 12 July 1927, during Plymouth Week, with the Atlantic Fleet moored in the Sound. The ceremony was presided over by The Right Worshipful the Mayor of Plymouth, Alderman J.J. Hamlyn Moses, with the naming of the boat being conducted by the Countess Jellicoe of Scapa. The *Western Daily Mercury* reported:

"I name thee Robert and Marcella Beck. *God bless you and all who sail in you." With these words Lady Jellicoe performed the ceremony of naming Plymouth's new motor lifeboat. Constructed at a cost of over £14,500 the boat is capable of carrying to safety 150 persons, exclusive of crew, in even the worst weather.*

This practically unsinkable super-boat was the centre of attraction for huge crowds who thronged the Pier and front to watch the proceedings which were opened by the Mayor. Among the company were Mr. George F. Shee, general secretary of the National Lifeboat Institution, and Chief Inspector Capt. Howard F. J. Rowley who gave a description of the craft. The boat was dedicated by the Bishop of Exeter, and others present included Lady Astor M.P., Sir Arthur Shirley Benn M.P. and the Commander-in-Chief at Devonport Admiral Sir Rudolph Bentinck. A special choir, conducted by Mr. David Parkes, and a naval band helped to make the ceremony all the more impressive. It was an inspiring moment when the lifeboat, having been named and dedicated, sprang into life and moving swiftly out into the harbour, fired her guns and rockets. Meanwhile the great crowd cheered lustily and the ships in the Sound and pleasure craft sounded their sirens and hooters. When the jubilation ceased there could be heard the voices of Mr. Parkes' choir singing a sea shanty. The Mayor spoke of the importance of the event to the town and referred to the great strides that science had made in the construction of lifeboats. The hymn "Eternal Father, strong to save" followed.

Mr George Shee, General Secretary of the RNLI, in the absence of Sir Godfrey Baring, Bart. (Chairman of the Institution's Committee of Management), presented the boat to the Plymouth branch and had no hesitation in saying that it was the finest lifeboat in the world. The lifeboat was accepted by Chairman of the branch, Admiral Hutchison, who undertook that it would, at all times, be ready for immediate service, so far as was humanly possible. Captain Howard F.J. Rowley, Chief Inspector, gave the following description of the qualities of the new lifeboat:

A lifeboat must be a superboat. She must be self-baling, unsinkable, and her motors must be amphibious. Her length was 60-feet, with a 15-feet beam, and she drew 4ft. 4" of water, her displacement being 44-tons. She was driven by two 6-cylinder internal combustion petrol engines of 76 b.h.p. giving a speed of 9.5 knots. She was built of two thicknesses of teak, worked diagonally, divided into five watertight compartments, these again being sub-divided by buoyant air cases. There were 15 main compartments and 100 minor compartments. Even if severely damaged, and badly holed, she would remain afloat and manageable and her engines would continue functioning although submerged, provided, of course, the air inlets remained above water.

In a heavy sea, the *Robert and Marcella Beck* was taken out to the lighthouse and, reportedly, 'cruised about in such a way as to give every satisfaction to the coxswain and crew.'

A strong south-westerly breeze and rain squalls were whipping up a rough sea on Tuesday 14 February 1928, when, at 12.40 hours, the following telephone message was received from the stations at Looe and Penzance:

Following received from British steamer Leighton, *begins – "Steamer* Burnside *in distress position 66 miles south and 16 miles west from Eddystone wishes tugs to stand-by for the present."*

At 13.23 hours a further message was received from Penzance:

Following from S/S Leighton – Burnside *reports forward Top Tank leaking – considerably down by the head.* Burnside *not under control but is steaming – appears unable to steer.*

A third message, received at 13.30 hours, read: 'From Commander-in-Chief at Looe – *Burnside* appears to be in sinking position.'

The *Robert and Marcella Beck* left her moorings at 13.50 hours, reaching a position 16 miles south-west of the Eddystone at 17.00 hours. The exact course of the *Burnside* being unclear, the lifeboat had been launched, with the authority of the Hon. Secretary, in order to intercept the steamer, assuming that she had been steaming towards Plymouth. This, however, was not the case and the *Robert and Marcella Beck* returned to her station at 20.45 hours without having rendered service.

On Wednesday 24 October 1928, Sir Godfrey Baring, Bart., Chairman of the Committee of Management of the RNLI, presented to the Mayor, Mr W.H.J. Priest, on behalf of the local branch of the Institution, a framed Vellum commemorating 100 years of service of the Plymouth lifeboats. Alderman R.R. Oke, Chairman of the Public Libraries and Art Gallery Committee, accepted the Vellum, which had been signed by the Prince of Wales. The Vellum was to be hung in the City Library. Sir Godfrey Baring read a memorandum sketching the history of the Plymouth lifeboats, saying:

There have been seven lifeboats in the port, they were launched for service 73 times, and effected the rescue of 134 lives. One of them, the Prince Consort, *was the means of saving 60 lives at various times.*

The Mayor, acknowledging the gift of the Vellum, expressed his admiration of the work of the Institution, and said: 'Even in Plymouth there are people who ask, "What is the use of a lifeboat?"'

The first effective service to be provided by the *Robert and Marcella Beck* took place on Friday 16 November 1928, when she went to the assistance of the 758-ton steamer *Kentish Town*, which was bound from Teignmouth to Bristol, with 13 people aboard. It was at 12.45 hours that a report was received from the harbourmaster, stating that in a strong south-westerly gale a steamer belonging to Coast Lines Ltd was in difficulty in Jennycliffe Bay. Within five minutes of this report being received at the lifeboat station, the *Kentish Town* put up a distress signal. The lifeboat crew were summoned, and slipped moorings at 13.00 hours. The *Robert and Marcella Beck* set out into the gale and heavy rain, arriving at the stranded vessel at 13.45 hours. Due to the shallow depth of water, on an

ebbing tide, the lifeboat experienced great difficulty in approaching the steamer. Coxswain Eagles found it necessary to deploy both his port and starboard anchors and by letting out 50 fathoms of cable veered the lifeboat down on to the *Kentish Town*. The *Robert and Marcella Beck* was within 10 feet of the casualty when her starboard anchor cable parted. By skilful boat handling, Coxswain Fred Eagles held the lifeboat on her port cable and prevented a collision between the two vessels.

At the same time, a local rocket-apparatus team established a line and, with the use of a Breeches buoy, took off six members of the crew, leaving the captain and a further six crewmen to be rescued. Coxswain Eagles eventually succeeded in manoeuvring the lifeboat right up to the steamer, allowing the crewmen to leap into the lifeboat's jumping net. The captain, for his part, attempted to jump onto the gunwale of the lifeboat but in so doing he slipped and was in danger of dropping between the hulls of the two vessels. Fortunately his fall was broken by the lifeboat's Bowman Briggs, who sustained a nasty gash to the forehead as he caught him.

The *Robert and Marcella Beck* returned to her mooring at 14.45 hours but did not return from this service completely unscathed; she sustained damage to her starboard bulwark, starboard anchor and to the brake band on the cable wheel. Part of her starboard cable was lost, as was one L.T. gun projectile.

The Plymouth lifeboat rendered outstanding service on Tuesday 12 February 1929, when under the command of Coxswain Frederick Eagles she answered the distress calls of the SS *Deventia*. At 02.10 hours, Coxswain Eagles received the message from the Hope Cove Coastguard, 'Steamer ashore near Bolt Head.' This location is 18 miles to the east of the Plymouth boat-house. Coxswain Eagles immediately contacted the Hon. Secretary, Mr G. Scantlebury, who in turn communicated with the Hon. Secretaries of both the Hope Cove and Brixham Lifeboat Stations. The Secretary of the Brixham station informed Mr Scantlebury that he was doubtful as to whether the presence of the Torbay boat was required; the Secretary was also informed that the Hope Cove boat could not attend, as a crew could not be raised, due to sickness. After further discussion with Brixham, Mr Scantlebury authorised the launch of the *Robert and Marcella Beck*, the lifeboat slipping her mooring at 03.10 hours.

Coxswain Eagles and his crew took the lifeboat into heavy seas, which were fuelled by a strong, bitterly cold, east-south-easterly gale-force wind and accompanied by snow squalls. For over two-and-a-half hours the lifeboat fought her way doggedly through the raging seas, slowly gaining ground towards the stranded vessel. Having reached Bolt Head, due to the increasing ferocity of the weather, it was 05.45 hours before the *Deventia* was located.

The 800-ton SS *Deventia*, of Worthington, commanded by Master T. Kelly and carrying a crew of 13, was bound for London from Fleetwood, with a cargo of soda, when she was driven onto rocks below Bolt Head. A line to the *Deventia* had been established by the Hope Cove rocket-apparatus team, who took off three members of her crew. Now in truly horrendous weather and sea conditions, Coxswain Eagles commenced his approach to the steamer, which was sheltered to a degree by the lee of the headland, but filling rapidly with seawater and lying in a very dangerous and precarious position. The lifeboat was taken into the comparatively calm waters in the lee of the steamer, Coxswain Eagles holding the vessel steady in order to allow the remaining ten members of the *Deventia*'s crew to jump into the life-saving net. The crew were landed at Plymouth at 09.00 hours, when they were handed into the charge of the Shipwrecked Mariners Society. During the rescue the *Robert and Marcella Beck* performed 'splendidly throughout', although the boat sustained damage to one stanchion and a wire fastening was carried away. One deck rope was also lost.

For his outstanding leadership and seamanship, Coxswain Eagles received a Thanks on Vellum. It was noted at the Committee Meeting, of 10 June 1929, that a further monetary award, of £1, had been made to the Coxswain and each member of the crew, which consisted of: F. Eagles (Coxswain), C. Mallalieu, R. Parsons, A. Foot, S. Eagles, G. Freeman, O. Kerslake and F. Lang.

At the AGM of the Local Committee, held on Friday 11 October 1929, the newly appointed District Inspector, Lieut. Com. Wheeler, was introduced to the meeting. He said that he was endeavouring to have the Plymouth lifeboat equipped with wireless telephony:

The Plymouth lifeboat is one of four sister ships. On one of them wireless telephony has been installed, but it is at an experimental stage at present.

Frederick Eagles retired, upon reaching age limit as Coxswain of the Plymouth lifeboat, at the end of 1929. His departure was marked suitably:

Coxswain Eagles, I have the greatest possible pleasure in presenting you with the Certificate of Merit. May it bring to you in years to come happy memories which will remind you of the many years of faithful service rendered on behalf of those in peril on the sea.

With these words the Mayor of Plymouth, Alderman James Churchward, expressed the appreciation of the RNLI for the dedication of Frederick Eagles, who had completed 45 years' continuous service with the Plymouth lifeboat. When making the presentation, at the Council Chambers, the Mayor said:

Coxswain Eagles was an ideal man for his job – genial, conscientious, alive to the responsibility of his position, holding the respect of his crew, and yet maintaining that authority and discipline always particularly important in extreme and difficult circumstances.

Coxswain Eagles was also awarded an annual pension of £11.16s.3d. James Roach succeeded Frederick Eagles as Coxswain.

The first service to which Coxswain James Roach responded took place in the early hours of Sunday 10 August 1930. The Hon. Secretary received a telephone call from the harbour-master at 02.00 hours, reporting that two small launches belonging to RAF Mount Batten, which in turn were towing two whalers, were overdue. The small fleet of vessels had left the River Yealm the previous evening, since which time they had not been sighted. Signals were exchanged between the breakwater and the Forts until 03.30 hours when the Air Service Authority at Batten sent out a launch with instructions to carry out a search. The launch failed to locate the missing craft. There was that night a dense fog in the Channel and at 03.40 hours the lookout on the breakwater reported that the fog had lifted slightly and they had sighted what appeared to be distress signals off the Mew Stone. The *Robert and Marcella Beck* was launched at 04.00 hours and made her way directly to the Mew Stone, where the missing fleet was located, anchored in a very dangerous position, but safe and well. The lifeboat escorted the small craft, with their party of 40 persons, into the safety of RAF Mount Batten.

As was widely predicted, during 1930 the RNLI closed the stations at Hope Cove and Looe. The area of operation of the Plymouth lifeboat now extended from Bolt Head in the east to Fowey in the west. With a full-speed radius of 200 miles, this was well within her capabilities.

Coxswain James Roach and his crew were at the forefront of an excellent service that took place on Saturday 20 September 1930, and which culminated in the rescue of 18 persons from the 4,950-ton steamer, the *Umberleigh*, of London. Under the command of Captain Penn and owned by W.J. Tatum Ltd, Cardiff, she was in ballast from Antwerp to the Barry Roads, and making her passage in south-south-westerly winds that were reported to have reached 80 miles per hour. The seas were exceptionally heavy and visibility was poor in torrential rain.

At 03.10 hours the police received a report that distress signals had been seen off Bovisand. The lifeboat crew were immediately placed on stand-by and communication was established with the Breakwater Fort. There the lookout reported that they had not observed the distress signals, but they did report that their funnel was on fire and believed that this could have been mistaken for distress signals. The informant was contacted; he was so emphatic that he had seen distress signals that the Hon. Secretary authorised the launch of the lifeboat. The *Robert and Marcella Beck* left her mooring at 03.30 hours and, in the dark and extremely poor visibility, carried out a search for a possible casualty. It was not until 04.45 hours that Coxswain Roach located the *Umberleigh* stranded on the rocks of Bovisand Bay. Coxswain James Roach established communication with Captain Penn who asked the lifeboat to stand-by.

In 56–63-knot winds, heavy rain and mountainous seas, Roach and his crew held the *Robert and Marcella Beck* on station until daybreak. At that time Captain Penn suggested that the lifeboat should make for port and return to the *Umberleigh*, on the next tide, at 13.00 hours. The lifeboat commenced her journey to Plymouth.

At 09.30 hours a telephone message was received, from Land's End, stating that the *Umberleigh* was requesting the immediate assistance of the lifeboat as the ship was to be abandoned. Coxswain Roach and his crew once more put to seas into the teeth of the gale and returned to the stranded vessel, coming alongside at 09.45 hours. With great determination the lifeboat was manoeuvred into a position from which a line could be established between the lifeboat and the steamer. With the use of a breeches buoy, Coxswain James Roach and his crew successfully took off 18 members of the *Umberleigh's* crew, whom they landed at the Great Western Dock at 12.00 hours.

The lifeboat was launched once again to the *Umberleigh* at 16.30 hours. On this occasion she stood-by, as the steamer was refloated with the aid of tugs. *The Robert and Marcella Beck* finally returned to her mooring at 17.30 hours. In the Return of Service, the Hon. Secretary wrote the following entry:

Excellent service was rendered by every man. For four hours they were standing-by the vessel on a lee shore with terrific seas. It was impossible to anchor with safety but the boat was so well handled that practically no damage has to be recorded.

The crew of the Plymouth lifeboat saved three lives on the evening of Sunday 22 November 1931, when they went to the assistance of the yacht, the *Sus*, of Cowes. A cold, gale-force wind was blowing from the south-east when at 18.33 hours the Rame Head Coastguard telephoned the lifeboat station to report a vessel sending up flares and apparently out of control four miles west-south-west of Rame Head.

At 18.55 hours the lifeboat slipped her moorings and headed into the raging seas. One-and-a-half hours later, with the use of flares and her searchlight, the lifeboat located the *Sus*, a schooner yacht of 100-tons, on passage from Falmouth to Plymouth with three hands and commanded by its owner F.J. Brimley. The crew of the schooner were obviously suffering from exposure and exhaustion and, it subsequently transpired, had given up all hope of rescue.

In the angry seas, Coxswain Roach approached the yacht, as he suspected she was not under control and appeared to be totally waterlogged. Using the lifeboat's line-throwing apparatus, a line and tow were established. At one point, one member of the yacht's crew, the deck hand William Conister, fell overboard but was quickly pulled to safety. With the *Sus* in tow, Coxswain Roach set a course for Plymouth, landing the crew and mooring their vessel at 23.59 hours. Coxswain James Roach told a reporter of the *Western Morning News*:

It was a very stormy night at sea, and we had

a wild passage down Channel, there being a high following wind.

We fell in with the Sus *about ten miles west-south-west of Rame Head. At that time the yacht was rolling heavily, and her masts were at times nearly touching the water. Her canvas had been housed, and she was just able to keep her head to sea by her auxiliary engine.*

The sea was too rough for the lifeboat to venture alongside without the risk of damaging both craft so communication was effected by firing a rocket. Then we got a tow rope to her to bring the ship to Plymouth. So rough was the sea on the way up Channel, and in spite of all the care we exercised, the yacht's lifeboat swept away from its davits, and it was impossible to do anything to recover it. At 11 o'clock the Sus *was safely mooring.*

Crew of the Robert and Marcella Beck. *Left to right: J. Roach (Coxswain), George Stanbury, Arthur Foot, Sid Harris, ?, Walter Crowther.*

Paying tribute to the lifeboat crew, the skipper of the *Sus*, Mr Brimley, said:

I thought we were done, but we have wrestled through. Your lifeboat crew are great. I never thought they would be able to tow us home when our engine 'conked out'. It was a fine bit of seamanship.

The next service provided by the *Robert and Marcella Beck* also took place in the vicinity of the Eddystone. The harbour-master reported receiving a signal that Hope Cove Coastguard had sighted flares two miles inshore of the Eddystone, at 20.35 hours on Thursday 27 October 1932. As Coxswain Roach was assembling his crew, at 20.50 hours, a second message was received from the Hope Cove lookout reporting distress signals five miles 'south-½-east' of Stoke Head. The Plymouth lifeboat was launched at 21.05 hours into a west-north-westerly gale that carried heavy rain. For one-and-a-half hours the *Robert and Marcella Beck* battled her way through violent seas, which were running on an ebb tide, eventually reaching the wreck at 22.35 hours. The casualty was the 150-ton auxiliary ketch, the *Millom Castle*, under the

command of Captain Thomas from Swansea, with a cargo of loam; she carried a crew of three. It immediately became apparent to Coxswain Roach that the vessel was waterlogged and in danger of foundering, the vessel's engine had failed, her mast had broken and her sails had been carried away. The *Millom Castle* was totally at the mercy of the sea. Captain Thomas requested that all persons be taken off the vessel by the lifeboat.

In terrific seas, which swept over the lifeboat drenching the crew, James Roach approached the *Millom Castle* only to find that the tangle of mast, rigging and spars prevented a rescue attempt from being made on the lee side of the vessel. He was therefore compelled to approach the casualty from the windward side. As the lifeboat closed on the ketch, the sea threw the two vessels together, the lifeboat having her portside bow fender ripped off. At great personal risk to both himself and his crew, in exceedingly difficult conditions, Coxswain Roach held his boat steady as the three-man crew leapt from the ketch to the safety of the *Robert and Marcella Beck*. The *Millom Castle* was abandoned.

On the return journey the lifeboat had to head into the teeth of the gale, the boat constantly being swept from bow to stern by the heavy seas, which at times threatened to overwhelm her. The *Robert and Marcella Beck* withstood her trial and regained her mooring at 00.45 hours. For this excellent service, the RNLI awarded Coxswain James Roach their Thanks on Vellum.

It was at 07.45 hours on Saturday 18 February 1933 that a report was received from the harbour-master stating that the Yealm Coastguard had reported a vessel apparently flying distress signals three miles south-west of the Mew Stone. The Plymouth station's Hon. Secretary immediately contacted the Yealm, breakwater and Rame lookouts, all of whom stated that they were uncertain of the nature of the flags. At 08.15 hours the Direction Finding Station, at Wembury, reported that they could see a vessel, which was in considerable trouble, with her mainsail lying over the side. The lifeboat crew was assembled and, on an exceedingly cold day with a snowstorm being carried on an east-north-easterly gale-force wind, the lifeboat slipped her mooring at 08.40 hours. Upon reaching the distressed vessel at 09.40 hours, it was found that she was the ketch *Ethel Edith* of Faversham, under the command of Captain R.G. Jackson. The 93-ton vessel, which was carrying a crew of four plus the captain's wife, was riding at anchor, her sails being totally blown out. As the crew of the ketch were totally exhausted Captain Jackson requested Coxswain Roach to place members of the lifeboat crew on board his vessel to assist his crew. The lifeboat men who were placed upon the ketch found the working conditions very difficult indeed, on account of the very heavy seas that were running. Two anchors had to be raised, one with 60 fathoms of cable and the other with 40 fathoms, this operation alone taking three hours.

The *Ethel Edith* was towed to Plymouth by the *Robert and Marcella Beck*, and after an exhausting service the crew of five were landed safely at 13.45 hours.

Two members of the Plymouth lifeboat crew had a very lucky escape on Sunday 14 January 1934, following a report of distress rockets being sighted six miles south-east of Rame Head. On a bitterly cold night, in strong south-westerly, gale-force winds, the *Robert and Marcella Beck* was launched at 23.50 hours and proceeded to the casualty in very heavy seas. When east of the Eddystone, at about 01.00 hours, Coxswain Roach and his crew sighted a flare about two miles south-east of the lifeboat. A search made of the area revealed surface litter but no vessel was found. The search continued for a further one-and-a-half hours but the source of the flare was not located.

It was on the return journey, in mountainous seas, that the *Robert and Marcella Beck* was swamped and two of her crew members washed overboard. Thankfully, their colleagues quickly rescued the men and the lifeboat safely reached port at 03.30 hours.

Over the next two years the Plymouth lifeboat was launched for service on only three occasions, her next service of note taking place on Thursday 9 January 1936. The vessel requiring assistance was the Dutch motor boat, *Zeehond*, bound with a crew of six from Southampton to Plymouth, with a cargo of timber. The first indication of trouble came at 16.30 hours when the vessel was sighted, showing distress signals, off Bolt Head. The Salcombe, and former Torbay,

motor lifeboat, the *Alfred and Clara Heath* (ON 672), was launched at 17.00 hours but, in the prevailing weather conditions, a strong south-westerly gale accompanied by heavy rain, found that she was unable to safely cross the infamous Salcombe Bar. At 17.25 hours the Plymouth lifeboat, the *Robert and Marcella Beck*, and the Torbay Barnett Class lifeboat, the *George Shee* (ON 734, Coxswain W. Mogridge, see *A History of the Torbay Lifeboats*) were launched. Having battled through violent seas, with a following sea, the *Robert and Marcella Beck* was the first lifeboat to reach the casualty, exactly two hours later.

The 250-ton *Zeehond* had lost her engines and her captain requested that his crew should be taken off. The lifeboat made several approaches with a view to carrying out this request, but the captain subsequently changed his mind and further approaches were abandoned. In exceedingly demanding conditions, James Roach held the lifeboat on stand-by until 07.10 hours the following morning, by which time the *Zeehond's* engineers had succeeded in repairing her engines. Having effected the repairs, her captain indicated his intention to make for Salcombe Harbour but in raising his anchors both cables parted and the anchors were lost. The Plymouth lifeboat escorted the *Zeehond* to the entrance of Salcombe Harbour, where she was safely moored. The *Robert and Marcella Beck* was back on station at 10.10 hours on Friday 10 January, the service having lasted some 17 hours. The Hon. Secretary made the following entry in the Return of Service:

Our lifeboat had a very trying experience. The weather conditions were exceptionally bad and after 12 hours buffeting in terrific seas alongside the distressed vessel they started their return journey in the teeth of a strong gale and tremendous seas. Coxswain and Crew are to be congratulated on a magnificent piece of work under most extreme conditions.

Signalman Saegent had a narrow escape from being washed overboard but was grabbed just in time by the Coxswain.

The crew on this occasion were: J. Roach (Coxswain), W. Crowther (Second Coxswain), F. Crowl, S. Harris, F. Harris, W. Saegent, A. Banham and J. Hignett.

In April 1937 a relief lifeboat, the *Hearts of Oak*, temporarily replaced the *Robert and Marcella Beck*. The relief boat's first recorded service launch took place on Friday 9 April 1937, when it went to the assistance of the yacht *Janette*. The Yealm Coastguard raised the alarm at 21.40 hours when the *Janette* was reported overdue. It was known that the vessel had passed the breakwater at 17.55 hours, making for the Yealm, but since that time the yacht had not been seen. A strong southerly gale was blowing and a moderate sea was running.

As enquiries made with the breakwater, Cawsand and other coastal stations revealed that the yacht had not been located, the *Hearts of Oak* was launched and left Plymouth at 23.00 hours for the River Yealm. Given the conditions, Coxswain Roach was instructed to search Cawsand and the adjacent coastline. A seaward search was also carried out in case the yacht had drifted out to sea. The agreed search area failed to locate the missing vessel and the lifeboat returned to her mooring at 03.30 hours.

The *Janette* was located at daybreak when she was found, anchored, near Gara Point. She had suffered engine failure but had been unable to indicate her position, as she had not been carrying lights.

In 1939, upon the retirement of James Roach, Walter Crowther was promoted from Second Coxswain to Coxswain of the Plymouth lifeboat.

The first service performed by the Plymouth station during the Second World War occurred on Thursday 7 December 1939 when the *Hearts of Oak* was launched in support of the Salcombe lifeboat, the Watson Class *Samuel and Marie Parkhouse* (ON 805). Early on that December morning, the 6,000-ton steamer *Louis Sheid*, belonging to the Belgian National Shipping Line, was homeward bound for Antwerp. The steamer carried a crew of 46 and a cargo of grain. Whilst off the coast of South Devon the crew of the *Louis Sheid* saw the Dutch passenger liner, the *Tajandoen*, sinking, the vessel having either been the target of a U-boat attack, or having struck a mine. Some of the crew and passengers of the *Tajandoen* had taken to the ship's boats and the steamer rescued 62 such survivors. The *Louis Sheid* then sought the shelter of the coastline, in an attempt to distance herself from prowling U-boats, but with the absence of shore lighting, and in poor visibility brought about by heavy rain squalls, she ran onto rocks near Thurlestone. Mr J.H. Jarvis, former Coxswain of the Hope Cove lifeboat, witnessed the grounding and immediately raised the alarm at Salcombe. The Salcombe lifeboat, the *Samuel and Marie Parkhouse*,

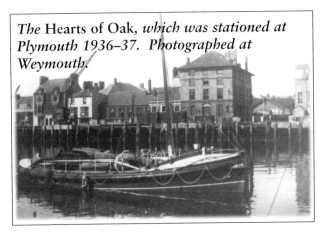

The Hearts of Oak, *which was stationed at Plymouth 1936–37. Photographed at Weymouth.*

was launched under the command of Coxswain Edwin Distin and, at 21.18 hours, the *Hearts of Oak*, under the command of Coxswain William Crowther, was launched at Plymouth. The Plymouth lifeboat reached the casualty at 23.15 hours.

The Salcombe lifeboat was first to reach the *Louis Sheid* and found her to be stuck fast on a reef, although her captain had her engines turning full ahead in an attempt to refloat the vessel. In atrocious seas and weather conditions, the *Samuel and Marie Parkhouse* anchored and Coxswain Distin veered the lifeboat down on to the *Louis Sheid*, but attempts to come alongside the windward side of the vessel were thwarted by rocks. By veering down on her port side Coxswain Distin discovered a small amount of shelter, and tied up alongside, the lifeboat rising and falling an estimated 25 feet on the seas. It was then that Coxswain Distin dicovered the true scale of the rescue that was to be undertaken. Realising that several journeys would be required, Distin signalled his intention to land the survivors at Hope Cove. The first 40 persons were taken off, all of whom came from the *Tajandoen*. Distin was met by a party of local fishermen, in a 16-foot boat, in which the survivors were ferried ashore.

Upon returning to the casualty, it was found that she had moved her position and was now head-on to the waves, providing no shelter whatsoever for the lifeboat. Showing great skill and determination Distin made another approach to the steamer and, with great difficulty, took off the remaining 22 Dutchmen, all of whom were landed in the same way. When the Salcombe lifeboat returned to the *Louis Sheid* for a third time it was found that a line had been established by the local rocket-apparatus team and the ship's captain had decided that, if it proved necessary, his crew would be taken off by this method.

Throughout this rescue the *Hearts of Oak* and the Plymouth lifeboat crew had supported the Salcombe lifeboat. Both lifeboats stood-by the *Louis Sheid* until morning when, with an improvement in the weather conditions, they returned to their respective stations, the *Hearts of Oak* regaining her mooring at 11.00 hours.

For his part in this difficult and protracted rescue, Coxswain Edwin Distin of Salcombe was awarded the RNLI's Silver Medal, and each member of his crew was awarded a Bronze Medal. The crew of the Plymouth boat were: Coxswain Crowther, Second Coxswain Holmes, Bowman Curtis, G. Stanbury, A. Banham, ? McMoran and A. Foot.

The *Robert and Marcella Beck* was launched at 03.38 hours on Thursday 13 January 1942, following a report from the harbour-master that distress flares were being seen in Jennycliffe Bay. Coxswain Crowther took the lifeboat out into heavy rain and a very rough sea, which was being aggravated by a strong south-south-westerly wind. On reaching Jennycliffe Bay, at 04.00 hours, Coxswain Crowther found that a Sunderland Flying Boat, of the Royal Australian Air Force, based at RAF Mount Batten, had fired the distress flares. The Sunderland lay in an exceedingly dangerous position, very close to the Batten reef, with waves rebounding off the cliff face and breaking over her fuselage. The aircraft had been carried away from her mooring by a motor coaster, which in the surging seas had dragged her own moorings. Wireless communication with the Naval authorities revealed that there were in fact two crewmen aboard the seaplane. The authorities requested that the lifeboat should, if possible, tow the aircraft to a safe anchorage. With great difficulty, Coxswain Crowther approached the seaplane but, as he could not communicate with the crew, he returned to Mount Batten and took on a Royal Air Force officer.

Returning to the Sunderland, which was now in imminent danger of breaking up, with great skill and in horrendous conditions, Coxswain Crowther approached the aircraft on three separate occasions, each time allowing a crewman to throw the weighted heaving line to the aircraft crew. On two occasions the line parted and on the third the rough seas prohibited the aircraft's crew from holding onto it. However, a line was established and with the aircrew remaining on board, the *Robert and Marcella Beck* towed the flying boat to the safety of the Cattewater. The lifeboat returned to her station at 07.12 hours.

The Wing Commander of RAF Mount Batten expressed his gratitude for the service provided by the Plymouth lifeboat, wishing to put on record his admiration for the work carried out by the crew. The Wing Commander acknowledged that the RAF launches could not possibly have carried out the work.

For this outstanding service, Coxswain Walter Crowther was awarded the RNLI's Bronze Medal, with the Thanks of the Institution on Vellum being awarded to each of his eight-man crew, which included: A. Sleeman (Second Coxswain), W. Lillicrap (Bowman), E. Curtis, G. Stanbury, F. Fowler, A. Banham (Mechanic), A. Foot and L. Holmes. HRH The Duke of Kent, President of the RNLI, presented the awards at the Guildhall, Plymouth, on Saturday 11 July 1942. Sadly, this was the last meeting between the Duke and the lifeboat service, for he was killed in a car crash just seven weeks later.

Not surprisingly, given the fact that it was wartime, the next two launches of the *Robert and Marcella Beck* were to assist aircraft in distress. The first launch took place on Monday 2 March 1942, when, at 07.14 hours, in thick fog, an RAF Sunderland flying boat was reported to have been 'forced down', six miles south of the Plymouth breakwater. The lifeboat proceeded to the given location at 07.35 hours, but whilst en route, received a wireless message amending the location of the casualty to eight miles south of Stoke Point. At 08.25 hours a second message was received, from the harbour-master, ordering the lifeboat to return to port. It was subsequently made clear, unofficially, that a second seaplane had undertaken the rescue.

Only eight days later, the *Robert and Marcella Beck* was launched, at 05.15 hours on Tuesday 10 March, upon the receipt of a message from the Duty Commander, Mount Wise, reporting that a damaged aircraft, type unknown, was to attempt to 'land' in the Sound. One can assume that the aircraft was probably a seaplane. At 07.50 hours Coxswain Crowther received a wireless message instructing him to return to his moorings. No explanation was given for this order but it was believed that the aircraft had 'landed' elsewhere.

On 21 March 1943, the *Robert and Marcella Beck* left Plymouth for an overhaul. Upon completion of this work, she was requisitioned by the Royal Navy and sent to Iceland to carry out rescue duties on the hazardous northern convoy route to Russia. She was not to return to her home station of Plymouth for nearly four years.

9

MINISTRE ANSEELE

MAY 1943–APRIL 1946

Class: Watson (modified)   **Propulsion:** 2 x 60hp 6cyl Maybach petrol engines (with auxiliary sails)

Speed: 9 knots   **Length:** 14m   **Beam:** 3.82m   **Displacement:** 16.15 tons

Official number: 845   **Built:** 1926, Germany   **Crew:** 8

Service Launches: 6   **Lives Saved:** 6

Coxswain: Walter Crowther
Mechanic: Arthur Banham

The *Ministre Anseele* was a Watson Class 'cabin type' lifeboat, which had been built in Germany to modified specifications for the Belgian lifeboat service. In September 1940 the lifeboat was found by one of His Majesty's ships, derelict and drifting off Weymouth, and was taken into Portsmouth. The vessel had apparently escaped from German-occupied Ostend, but the fate of her crew is unknown. The matter was communicated to the exiled Belgian Government, who placed the *Ministre Anseele* at the disposal of the RNLI, free of charge, for the war years.

Following repair in January 1941, the lifeboat was sent, in April, to Douglas, Isle of Man, on temporary duty. In September 1941 she was transferred to Donaghadee (Northern Ireland), once again returning to Douglas in a temporary capacity during November 1941. In December 1941 she was refitted and subsequently, in 1942, carried out temporary duties in Wales at Pwllheli and Holyhead. For her last period of temporary duty she was placed on station at Appledore, North Devon. The lifeboat underwent a further overhaul in October 1942 and in February 1943 the *Ministre Anseele* took up permanent duties at Plymouth.

During the period of the Second World War, Plymouth, in common with all Naval bases, saw a vast increase in shipping. Ships of many Allied nations used the port and there was a constant flow of small craft and patrols criss-crossing the Sound. Many minor rescues were carried out by these craft, alleviating the necessity of launching the lifeboat. Information relating to lifeboat rescues for this period is somewhat scant, primarily due to reporting restrictions, but some records have been traced, which provide a flavour of wartime service.

The first call to be undertaken by the *Ministre Anseele* took place on Sunday 13 August 1943, when in a south-westerly wind and heavy swell the lifeboat responded to a report of a boat and two men being marooned near the Mew Stone on the Rennie Rocks. The lifeboat slipped her mooring at 00.20 hours under the command of Coxswain Walter Crowther, who, having local knowledge of the rocky foreshore at the given location, decided to take the boarding boat in tow. Upon reaching the casualty, at 01.00 hours, the lifeboat crew found Army engineers from the War Department vessels, *Brigadier* and *Grey Lady*, stranded on the rocks. The engineers had been in the process of salvaging a small boat when they became trapped.

The lifeboat crew used the boarding boat to veer down from the lifeboat to the stranded men. In a heavy swell, which was breaking on the rocks, the lifeboat men managed to establish a line between the boarding boat and that of the engineers. The line being secured, they were pulled clear of the rocks by the *Ministre Anseele*, the men and their craft being reunited with their parent vessels at the Barbican at 03.00 hours. The crew for this rescue were: W.D. Crowther

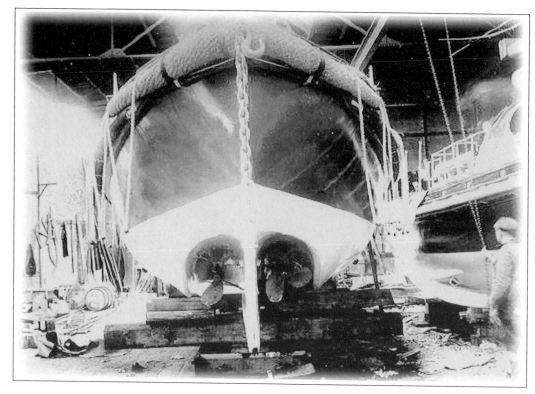

Above: *The fitting out of the German-built, modified 'Watson' type lifeboat, the* Ministre Anseele, *c.1926.*

Right: *Coxswain Walter Crowther.*

Below: *The wartime crew of the former Belgian lifeboat the* Ministre Anseele.

(Coxswain), A. Sleeman (Second Coxswain), W. Lillicrap (Bowman), E. Curtis, F. Fowler, G. Stanbury, A. Banham and L. Holmes.

The hand of fate dictated that, on Sunday 11 February 1945, the *Ministre Anseele* would be launched to go to the assistance of a fellow countryman, the Belgian vessel, SS *Persier*. Built at Newcastle in 1918 by the Northumberland Ship Building Co., she was originally named the *War Buffalo*, the name change occurring when she was acquired by the Belgian Maritime Co. During the years 1918–39, the 5,030-ton vessel undertook 74 voyages, trading throughout the world. In May 1940, the *Persier* was requisitioned for duties at Dunkirk.

The change in her duties, from cargo ship to transport ship, brought with it a change in her fortunes. At Christmas 1940, whilst moored at Oban, Scotland, she was bombed by German aircraft. Two bombs exploded close to her stern, inflicting damage to her hull. Unfortunately the extent and seriousness of the damage was not identified until leaks occurred during a passage to Baltimore, USA. During her return voyage, whilst laden with steel, she fell behind the convoy. Alone in the Atlantic, her cargo shifted, leaving her at the mercy of the heavy seas which, having caused extensive damage to the vessel, finally drove her ashore on the Icelandic coast. The *Persier* was in Iceland for 14 months, whilst temporary repairs were made. Once seaworthy, she was towed to Yarrow. Fully repaired, the *Persier* returned to service, only to face the proposal of being sunk as a block ship for the Normandy landings in 1944; however, she received a last-minute reprieve and was restored to her former glory.

The *Persier* left Cardiff docks on Thursday 8 February 1945 as a member of a small convoy, with a cargo of food, bound for Belgium. She had 63 people on board. At a point off Plymouth she came under attack from a German U-boat. A torpedo struck the *Persier* in her No.2 hold, causing her to list alarmingly. Of the four lifeboats carried by the *Persier*, only one was successfully launched and managed to get away. Local shipping recovered the survivors.

The alarm was raised at 18.31 hours when a message was received from the Admiralty requesting the lifeboat to attend the *Persier*, which was reported to be sinking four miles south of the Eddystone. The *Ministre Anseele* was launched at 06.45 hours into a westerly gale, heavy rain and a rough sea, and immediately made her way to the scene of the tragedy.

Coxswain Walter Crowther carried out a methodical search but failed to locate further survivors. The lifeboat was recalled to port by wireless at 21.03 hours. It is possible that, whilst sinking, the ship's engines continued to function and drive her onwards towards the shore as, 24 years later, divers working on a wreck in Bigbury Bay recovered the ship's bell from the *Persier*. On the night of this terrible disaster, 20 lives were lost.

The *Ministre Anseele* was launched at 03.05 hours, the following day, when the Admiralty reported the sighting of a raft believed to be carrying survivors from the *Persier*. In the continuing gale, the lifeboat made her way to a point five miles south-east of Stoke Point, this being the reported position of the raft. Coxswain Crowther carried out a search, eastwards, towards Bolt Head. At 08.10 hours the lifeboat crew sighted a raft but, as they made their approach, it became evident that it was empty. The lifeboat retraced her course, searching the coastline between Bolt Head and Plymouth. As no trace of another raft, or survivors, could be found, the lifeboat returned to Plymouth, regaining her mooring at 11.30 hours. The crew were: W.D. Crowther, A. Sleeman, W. Lillicrap, E. Curtis, F. Fowler, G. Stanbury, A. Banham and L. Holman.

On Wednesday 21 March 1945, the station's Hon. Secretary received a request from the Admiralty to dispatch the lifeboat to assist a vessel which, as the result of enemy action, was sinking five miles north-east of the Eddystone. At the time there was a southerly wind blowing and a moderate sea running. Visibility was poor in fog patches. The *Ministre Anseele* was launched at 16.23 hours and made for a position eight miles south of the breakwater, arriving on location at 17.45 hours. On this occasion the lifeboat was under the command of Albert Sleeman, as Coxswain Crowther had suffered an accident. The vessel in need of assistance was found to be the 10,000-ton United States 'Liberty' Ship, the *James Eagan Layne*, which was already in tow of a tug. A small fleet of tugs and patrol vessels that were in the area had rescued the ship's crew. A rescue tug informed acting Coxswain Sleeman that 'all hands had been accounted for' and sent the following message: 'Captain of distressed ship is aboard this tug and wishes to thank lifeboat for prompt offer of assistance.'

Finding two undamaged rafts belonging to the *James Eagan Layne*, the *Ministre Anseele* towed them in to port, arriving back at 21.20 hours.

The *James Eagan* was eventually beached. The lifeboat crew had been: A. Sleeman (Coxswain), W. Lillicrap, E. Curtis, G. Stanbury, F. Fowler, R. Chown, L. Holmes and A. Banham.

The next launch of the *Ministre Anseele* took place on Sunday 16 December 1945, when in moderate to rough seas, whipped up by a south-westerly gale, she undertook a search for the crew of a Naval motor boat. The alarm was raised at 21.48 hours when a message was received from the harbour-master who reported that eight men were missing from a boat belonging to the sloop *Temby*, the craft having foundered in the Hamoaze. The lifeboat left her mooring at 22.05 hours and made her way into the Hamoaze. Whilst searching for the missing men, Coxswain Walter Crowther kept in, by means of wireless, with Mount Wise. However, it was not until 23.00 hours that Crowther and his crew were informed by the sloop *Temby* that the motor boat that they sought had in fact foundered at 18.10 hours, some 3 hours and 38 minutes before the lifeboat was first alerted. In the slim hope that survivors might have reached safety, the lifeboat crew commenced a search of buoys and barges along the Hamoaze.

At 23.38 hours Coxswain Crowther was informed by the *Temby* that there had been nine men in the missing motor boat, one of whom had succeeded in reaching the shore. There being no sign of the eight missing men, Crowther was requested to continue his search until 08.00 hours, but at 01.03 hours he received instructions from Mount Wise to abandon the search.

The *Ministre Anseele* regained her mooring at 01.50 hours. The eight missing men were lost. The crew were: W.D. Crowther, A. Sleeman, W. Lillicrap, G. Stanbury, F. Fowler, E. Curtis, S. Harris and A. Banham.

The last recorded service launch of the *Ministre Anseele* at the Plymouth station took place on Monday 11 February 1946, in response to the possible sighting of distress signals. The initial call from the harbour-master was received at 21.30 hours, requesting that the lifeboat be placed on stand-by. The Coastguard at Portwrinkle had reported sighting 'flash-lights', possible distress signals, about five miles south-west of his lookout post. Like reports were also received from two other Coastguard stations, but they could not confirm that the lights were distress signals. The harbour-master then reported that it was thought likely that the lights were signals between vessels of the fishing fleet. The Plymouth Lifeboat Station's Hon. Secretary was not convinced by this explanation and authorised the launch of the lifeboat in order to investigate the matter further. The assembly signal was made at 21.49 hours and the lifeboat launched at 22.00 hours.

It was just after midnight, in a westerly force 2 wind that carried heavy drizzle, that members of the lifeboat crew saw the faint glow of a light; they steamed towards it and, at 00.08 hours, located the 33-foot open motor boat, the *Three Brothers*, which was drifting helplessly, the engine having broken down. The two crew members were in a very poor physical state, suffering from exhaustion and exposure.

The 'flash-lights' that had been reported by the Coastguard were in fact signals made by the crew of the *Three Brothers*, not by torches, as suspected, but by the striking of matches. It was therefore with the utmost good fortune that the lifeboat crew had spotted the light emanating from the motor boat, as this signal had literally been made with the very last match in the possession of the two-man crew!

The *Ministre Anseele* could not be used to undertake a service requirement on Sunday 2 June 1946, when, at 19.20 hours, a report was received of the capsizing of a Royal Navy dinghy and difficulties being experienced by a whaler. The assembly signal summoning the lifeboat crew was made at 19.30 hours; they had all mustered by 19.45 hours, with the notable exception of the mechanic. In the absence of this vital member of the crew, the lifeboat could not put to sea. It was therefore decided that the lifeboat crew would man a motor boat, the *Golden Hind*, of which William Crowther was also the Coxswain.

The *Golden Hind* was launched into a strong west-south-westerly wind and a confused sea on a flood tide, and reached the scene of the incident, south-west of the Mew Stone, at 20.05 hours. Upon arrival it was established that the two-man crew of the dinghy had been rescued by a passing motor boat but information was later gained that only one man had been rescued, the other being reported as 'missing'. The *Golden Hind* searched the area without success, returning to port at 21.15 hours. The crewman was not found. The crew members were: W.D. Crowther (Coxswain), A. Sleeman (Second Coxswain), W. Lillicrap, E. Curtis, F. Fowler and R. Chown.

Later that year, following an overhaul, and after having proudly served as the Plymouth lifeboat for three years, the *Ministre Anseele* was returned to the Belgian Government.

10

THE BROTHERS

APRIL 1946–FEBRUARY 1947

Class: Watson   *Propulsion:* Motor   *Crew:* 8

Length: 45' 0"   *Beam:* 12' 6"   *Displacement:* $17^T 16^{Cwt}$

Official number: 696   *Builder:* J.S. White, Cowes, 1922

Service Launches: 2   *Lives Saved:* 0

Coxswain: Walter Crowther
Mechanic: Arthur Banham

The lifeboat which replaced the *Ministre Anseele* was the 45-foot Watson Class boat, *The Brothers*. She had been built in 1922 for the Penlee Lifeboat Station. The lifeboat had been donated by Miss Eddy of Torquay, and had cost £13,214. *The Brothers* was placed on 'temporary duty' at Plymouth in 1946, for a one-year period, during which she was launched for service on only two occasions.

The first service for *The Brothers* took place on Monday 12 August 1946 when, in very rough seas, heavy rain and squalls, carried by a south-westerly gale, she went to the assistance of two ocean-going yachts and a motor yacht. It was at 04.05 hours that the Secretary received a telephone call from the harbour-master stating that a yacht was dangerously close to rocks on Plymouth's southern shore. The assembly signal was immediately made and the lifeboat slipped her mooring lines at 04.15 hours. As *The Brothers* was leaving her mooring, the Secretary received a second message informing him that a second yacht was also in difficulty. The Secretary intercepted the lifeboat and passed this additional information to Coxswain Crowther.

On reaching the first vessel it was discovered that the yachts were in fact competitors in a race, having left Cowes, Isle of Wight, bound for Plymouth Sound. This vessel, a Dutchman, was stranded on the rocks, but fortunately, as the wind veered, the vessel refloated and was escorted by the lifeboat into the Barbican where she was beached. Coxswain Crowther immediately returned to the Sound and went to the assistance of the second vessel, the yacht *Valeria*, of Glasgow, which the lifeboat escorted to the Great Western Dock.

The Brothers returned to the Sound for a third time, on this occasion assisting a 30-ton motor yacht that had anchored perilously close to the breakwater.

The master of this vessel, the *Ellora* of Glasgow, was given advice and the vessel was moved to a safe anchorage. *The Brothers* regained her mooring at 07.15 hours. The crew were: W. Crowther, A. Sleeman, W. Lillicrap, F. Fowler, E. Curtis, R. Chown, L. Holmes and G. O'Dell (Relief Mechanic).

On Friday 22 November 1946, *The Brothers* was launched at 00.20 hours to go to the assistance of the vessel the *Baron Ailsa*. The alarm was raised at 23.45 hours (21st inst.), when a message was received from Land's End Radio; it read: 'Vessel in distress of Start Point. Requires immediate assistance.' The message was immediately relayed to the Torbay Lifeboat Station and at 00.05 hours (22nd inst.) the Plymouth station's Hon. Secretary received a second message, this one from the Hope Cove Coastguard: 'Vessel in distress 2½ miles east Eddystone and requesting lifeboat be dispatched immediately.'

Having satisfied himself that the two messages related to the same vessel, the Hon. Secretary authorised the launch of the lifeboat, under the command of Coxswain Walter Crowther. In violent rain squalls, mountainous seas and winds that were reaching speeds in excess of 64 knots (hurricane force 12) in the Channel, *The Brothers* was set on a course for the Eddystone. In the vicinity of the Eddystone, with approximately 12 miles' visibility, Coxswain Crowther conducted a search pattern over a radius of 12 miles. The casualty was not found and *The Brothers* returned to her mooring at 05.40 hours. It was later established that the *Baron Ailsa* had been located by a Royal Navy destroyer, 185° south-west of Start Point and had been taken in tow to Torbay. The crew of the lifeboat on this occasion were: W. Crowther (Coxswain), A. Sleeman (Second Coxswain), W. Lillicrap, L. Holmes, F. Fowler, E. Curtis, R. Chown and G. O'Dell (Relief Mechanic).

11

THE *ROBERT AND MARCELLA BECK*

FEBRUARY 1947–30 MARCH 1952

Class: Barnett   *Propulsion:* 2 x 76hp petrol engines   *Crew:* 8
Speed: 9.5 knots   *Length:* 60' 0"   *Beam:* 15' 0"   *Displacement:* 44^T 4^{Cwt}
Official number: 696   *Builder:* J.S. White, Cowes
Launches: 14   *Lives Saved:* 2
Coxswain: Walter Crowther
Mechanic: Arthur Banham

After being placed under Naval orders in 1943, the *Robert and Marcella Beck* was immediately sent to Iceland where she spent three months with the Fleet Salvage Officer as a rescue vessel. Her role was subsequently changed to that of convoy rescue and general duties. In addition to her time spent in Icelandic waters, she was additionally stationed in the Faeroes and at Wick, Scotland.

In July 1945 the *Robert and Marcella Beck* was posted to the River Clyde before carrying out further duties at Blyth, and later that same year, Grimsby. She remained under Naval orders until 9 April 1946. Following her wartime service, the *Robert and Marcella Beck* underwent a major refurbishment and refit before being returned to the RNLI. In February 1947 she arrived in her home waters off Plymouth.

The first call to which the newly refurbished *Robert and Marcella Beck* responded took place in exceptionally violent seas, which were aggravated by 60–65-mile-per hour winds that blew from the south-south-west. A request was received from the Rame Head Coastguard at 16.45 hours on Saturday 5 April 1947 for assistance to be sent to the 5,684-ton steamer, the *Empire Chamois*, of London, the vessel having suffered engine failure three miles west of Rame Head. She had signalled that she was out of control and drifting towards the shore. In heavy rain, the lifeboat slipped her mooring at 17.17 hours and headed for the casualty. After

steaming for just short of one hour, in truly horrendous seas, the lifeboat reached the *Empire Chamois* at 18.10 hours. The steamer was found to be dragging her anchors and continuing her slow drift shorewards.

Prior to the arrival of the lifeboat, the Captain of the *Empire Chamois*, realising his precarious position, had requested the assistance of tugs to prevent his vessel drifting onto the shore. Indeed, an Admiralty tug had been ordered out from the Plymouth dockyard but reported the sea conditions to be too bad for contact to be made with the steamer and returned to port. Unlike the Plymouth lifeboat, the tug had failed to reach the casualty having steamed an almost identical course through the same treacherous seas. Acting upon the request of the *Empire Chamois'* captain, Coxswain Crowther and his crew stood-by to await the arrival of a second tug, which was steaming towards the casualty from the port of Falmouth. The wind began to abate in ferocity and there was a noticeable calming of the sea by the time the Falmouth tug reached the *Empire Chamois* at 01.30 hours the following morning. The tug successfully established a hawser link and towed the steamer to the relatively sheltered waters of Plymouth Sound. The lifeboat returned to her mooring at 02.25 hours. It was noted in the Service Report that throughout the service 'The *Robert and Marcella Beck* behaved splendidly.' The crew were: W.D. Crowther, A. Sleeman, W. Lillicrap, E. Curtis,

F. Fowler, R. Chown, L. Holmes and A. Banham.

A strong south-westerly gale, which was accompanied by blustery rain showers and a turbulent sea, was blowing on the morning of Friday 30 January 1948 when a message was received, at 09.35 hours, that a vessel was in extreme difficulty and required immediate assistance. The message, relayed by the harbour-master, reported the Russian sailing ship, the *Jemchooc*, to be in a dangerous position and being driven towards rocks, three miles south-west of Bolt Head.

The *Robert and Marcella Beck* was launched at 09.48 hours and set off for the stricken vessel. Coxswain Crowther was notified that a tug, and a Royal Navy destroyer, had also been dispatched to the scene. The lifeboat maintained communication with both the casualty and the tug, reaching the given position of the sloop at 11.45 hours. The three rescue vessels searched the area for two hours but could not find any trace of her. At about 13.00 hours, after the destroyer had searched a further ten miles along the coast, without success, the tug received another message from the *Jemchooc* stating: 'No danger now - wind changed - help not required – proceeding.' The lifeboat returned to port, regaining her mooring at 14.35 hours.

Throughout her years of service as the Plymouth lifeboat, the *Robert and Marcella Beck* undertook several launches when a direct service was not provided. One such launch took place on Thursday 2 February 1950, when a request for the launch of the Plymouth lifeboat was received from the Hon. Secretary of the Fowey Lifeboat Station. A message was also received from the Rame Head Coastguard, at 18.02 hours, that a rocket had been observed at 16.15 hours off Windsworth, about one mile west of Seaton, Cornwall. At 18.11 hours, the assembly maroons were fired, summoning the crew. No further useful information could be obtained and the lifeboat slipped her mooring at 18.28 hours to head for the general location indicated. The *Robert and*

Marcella Beck set out into a south-south-westerly gale and heavy rain squalls, between which visibility was surprisingly good. The sea, however, was very extremely wild and the Coxswain, Walter Crowther, subsequently reported that, on the way out, the weather had been some of the roughest he had ever experienced. A search was made along the coastline as far as Looe Island but it proved fruitless. Shore parties searched the coastline from Portwrinkle to Looe, their efforts also found nothing. When these teams withdrew, the lifeboat was recalled, at 22.00 hours, returning to her mooring at 22.30 hours.

After the search, the following signals were received: From the Commander-in-Chief, Plymouth to Mr Hicks, the Hon. Secretary of the Plymouth Lifeboat Station: 'I congratulate you most heartily on promptitude of your lifeboat putting to sea last night', and from the harbour-master at Plymouth to the Hon. Secretary: 'May I add my personal congratulations to those of the Commander-in-Chief – a good show.'

Mr Hicks received the following message from the Yealm Coastguard at 16.46 hours on Saturday 24 June 1950: 'Explosion on yacht off Blackstone Pt about 2 miles E of Gara Point.'

The *Robert and Marcella Beck* left her moorings at 17.10 hours with Mr Hicks taking his place as a member of the crew. The lifeboat headed out into a moderate sea and heavy rain that was being carried on a moderate south-westerly breeze. Radio contact was maintained with Polruan Radio, but no further information as to the seriousness of the reported explosion was available. At 17.55 hours the lifeboat reached the casualty, off Stoke Point, and found her to be the *Edford*, a 5½–ton yacht belonging to Major H.E. Shore of the Royal Dart Yacht Club. The lifeboat crew immediately picked up the two occupants of a small dinghy, one of whom was supporting a woman in the water, whilst the other was using a bottom board as a paddle. Both men were exhausted and, on reflection, given that an ebb tide

Crew members of the Robert and Marcella Beck.
Left to right, back: *L. Holmes (Bowman), W. Crowther (Coxswain), A. Banham (Mechanic),*
A. Foot; front: *Sid Harris (Second Mechanic), N. Carter (Second Coxswain), F. Amos, Mr Hicks*
(Hon. Secretary), T. Keane, F. Fowler, B. Sleeman, A. Holmes.

was running, it was thought very unlikely that they would have reached the rocks or landed safely.

It was learned from the two men in the dinghy that a male person from the yacht who had been badly burned had landed safely in his dinghy. His wife, it would appear, had jumped overboard and disappeared below the surface. The two men had spotted her from the cliff top and they, in turn, had put out in their dinghy to rescue her. At this time the *Edford* was a blazing inferno and, having established that no other person was on board the yacht, the lifeboat kept well clear of the vessel.

A doctor and an ambulance were requested to meet the lifeboat upon its return to Plymouth. Artificial respiration was immediately commenced upon the woman with members of the lifeboat crew maintaining respiration until the casualty was handed into the care of the medical authorities. Unfortunately, the efforts of the crew were in vain as the woman was pronounced 'dead on arrival' at hospital.

In his Return of Service Report the Hon. Secretary, Mr Hicks, recorded that:

The two men who went out in the dinghy, John Stitson and Jack Shepherd, of Noss Mayo, S. Devon, undoubtedly did a brave job of work. It is understood that their action will be reported by Station Officer Harris, of Yealm C.G. and the Coxswain and crew will gladly confirm their plucky effort.

Yealm Coastguard duly commended the 'prompt action' of the men and their calling of the lifeboat. They also deemed the 'efficient handling of incident from start to finish' to be 'worthy of a special mention'. The lifeboat crew on that occasion were: W.D. Crowther (Coxswain), J. Carter (Second Coxswain), L. Holman (Bowman), F. Fowler, T. Keane, A. Foot (First Asst. Mechanic), S. Harris and A.J. Hicks (Hon. Sec.).

Plymouth had been battered by a south-westerly gale for much of Sunday 4 February

1951, the gale culminating in the grounding of the 410-ton MV *Drakedene*, of Cardiff, with nine persons on board. At 21.22 hours, the Lifeboat Station's Hon. Secretary received a message from the harbour-master, Commander M.H. Brown, relating that the vessel had dragged her anchors and gone aground on rocks near Jennycliffe. At the time of the alarm, the Naval tug *Careful* was also sent to assist the stranded vessel and the RAF authorities at Mount Batten sent a lorry to transport life-saving apparatus to the scene.

The vessel, formerly the *Empire Farjeon*, had been built in 1924 and was owned by Messrs W.J. Reynolds Ltd of Torpoint, her master being Captain W.H. Caple. She was bound from Antwerp to Gaston with a cargo of potash. The lifeboat was launched into a rough sea and squally rain at 21.46 hours and reached the wreck only 12 minutes later. The MV *Drakedene* had grounded approximately 200 yards from the shore, at a point between Batten and Jennycliffe. The ship appeared to be swinging by the bow and stern, apparently stuck amidships. She was illuminated by two searchlights from the cliff top, and by the headlamps of cars belonging to officers from the nearby RAF Officers' Mess.

In the continuing gale, Coxswain Crowther manoeuvred the *Robert and Marcella Beck* into a position where he could anchor and veer down on to the cargo vessel. The lifeboat approached to within hailing distance and, following a conversation, was able to establish radio contact. Captain Caple was able to assure Coxswain Crowther that, although stranded on rocks, the *Drakedene* was not taking in water. The harbour-master attended the scene and informed Coxswain Crowther that a further two tugs, the *Tactful* and the *Anthony*, were on their way. The tugs arrived at 23.00 hours but were unable to approach the *Drakedene*. The lifeboat was, however, in a position to be able to establish a line between the casualty and the tugs, if so required. The crew also acted as a relay station

between the vessels as the tugs were not fitted with radio-telegraphy equipment. Using their new rocket equipment, from a range of about 250 yards, the Turnchaple Life-Saving Apparatus Co. accurately fired a line across the casualty; although not used it proved a good demonstration of accuracy under severe conditions.

All vessels stood-by until about 02.00 hours when the *Drakedene* refloated under her own steam. At the request of Captain Caple, the lifeboat escorted the casualty to a safe berth at North Quay. The *Robert and Marcella Beck* returned to her mooring at 02.55 hours. The crew were: W.D. Crowther (Coxswain), J. Carter (Second Coxswain), L. Holmes (Bowman), F. Fowler, T. Keane, A. Sleeman, S. Harris, A. Banham and A. Hicks.

James Roach oversees Mr Blowey adjusting the compass on the Robert and Marcella Beck.

Mr A. Hicks, Hon. Secretary, received the following anticipatory message from the Yealm Coastguard at 12.02 hours on Friday 28 December 1951, the message having been relayed from Prawle Coastguard via Hope Cove: 'Schooner W/SW Prawle making slowly W, a large steamer and a coaster in neighbourhood.' Mr Hicks contacted Coxswain Walter Crowther and requested him to stand-by and await further contact. At 12.29 hours, the Yealm Coastguard reported: 'Schooner *Nellie Bywaters* with French trawler and British steamer *British Birch* standing-by and Dockyard tug *Careful* dispatched.'

The casualty was the 113-ton topsail schooner, *Nellie Bywaters*, commanded by Captain Richard England and carrying a crew of 11.

The weather at the time was overcast, with heavy rain, and a full gale was blowing from the south-south-east. The harbour-master made the assembly signal at 12.45 hours and the *Robert and Marcella Beck* was launched into a very rough sea with a full crew, plus two 'reserves', at 12.58 hours. The time of the launch was one hour after low water, on a very low spring tide, and Mr Hicks knew that although the Salcombe boat was closer to the casualty, in all probability, due to the state of the wind and tide, she would be unable to cross the Salcombe Bar.

At 13.12 hours Mr Hicks informed the Yealm Coastguard: 'Lifeboat cleared Breakwater and proceeding to casualty.' At 13.15 the *Robert and Marcella Beck* was at a position between the Shag Stone and the Mew Stone. The following radio signals were then recorded:

13.13 hours. Yealm CG – Hon. Sec.
'According to Hope Cove casualty now SSE ³/₄ E. 10 miles from Mew Stone.'
13.34 hours. Polruan – Hon. Sec.
'Land's End Radio report message from British Birch *and French trawler, position 188° 4 miles Bolt Tail. Schooner in tow proceeding towards Plymouth. Tug in sight.'*
13.42 hours. Mount Wise – Hon. Sec.
'Schooner capsized. Tug and British Birch *standing-by to pick up survivors.'*
13.58 hours. Hon. Sec. – harbour-master
'Can you verify all accounted for?'
14.01 hours. harbour-master – Hon. Sec.
'Two of Nellie Bywaters *still missing – tug returning to search.'*
14.10 hours. harbour-master – Hon. Sec.
'Careful now returning with 9 survivors.'
1415 hours. Polruan – Hon. Sec.
'From British Birch *– Tug* Careful *picked up ALL survivors and proceeding to Plymouth.'*

Concern now began to mount for the lifeboat and her crew, as radio contact had been lost at 13.30 hours. At 14.21 hours Mr Hicks asked Yealm Coastguard, 'Can you see lifeboat?' The following reply was received, 'No – visibility bad. Polruan cannot contact lifeboat will ask if Land's End can do so.' Polruan also failed to raise the lifeboat. The communication continued as follows:

14.35 hours. Hon. Sec. – harbour-master
'Having failed to contact lifeboat through Polruan and Rame will you try if Careful *can do so and request "Return to station" please.'*
14.45 hours. harbour-master – Hon. Sec.
'Tug Careful *on way back and left lifeboat searching.'*
Hon. Sec. – K.H.M.P.
'Repeat – will you try and contact lifeboat request "return to station".'

Following a frantic period of radio traffic, all heaved a sigh of relief when, at 14.45 hours,

Rame contacted the lifeboat and the following signals were received:

14.47 hours. harbour-master – Hon. Sec.
'Lifeboat now following tug back,' and at
14.50 hours. Yealm Coastguard – Hon. Sec.
'Lifeboat in sight about 2¹/₂ miles Stoke Point.'

It was subsequently established that, at 13.30 hours, the *Robert and Marcella Beck* had lost all radio transmission. Whilst still at sea the fault was traced to a damaged lead, between the aerial and transmitter, and rectified.

Upon leaving Plymouth, the *Robert and Marcella Beck* had maintained a steady 9 knots, but the casualty had foundered prior to her arrival at the search area, at 14.20 hours. Although a message had been received that the tug, *Careful*, had picked up all survivors, two members of the *Nellie Bywater*'s crew had in fact been lost.

Upon returning ashore at 16.35 hours, Coxswain Crowther and his crew had nothing but praise for the magnificent behaviour of their boat, having been at sea in what was described as being 'the worst gale recorded in the district for 22 years.' The crew were: W.D. Crowther, J. Carter, L. Holmes, F. Fowler, T. Keane, A. Banham, A. Foot, S. Harris, A. Holmes (reserve) and F. Amos (reserve).

A typically routine launch took place on the morning of Saturday 15 March 1952, following a report from the Rame Coastguard that he had sighted flashing lights, which he took to be distress signals. The Coastguard had seen the lights at 01.23 hours, south-south-east of Rame Head. Sea conditions were rough and cloud reduced visibility to five miles. Confirmation of the sighting of the distress signals was sought from both Breakwater Fort and the harbour-master at Plymouth, but the sightings could not be confirmed. The Rame Coastguard, however, stood firm regarding his original report. Authorisation was given for the lifeboat to launch.

Bitterly cold, force-6 winds blew from the south-east, as the *Robert and Marcella Beck*, with a full crew, plus the Hon. Secretary and a 'reserve', slipped her mooring at 01.55 hours. Taking a bearing from Rame Head, Coxswain Crowther searched in the direction indicated, maintaining radio contact with Polruan throughout the duration of the search. The lifeboat passed a solitary trawler, approximately five miles from Rame Head, and it was thought possible that her deck lighting, used during night trawling, may have been mistaken for distress signals as she was too far from Rame for her other lights to have been visible. As a casualty was not located, the lifeboat returned to Plymouth, regaining her mooring at 06.10 hours. The crew on this occasion were: W.D. Crowther (Coxswain), J. Carter (Second Coxswain), L. Holmes (Bowman), F. Fowler, T. Keane, A.W. Banham (Mechanic), A. Foot (First Asst. Mechanic) S. Harris (Second Asst. Mechanic), F.W. Amos (reserve) and A.S. Hicks.

In the Royal National Lifeboat Institution's official Service Report for that date, the Hon. Secretary, Mr A.S. Hicks, made the following entry:

A "wild goose chase" it may have been, bitterly cold & rough it certainly was, but on return to Station every man was glad to have had the opportunity of turning out in what may be the last service with their faithful "Robert and Marcella Beck" – and that goes for the Hon. Sec. as well.

These words were well founded, for it proved to be the last service launch of the *Robert and Marcella Beck*. This proud boat, having served the Plymouth station for 23 years, was credited, in total, with no less that 50 launches upon which she rendered active service. The boat, her Coxswain and crew were also credited with saving an outstanding 72 lives.

Later in 1952, the *Robert and Marcella Beck* was sold to the Irish Lights Board, where she was to be renamed to serve as the tender *Blaskbeg*. It is understood that some 12 years later she was returned to Weymouth where she was converted into a yacht.

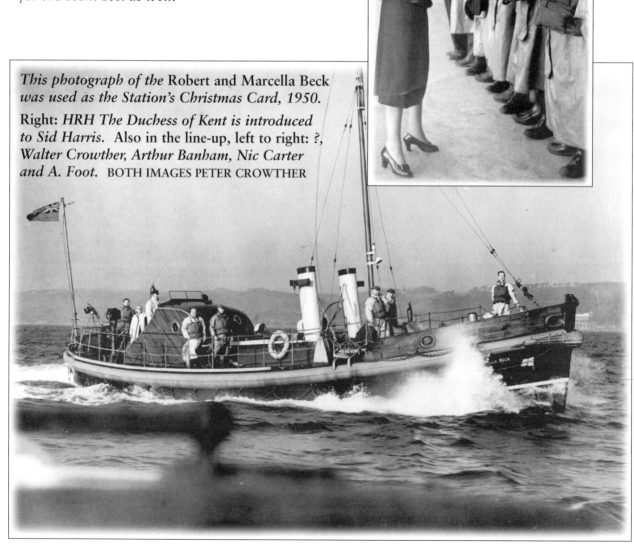

This photograph of the **Robert and Marcella Beck** *was used as the Station's Christmas Card, 1950.*

Right: *HRH The Duchess of Kent is introduced to Sid Harris. Also in the line-up, left to right: ?, Walter Crowther, Arthur Banham, Nic Carter and A. Foot.* BOTH IMAGES PETER CROWTHER

12

THOMAS FOREHEAD AND MARY ROWSE
30 MARCH 1952–22 MAY 1974

Class: *Barnett Stromness*   **Propulsion:** *Twin 60hp engines and screws*   **Crew:** *8*

Length: *52' 0"*   **Beam:** *13' 6"*   **Displacement:** *27^T 5^{Cwt}*

Official number: *890*   **Builder:** *J.S. White, Cowes, 1952*

Service Launches: *169*   **Lives Saved:** *63*

Coxswains: *Walter Crowther (1952–61), Nic Carter (1961–63), Peter White (1963–71), John Dare (1971–4)*   **Mechanics:** *Arthur Banham (1952–7), William Rogers (1957–67), Cyril Alcock (1967–74)*

The *Robert and Marcella Beck* was replaced, in 1952, by a new 52-foot Barnett Stromness Class lifeboat, which was powered by two 60hp 'Ferry' diesel engines. She was slightly smaller in length, her top speed being half a knot slower than her predecessor. The RNLI journal recorded:

Though the life-boat isn't fast – especially when compared with the powerful craft of the 19th Group Search and Rescue Station, R.A.F., Plymouth – she can do her nine knots in nearly any weather and when it's too rough outside for fast craft it is the plodding, steady boat that is needed for rescue work.

The Plymouth Lifeboat Station received a royal visit by the Duke and Duchess of Kent on Friday 16 May 1952, the occasion being the dedication and naming ceremony of the new lifeboat. The ceremony took place at 12.00 hours at the Princess Royal Pier, Great Western Docks, Plymouth. The dedication was presided over by the Earl of Mount Edgcumbe, who opened the proceedings. Commander T.G. Michelmore, RD, RNR, Chief Inspector of Lifeboats, described the new vessel and her operational capabilities to the congregation. On behalf of the donor, Commodore the Earl Howe, CBE, VRD, PC, RNVR, Deputy Chairman of the RNLI, then entrusted the lifeboat to the Plymouth branch. Mr A.S. Hicks, MBE, Hon. Secretary, accepted the lifeboat on behalf of the Port of Plymouth.

The hymn 'O God, our help in ages past', was sung and the Bishop of Exeter, the Rt Revd R.C. Mortimer dedicated the lifeboat:

To the honour and glory of Almighty God and for the noble purpose of rescuing those in peril on the sea, we dedicate this Life-boat, in the Name of the Father and of the Son and of the Holy Ghost.

Amen

Following the traditional singing of the lifeboat man's hymn, 'Eternal Father strong to save', HRH The Duchess of Kent named the lifeboat *Thomas Forehead and Mary Rowse*. A vote of thanks was proposed by Vice-Admiral Sir Maurice Mansergh, KCB, CBE, and seconded by Sir John Carew-Pole, Bt., DSO, TD. Throughout the ceremony accompaniment was provided by the band of HM Royal Marines, Plymouth, by kind permission of Major-General R.F. Cornwall, CBE, Royal Marines Plymouth Group.

The *Thomas Forehead and Mary Rowse*, which cost £30,857, was given, and endowed in perpetuity, from a gift of Miss A. Charlton Rowse of Birmingham. Miss Rowse made a second gift to the RNLI; the total sum of over £40,000 being one of the largest bequests that the Institution had received to date.

The first recorded launch of the *Thomas Forehead and Mary Rowse* took place on Saturday 13 September 1952 when she took part

Left: *Dressed in oil-skins and sou'westers, and wearing the old-style kapok-filled life-jackets, are the crew members of the* Thomas Forehead and Mary Rowse, *1964: Left to right:* Albert Holmes, Fred Amos, Ron Cottrell, Peter White, Danny Biscombe, John Dare, John Sheldon, Bill Rogers, Fred Fowler, Tom Keane, Mike Keane.

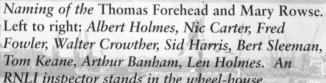

Naming of the Thomas Forehead and Mary Rowse. *Left to right:* Albert Holmes, Nic Carter, Fred Fowler, Walter Crowther, Sid Harris, Bert Sleeman, Tom Keane, Arthur Banham, Len Holmes. *An RNLI inspector stands in the wheel-house.*

This image: *The* Thomas Forehead and Mary Rowse, *stationed at Plymouth from 1952–74.*

Above right: *The naming of the* Thomas Forehead and Mary Rowse, *16 May 1952.*
Left to right: *Walter Crowther, Bob Jones, Len Holmes, Arthur Banham, A. Foot, Sid Harris, Nic Carter.* PETER CROWTHER

in a search to locate the *Royal Navy Dinghy, No. 178*, of Devonport. At 22.08 hours, a message was received from Longroom Signal Station that a Service dinghy, containing two men, was missing. Various Service craft were already engaged in a search for the missing vessel, the possible whereabouts of which was unknown. At 22.10 hours, Mr A.S. Hicks telephoned Longroom and requested that maroons be fired to summon the lifeboat crew; he was, however, informed that the message that he had received was for 'information only' and that they did not wish the lifeboat to turn out. Mr Hicks contacted the Duty Commander, Mount Wise, and explained that the lifeboat could be away within 20 minutes and was equipped with an excellent searchlight with which they would search any area designated. The offer was accepted and the maroons were fired by the harbour-master at 22.20 hours. On a calm, clear night, under the command of Coxswain Walter Crowther and with a full crew, the *Thomas Forehead and Mary Rowse* slipped her mooring at 22.23 hours, with instructions to search the Western Approaches and Great Mew Stone areas. As the search for the dinghy proved fruitless, at 23.50 hours the Duty Commander, Mount Wise, called the search off, at the same time requesting the lifeboat to resume at first light. Eight minutes later, at 00.01 hours, Longroom reported that the overdue dinghy had arrived back, safe and sound. The lifeboat returned to her mooring at 00.30 hours.

All did not go smoothly on this, the first launch of the *Thomas Forehead and Mary Rowse*, for in his Service Report the Hon. Secretary drew attention to the following points:

Steering most unsatisfactory at slow speeds.
Noise from exhaust makes loudspeaker in cockpit useless & cabin door must be shut & curtain over when transmitting or receiving.
In after cockpit impossible to hear any orders from Coxswain or for those aft to call [him]. Great handicap as when searching tonight.
Cabin & Cockpit awash although only moderate sea – water entering through relieving valves.

These teething problems were soon addressed by the RNLI. The crew were: W.D. Crowther (Coswain), J. Carter (Second Coxswain), L. Holmes (Bowman), F. Fowler, T. Keane, A. Banham (Mechanic), A. Foot, S. Harris and 'reserves' A. Sleeman, A. Holmes and F. Amos.

The first effective service undertaken by the *Thomas Forehead and Mary Rowse* took place on the evening of Sunday 10 May 1953. A warning was received, at 18.46 hours, from the Yealm Coastguard, that a 15-foot sailing dinghy, with two men on board, was overdue. The dinghy had last been seen outside the Great Mew Stone. On a strong ebb tide, and with a fresh east-north-east wind, the Coastguard was of the opinion that the craft would be unable to return safely to shore. Leaving her mooring at 19.02 hours, the lifeboat cleared the breakwater at 19.17 hours and made her way to within four miles of the Eddystone, from which point the lifeboat continuing to search in the direction of the Great Mew Stone. A helicopter from HMS *Illustrious* was also engaged in the search, as were Royal Navy launches and RAF launches from RAF Mount Batten.

At 20.32 hours, Rame Coastguard reported to the lifeboat, via Polruan, that they had sighted the missing craft near the Shag Stone Rock. Coxswain Crowther closed on the position and came alongside the dinghy, at 20.50 hours, between Wembury Point and the Great Mew Stone. The two crewmen were taken aboard the lifeboat and cared for while the dinghy was taken in tow to the Yealm.

On this occasion it was the radio that had caused concern, the Hon. Secretary recording:

R.T. on 137.5 metres had so far been unsatisfactory. Testing on Thur. 7th May could not get or receive Polruan though we were answered by Land's End clearly. On exercise this morning no contact was made until clear of Sound when contact was made but lost again when returning to station inside the Breakwater. During test and exercise much jamming from trawlers etc.
Peter Crowther, son of Coxswain, made his first trip as one of crew in absence of others and needless to say acquitted himself well – taking charge of the dinghy while in tow etc., and was later thanked by [myself].

The crew were: W.D. Crowther, J. Carter, F. Fowler, A. Banham, S. Harris, T. Keane, P. Crowther and A.S. Hicks.

The old saying 'There's many a slip twix cup and lip' can, in some instances, be applied to messages received by lifeboat stations. An unclear message, or signal, can potentially have a serious effect upon the efficiency of any subsequent rescue. Such could have been the case on

Saturday 20 June 1953. The casualty on this occasion was the Belgian MY *Krack*, with five persons on board.

The Hon. Secretary, Mr A. Hicks, received the following message, at 06.02 hours, from the harbour-master, Plymouth, which had been relayed from the office of the Commander-in-Chief (MHQ) via Land's End Radio:

Following message from British Ship Scholar – *0411 – Begins* "Captain V. Devose confirms he is master of M.Y. Krack – vessel nearly sunk – water on bridge – approx position of M.Y. Krack at 0100 G.M.T. – 4 miles N. Eddystone Light." – *(received 0552).*

The signal to assemble the crew was made at 06.05 hours, the *Thomas Forehead and Mary Rowse* slipping her mooring at 06.20 hours. On two occasions Mr Hicks attempted to obtain further information from Rame Coastguard, but their telephone was engaged. The harbour-master was informed of the lifeboat's launch as she headed out into a south-westerly wind, force 5–6, with poor visibility and a very confused sea.

At 06.20 hours the following signal was received from Polruan R/T Station: '5 men picked up 49°25' N 04°14' W (S by W 56 miles Rame Head).' Mr Hicks, having established that both HMS *Protector* and HMS *Orwell* had been dispatched to the scene, immediately requested the recall of the lifeboat. The *Thomas Forehead and Mary Rowse* returned to her mooring at 07.40 hours. In his report, the Hon. Secretary made the following observations:

If at 0100 M.Y. Krack *appeared to have been abandoned 4 miles N. Eddystone Light, how could survivors have been picked up 56 miles S by W Rame? To clear up what on face of things seemed impossible, I have personally visited Coastguard Rame and Polruan, also Q.H.M.P. Coastguard at Polruan received* three *messages from D.O. St. Just relating to above which, read in correct sequence indicated No Life-boat required. I received from Q.H.M.P. message III only and being unable to contact Rame to confirm at once, sent lifeboat away immediately and recalled when informed all had been saved. Further, at commencement of message III – 01.00 (GMT) should have read 1100 (GMT).*

Chinese whispers also prevailed in respect of the name of this casualty, the vessel's name varying between *Krack* and *Track*.

Fortunately, in this instance, the lack of clarity in communication did not cost lives. The crew were: W.D. Crowther, J. Carter, L. Holmes, F. Fowler, A. Holmes, S. Harris, T. Keane, A. Banham and F. Amos (reserve).

The *Thomas Forehead and Mary Rowse* was launched at 21.55 hours on Thursday 12 November 1953, following the report of a Royal Marines 'Dory', with seven men on board, having capsized in the Sound. Yealm Coastguard raised the alarm at 21.36 hours, Mr Hicks informed the harbour-master that the lifeboat crew would be placed on immediate stand-by, and would be prepared to assist and fit in with any arrangements that the Armed Services might make. No further information of the mishap was available but having local knowledge that the Royal Marines regularly carried out landings and climbing exercises in the Jennycliffe area, it was agreed that the lifeboat would commence her search in this locality.

Communication was maintained between the lifeboat, the Royal Marines, the harbour-master, the Duty Commander, Mount Wise, Group 19 Mount Batten, and the Coastguard at Yealm and Rame Head. The lifeboat was not successful in locating the casualty or its crew, but by 03.10 hours five of the missing Royal Marines had been accounted for, four having swum ashore and one having been picked up by another craft. Unfortunately, in this tragic accident, which occurred on a cloudy night, with moderate visibility and a near gale-force west-south-westerly gale, two Royal Marines lost their lives.

For their quick actions that night, the Coxswain and crew of the Plymouth lifeboat received the personal thanks of Colonel E.C.E. Palmer, Commandant, Royal Marines, Commander R.T. Gardiner, Royal Navy, and the harbour-master, Plymouth. A letter of thanks was also received from Colonel Houghton, Headquarters, Royal Marines, Plymouth. The crew were: W.D. Crowther, J. Carter, F. Fowler, A. Holmes, F. Amos, A. Banham, S. Harris, T. Keane and P. Crowther (reserve).

A commemoration ceremony was held at the Baptist Church Hall, Mutley Plain, on Tuesday 15 December 1953, to mark the 150th Anniversary of the Plymouth Lifeboat Station. In the absence of the Earl of Mount Edgcumbe, the Queen's Harbour-Master, Com. R.T. Gardiner, presided. The RNLI awarded a commemorative Vellum to the Plymouth Lifeboat Station which was signed by the Duchess of Kent. Captain Guy D. Fanshawe, a Vice-President of the Institution and a member of the Committee of Management, presented the Vellum to the Lord Mayor of Plymouth, Alderman Sir Clifford Tozer. It read:

The Institution gratefully recognises the services of the Plymouth lifeboat station, started in 1803, in the great cause of lifesaving from shipwreck, and on the occasion of the 150th year of the establishment, desires to place on record its appreciation of the voluntary work of the officers and the devotion and courage of the lifeboatmen, who have never failed to maintain the high traditions of the lifeboat service.

Captain Fanshawe said:

Whenever there is trouble at sea, Westcountry seamen have always been prepared to go on the waves, look into the trouble, and help people in need.

In paying tribute to the Coxswain and crew, Captain Fanshawe said that he knew Mr Crowther and the crew were very sorry, last year, to lose their old lifeboat, the *Robert and Marcella Beck*, but the vessel was not everything that could be desired in the way of a modern lifeboat.

Sir Clifford, who was accompanied by the Lady Mayoress, Lady Tozer, suggested that the Vellum might best be kept in the City Art Gallery.

Plymouth Sound was being subjected to a south-westerly gale, with gusts that the local Meteorological Office recorded as reaching 50–60 miles per hour, and a rough sea, when a MAYDAY call was intercepted by Mr G. O'Dell, the Mechanic of the RNLI's Fowey lifeboat. The message, which was monitored at 21.40 hours read: 'MAYDAY, MAYDAY, MAYDAY. Anchored in Plymouth Sound. Dragging ashore, asking assistance immediately.'

At 21.52 hours, Rame Head Coastguard relayed the message to the Hon. Secretary at his home address. Fortunately, at that precise time, Coxswain Walter Crowther was visiting Mr Hicks and an immediate request was made for the sounding of the maroons. With a full crew on board, the *Thomas Forehead and Mary Rowse* left her mooring at 22.07 hours.

The vessel from which the MAYDAY had been transmitted was the 1,221-ton British tanker, the *Atonality* of London. The tanker, owned by Everard & Sons of London, was under the command of Captain Edward Overton. The vessel, which carried a crew of 13, was bound from Fawley to Plymouth laden with a cargo of 380,000 gallons of high-octane petrol. The vessel had been riding at anchor in the Sound, but in force 7 south-westerly winds and a rough sea, on a rising tide, had dragged her anchors and was now aground, on rocks, approximately 200 yards offshore in Jennycliffe Bay.

Radio contact had been established between the casualty, the lifeboat and Rame Coastguard; the first message, from the casualty, advising: 'Tank leaking and surrounded by petrol – use no flares.' The *Atonality* repeated the message. A further signal was received from Captain Overton, requesting Coxswain Crowther to take off 11 members of his crew, whilst he and his chief engineer would remain on board.

Owing to a large area of petrol, and a build-up of fumes on the lee side of the tanker, Coxswain Crowther informed the ship's captain that he would attempt to take off the crew from the port quarterdeck, which was on the weather side of the vessel. In heavy waves, Walter Crowther edged the *Thomas Forehead and Mary Rowse* towards the *Atonality's* port quarter, the lifeboat rising and falling alarmingly on each wave. With great skill and seamanship, Coxswain Crowther held the Barnett as steady and as close as he could to the tanker, allowing all 11 crewmen to jump and, with the assistance of the lifeboat's crew, scramble aboard the lifeboat. The 11 crewmen were landed at Plymouth where contact was made with the *Atonality's* agents, W.D. Tamblyn & Co. By this time, as the sea had moderated and the wind had dropped, the lifeboat returned members of the crew, together with representatives of their Agents, to the *Atonality*, which, some two hours after foundering on a rising tide, was pulled clear by the Admiralty tug, *Atlas*.

After the incident, the master of an Esso tanker, which had been moored nearby and witnessed the whole affair broadcast, on R/T, his appreciation of the promptitude of the Plymouth lifeboat's arrival on the scene, congratulating Coxswain and crew in the fine handling of the lifeboat in getting alongside and taking off the crew under difficult conditions.

Yet again Coxswain Crowther registered his dissatisfaction with the lifeboat's R/T contact:

R/T with Rame Head and casualty excellent, but being inside the Sound, Polruan was found impossible – cannot do without Rame Head

The relief lifeboat Hearts of Oak *with the motor boat* Apollo *in tow, 14 May 1954.*
The crew were: Tom Keane, Fred Fowler, Arthur Banham, Walter Crowther (Coxswain), Nic Carter and Albert Holmes.

and they are a good team there.

The crew were: W.D. Crowther, J. Carter, L. Holmes, F. Fowler, A. Holmes, A.W. Banham (Mechanic), S. Harris, T. Keane, A.S. Hicks (Hon. Sec.), and 'reserves' F. Amos and P. Crowther.

Plymouth was in a celebratory mood on Friday 14 May 1954, the occasion being a visit to the city by Her Majesty, The Queen. At 05.58 hours, Coxswain Crowther slipped the moorings of the relief lifeboat, the *Hearts of Oak*, and took up a position to await the arrival, at 07.00 hours, of HMY *Britannia*.

At 10.00 hours, after most of the armada of vessels that had greeted the Royal Yacht had dispersed, a motor boat was observed, in difficulty, about three miles south of the Great Mew Stone. The craft was the converted whaler the *Apollo*, of Plymouth, with eight persons on board. In a moderate sea, a fresh north-north-easterly wind blowing off the land, and an ebb tide, Coxswain Crowther assessed that as visibility was deteriorating, the position of those on board had the potential of becoming serious. The lifeboat approached the *Apollo* only to find that the motor boat had suffered total engine failure. It was indeed fortunate that the lifeboat crew had sighted the casualty as there were no other boats in the vicinity and the vessel could not be observed from the shore. The lifeboat crew established a line and the *Hearts of Oak* towed the *Apollo* and her crew of eight into Millbay Docks.

The *Thomas Forehead and Mary Rowse* was launched on Wednesday 23 March 1955, following the receipt of a message from Longroom Signal Station at 05.05 hours, reporting that the liner, the *Venus* of Bergen, required immediate assistance. The call from the liner, which had been monitored by Land's End Radio, stated that she was dragging her anchor and wanted the immediate attendance of a pilot and a tug. The 6,269-ton liner, under the command of Captain S.V. Johnsen of the Bergen Shipping Line, carried her crew only, but was due to embark passengers for Madeira. At 05.20 hours, Mr Hicks ascertained that the *Venus* had in fact grounded near the Batten breakwater, that no lives were in danger and that the harbour-master had called for the assistance of tugs. At 06.53 hours, the Hon. Secretary reported to the Coxswain that he had seen two small tugs proceeding across the Sound; they agreed that the lifeboat should be launched immediately and stand-by the casualty. The lifeboat launched at 07.14 hours, reaching the casualty at 07.20 hours. At the time of the launch a full south-south-westerly gale was blowing, with gusts of 70–90 miles per hour being recorded. It was two hours after high tide and the sea was extremely rough. The *Thomas Forehead and Mary Rowse* made her way across the Sound in mountainous waves and, on reaching the scene, found the Admiralty tugs *Freebooter*, *Careful* and *Masterful* in attendance.

The *Masterful* had fouled her propeller and was grounding, when she was pulled clear by the *Careful*. In atrocious weather conditions, the lifeboat stood-by until 09.00 hours when attempts to refloat the *Venus* were abandoned. Coxswain Crowther agreed to return to the casualty in the late afternoon, when further attempts were to be made to refloat the vessel. The *Thomas Forehead and Mary Rowse* returned to her mooring at 09.30 hours the following day but was launched into the teeth of the gale once again at 16.05 hours, and stood-by the liner whilst unsuccessful attempts were made to refloat her. The lifeboat returned to the Plymouth boat-house at 18.35 hours, the refloating of the *Venus* having been placed in the hands of a salvage company and Admiralty tugs. The R/T again caused concern, the Service Report recording:

We hope R/T strength for transmission and reception will be improved in the very near future when twin aerial is fitted. This service <u>again</u> demonstrated Polruan as primary R/T *cannot be relied upon with our set in its present state.*

The crew were: W.D. Crowther, J. Carter, L. Holmes, F. Fowler, A. Holmes, S. Harris, A.S. Hicks, A.W. Banham and P. Crowther.

The keen hearing of the breakwater lighthouse-keeper saved the lives of three men on the evening of Monday 27 June 1955. Hearing their cries for help, the keeper raised the alarm with the Breakwater Fort who contacted Longroom Signal Station. At 22.50 hours, the message was passed to the Plymouth lifeboat, which launched at 23.10 hours. Coxswain Walter Crowther headed the *Thomas Forehead and Mary Rowse* to the indicated location of the casualties, some 200 yards outside the breakwater. Using the lifeboat's powerful searchlight, the crew picked out a 24-foot motor boat, moored to the Panther Buoy, about 300 yards south by west, of the breakwater lighthouse.

The occupants of the boat, two men and a boy, had been out on a fishing trip when their engine failed. The craft was without both paddles and lights. The lifeboat towed the stricken vessel to a wharf above the Electricity Generating Station, at Prince Rock, where the men and boy were landed. The men reluctantly gave the name of the owner of the vessel and then left, without a word of appreciation for the lifeboat men. The crew were: W.D. Crowther, L. Holmes, F. Fowler, T. Keane, A.S. Hicks, S. Harris, A. Holmes and P. Crowther.

Yealm Coastguard contacted the Plymouth Lifeboat Station's Hon. Secretary at 00.05 hours on Monday 2 January 1956, to report: 'Mount Batten and Longroom have seen flares in direction of Picklecombe/Drake's Island. Admiralty MFV (motor fishing vessel) being sent to investigate.'

Mr Hicks kept in constant contact with both Rame Head and Longroom but no useful information was gained. At 00.35 hours he was informed by Longroom Signal Station that a craft, drawing less water than the MFV, had been sent to investigate, but still no further information was available.

At 01.55 hours Mr Hicks spoke to the harbour-master and suggested that the lifeboat should be launched immediately. He undertook to cooperate fully with any request of the Admiralty in conducting a search. This offer of assistance was accepted. The assembly maroons were fired at 02.00 hours and the lifeboat slipped her mooring at 02.15 hours. Exceptionally poor weather conditions prevailed with a full

north-north-westerly gale blowing, in turn whipping up very rough seas, as the *Thomas Forehead and Mary Rowse* set a course for Picklecombe. The casualty was located, at 02.38 hours, with the use of the lifeboat's searchlight. Her position was just outside Picklecombe, at a point known locally as 'The Bridge'. When found, the craft was at anchor, too far out for any life-saving apparatus team to operate, yet in dangerously shallow, rock-littered waters. The casualty was a 30-foot converted Naval liberty boat, now bearing the name the *Edna* of Plymouth, with five members of the Plymouth Sea Fishing Club on board. The *Edna* had suffered gear failure in St Germans River, the wind and strong tidal currents having carried her out to sea. In extremely demanding conditions, Coxswain Crowther and his crew made an excellent job of manoeuvring the lifeboat into a position from which the *Edna* could be taken in tow. The five anglers were landed safely at the Barbican at 03.50 hours.

The timing of the call-out of the Plymouth lifeboat on this service caused much consternation, as indicated in the Service Report, in which Mr Hicks commented:

Longroom (Q.H.M.P.), had seen and been told of the flares, at or before 11pm and although taking action, neither then nor at any time, advised me. My first intimation came from Yealm Coastguard at midnight. Had we been advised at once, three hours might well have been saved and the risk to five occupants and their boat minimalized. We could have had a good chance of getting under way and completing the service before the M.F.V. got out. Rame as primary R/T was excellent.

The crew were: W.D. Crowther, L. Holmes, F. Fowler, A.W. Banham, S. Harris, T. Keane, A. Holmes, P. Crowther and J. Keane.

Following the unfortunate breakdown in communications experienced in respect of the above service, the following resolution was drafted:

Service to Motor Launch Edna
2nd January 1956
Although given to understand by Longroom that all necessary was being done through Q.H.M.P. and Duty Commander, Mount Wise, as a result of unsatisfactory action and failure to advise us of such, we, the Coxswain and Hon. Secretary, have agreed that in future

we shall launch at once regardless of any such information or assurance being given.
5th January 1956.

A small coaster was observed by the Breakwater Fort, flying the 'not under command' signal, at 10.02 hours on Monday 23 July 1956. The vessel was at a position approximately two miles south-east of the Great Mew Stone and failed to acknowledge or respond to signals. The boathouse contacted the Breakwater Fort lookout direct and ascertained that the vessel was drifting up the Channel. The assembly maroons were fired at 10.14 hours and ten minutes later the *Thomas Forehead and Mary Rowse* slipped her mooring. At the same time the Yealm Coastguard was dispatched to the Gara Point lookout.

At 10.55 hours the Rame Head Coastguard notified the boat-house that it was in contact with the lifeboat and that the casualty was now about one-and-a-quarter miles west of Stoke Point. By 10.59 hours the lifeboat had passed Gara Point and the casualty was estimated to be five miles south of Burgh Island.

At 11.05 hours the harbour-master received a report from Tamlyns Shipping Agents, which read: 'M.V. *Adaptity* hopes to have repairs completed by noon.' This was the first communication by either the vessel or her agents. At 11.36 hours Coxswain Crowther closed on the coaster, which proved to be the 945-ton MV *Adaptity*, owned by Messrs Everards of London. It was confirmed that the ship had been undergoing engine repairs, her captain having not thought it necessary to advise the authorities of the vessel's position. Having completed repairs, the *Adaptity* got under way at 11.50 hours, and was escorted by the lifeboat to Plymouth. The crew were: W.D. Crowther, J. Carter, A. Holmes, F. Fowler, P. Crowther, A. Banham, S. Harris and F. Amos.

Gale-force winds caused havoc with local shipping on Sunday 29 July 1956, to such an extent that a 30-foot, twin-screw cabin cruiser was driven, broadside-on, onto the foreshore beneath The Hoe. Pounded by 8-foot waves, the vessel was reduced to matchwood within the hour. The engines were all that was subsequently salvaged from the wreckage. The 'Flying Fifteen' yacht *Winwillow* was driven aground from her mooring near the Royal South Western Yacht Club and a pulling boat also sank near The Hoe. The *Thomas Forehead and Mary Rowse* was launched at 07.00 hours, when Rame Coastguard reported sighting red distress flares

from outside the Sound. The lifeboat immediately proceeded to the location given and found the casualty to be the 8-ton yacht, *Isonda*. The crew of the vessel comprised Mr and Mrs Cape of Pinner, Middlesex, their ten-month-old baby and a family friend. The group had been on a sailing holiday when their yacht was swept out to sea by gale-force winds. Upon reaching the safety of land, Mr Cape explained:

We arrived in Cawsand Bay on Saturday from Dartmouth and moored there. Then the gale started and we tried to get into Plymouth for safety. But the light was failing so we ran back into Cawsand Bay.

We anchored under the lee of the land and were all right until 8a.m. when the wind suddenly veered north.

The anchor dragged and we just drifted to the mouth of the bay. We put up flares. By that time the anchor had caught something below and it held us.

The *Isonda* was taken in tow by the lifeboat and found safety at Millbay Docks.

At about 19.00 hours on the evening of Tuesday 5 March 1957, four men set out from Plymouth in the 50-ton motor schooner, *Olivia*, of Plymouth, for Jersey. As the vessel cleared the Sound, it became apparent that weather conditions were deteriorating. At about 21.45 hours, an amateur radio operator in St Peter Port, Guernsey, picked up a radio distress signal from the *Olivia*, which was at that time drifting helplessly in heavy seas, approximately four miles inside the Eddystone Light. The signal was subsequently monitored by the Polruan Coastguard who alerted the Plymouth Lifeboat Station.

The *Thomas Forehead and Mary Rowse* slipped her mooring at 22.05 hours into a heavy sea and a strong south-easterly wind. Coxswain Walter Crowther was at the helm. Visibility was extremely poor and he requested the burning of additional flares to help locate the casualty. Eventually, in difficult sea conditions, the lifeboat came alongside the *Olivia*, but it took three attempts before a tow could be established. On the first attempt, the lifeboat closed on to the casualty and successfully passed a line. This line was secured to a winch but, as the force of the sea corkscrewed the two vessels from each other, the strain upon the winch proved too great and it was ripped from its fixings. Coxswain Crowther described the rescue attempts:

Visibility was poor and the sea rough. The first line was heaved aboard and secured to the winch, which was dragged from its fixture. Finally, after two other mishaps, a line was rocketed aboard and made secure.

The skipper/owner of the *Olivia*, Mr Gerry Scali, gave his recollection of events leading up to the rescue by the Plymouth lifeboat:

Everything went wrong. If the radio had gone wrong too we would have been swimming and that would have meant drowning because it was not until we were taken in tow that we had time to realise that none of us had life-jackets on.

Mr Scali explained that his party had left Plymouth having received favourable weather reports. About four miles beyond the Eddystone, the mechanic, Mr Easton, had been taken violently ill, and the party decided to return to Plymouth. After travelling some six miles, the engine's oil pressure suddenly dropped and the engine totally seized up. In the strong south-easterly wind, the crew attempted to deploy the foresail but it split in three places. They then attempted to raise the mainsail in an effort to obtain steerage, but, not being prepared for night sailing, the crew found themselves unable to hoist the sail. Whilst trying to raise the sails, Mr Easton was thrown across the deck by a violent movement of the vessel, and injured. It was at this point that Mr Scali sent out a distress signal.

The *Olivia* was being towed by the Plymouth lifeboat, when at a point near the Draystone Buoy, off Penlee Point, the tow-line, having chaffed against the yacht's partially lowered anchor chain, parted. Fortunately the lifeboat crew quickly replaced the tow-rope and completed the tow into Millbay Docks, accompanied for the latter part of the journey by the Trinity pilot cutter, *Maker*.

Plymouth was struck by hurricane-force-12 winds on the night of Tuesday 10 December 1957, which wrought devastation on local shipping, particularly in the Hamoaze. The frequent violent squalls aggravated the already turbulent and exceptionally rough seas. At Saltash the 500-ton ferry was blown ashore and was left stranded in the roadway at the Saltash landing stage. Several other vessels were swept from their moorings; these included the reserve Torpoint ferry, which was carried some 400 yards upriver, and two tugs, the *Tactful* and the *Carbiel*, each of

about 250 tons, belonging to Messrs Reynolds, the Admiralty contractors.

The storm was of such ferocity that the 360-ton wooden minesweeper, HMS *Darlaston*, broke adrift in No.3 Basin, Devonport Dockyard. She first collided with a quayside before colliding with the South Torpoint ferry. The prow of the ferry was damaged but there were no personal injuries.

In truly horrendous conditions, the *Thomas Forehead and Mary Rowse* was launched at 21.55 hours. Initially she rescued two men who had been swept upriver, past the vessel that they were attempting to board. Having been swept from her mooring, the tug *Carbiel* became jammed in the entrance of No.5 Basin. The lifeboat took off her crew and, having put them ashore, stood-by while the *Carbiel* was towed clear by another tug. The lifeboat placed the crew aboard the tug *Alexandra*, which then took part in the salvage work. After an eventful two hours, during which the lifeboat rendered assistance to numerous craft, the Plymouth lifeboat regained her mooring at 00.10 hours.

A headline in the *Western Evening Herald*, of Monday 5 December 1960, proclaimed: 'COLLIER SAVED 10 FEET FROM DISASTER DURING HOWLING WEST GALE.' The gale, with winds that reached 50 miles per hour, had swept Plymouth for much of the previous day, Sunday, and at their height threatened to dash a collier on the rocks at Jennycliffe. At one time the vessel was reported to have been within ten feet of disaster. Simultaneously the Dutch liner, *Prins der Nederlanden*, was forced to raise her anchors and seek the safety of the open sea. Paradoxically, the city of Plymouth was left practically unscathed.

The collier was the 316-ton *Edenside* of Middlesborough, commanded by Captain George Smith of Aberdeen. Realising the plight of his vessel, Captain Smith broadcast a MAYDAY and, within 20 minutes, the Plymouth lifeboat was heading for the casualty. 'The conditions in the Sound were the worst I have experienced for years', said Coxswain Crowther. 'There was a howling gale; the rain was lashing down, and the sea a mass of confused water. Total darkness and flying spray did not help matters.'

With the *Thomas Forehead and Mary Rowse* heading to her rescue, the *Edenside* continued to send up distress flares and to make continuous, urgent requests for a tug to render assistance and

Left: *Walter Crowther on the cover of the RNLI's Life-Boat Magazine, March 1958.* PETER CROWTHER

Above right: *HRH Prince Philip, Duke of Edinburgh and Plymouth lifeboat crew members during his visit to the station, Thursday 22 July 1965.* Left to right: *Mr J. Hicks (Hon. Sec.), HRH Prince Philip, P. White (Coxswain), F. Amos, W. Rogers, T. Keane, D. Biscombe, F. Fowler, J. Dare.*

pull her out of danger. The *Edenside's* request was acknowledged by the Admiralty tug, *Camel*, which put out from Devonport. As the *Camel* reached the stricken vessel, her radio failed and for the next three hours all communications had to be relayed via the lifeboat.

The lifeboat stood-by as the *Camel* commenced the rescue operation, but the *Edenside* was straining so heavily at her anchors that it was feared the tow-rope would part. It was at this point that Captain Smith gave the order to cut through the anchor cables. The eight-man crew of the collier cut through the anchor cables with a hacksaw, an operation that took two hours, before the collier could be taken under tow and safely berthed at the Barbican's North Quay. Captain George Smith later commented: 'It was touch and go. Our safety was a matter of tide. If it had been on the ebb, we would have gone to the bottom.'

In 1961 Walter Crowther retired, having given 34 years of service to the RNLI's Plymouth lifeboats, the last 22 years as Coxswain. His retirement was marked on Thursday 9 November 1961, when the *Thomas Forehead and Mary Rowse* carried the crew and their wives, to Cremyll from where they made their way to Mount Edgcumbe House, the family home of the Earl of Mount Edgcumbe. Lord Mount

Edgcumbe paid tribute to Walter Crowther, recalling the occasion when, on 13 January 1942, a Sunderland flying boat was aground on rocks in Jennycliffe Bay. Two men were trapped aboard and the then Plymouth lifeboat, the *Robert and Marcella Beck*, went to the rescue, with Coxswain Crowther in charge. After attempts by gun had failed, he threw a line aboard. In expressing his thanks, Walter revealed a wartime secret. The area over which he had taken the lifeboat that day was heavily mined. Had he used the electric capstan to release the anchor, a magnetic mine could have blown the vessel sky-high.

Two of Walter's wartime crew, Second Coxswain Albert Sleeman and Motor Mechanic Arthur Banham, attended the ceremony. Lord Mount Edgcumbe then presented Walter Crowther with a cheque and a framed Certificate of Service from the RNLI, together with a clock from the crew and honorary officers of the station. For Mrs Crowther there was a presentation of a handbag and a bouquet of flowers.

Nic Carter (who in 1963 was in turn succeeded as Coxswain by Peter White) took over from Walter Crowther.

The year 1964 proved to be one of the busiest to date for the crew of the Plymouth lifeboat with 21 services being answered, and a total of 19 lives being saved. The month of August alone saw seven launches.

The Mayer family of Plymouth set out for Dartmouth on Friday 31 July 1964 to take delivery of a 40-foot cabin cruiser, *Nimrod II*, and cruise back to Plymouth. The passage went well for the family, Mr and Mrs Mayer and their three children, until they got into difficulties at 22.20 hours in Heybrook Bay. After the police at Plympton had received reports that flashing lights had been seen, and shouts for help heard, the Plymouth lifeboat was launched, at 23.25 hours, under the command of Coxswain Peter White. Upon the lifeboat's return to port, he told a reporter:

We had no trouble finding the cruiser. We fired a flare and were assisted by the headlights of cars on the shore. Mr Mayer was sending SOS with the aid of a bicycle lamp.

Two of the lifeboat's crew were placed aboard the *Nimrod II* and the vessel was taken in tow by the lifeboat. The Mayer family were landed at Millbay Docks at 01.15 hours and the *Thomas Forehead and Mary Rowse* was ready for service at 02.00 hours.

The relief fleet lifeboat, *Lloyds*, was placed on station at Plymouth for the summer of 1962, while the *Thomas Forehead and Mary Rowse* underwent a major refit. As part of the refit, a wheel-house was fitted over the previously open centre cockpit.

The *Thomas Forehead and Mary Rowse* sustained minor damage when she went to the assistance of the German freighter, the *Kremsertor*, on Thursday 20 January 1966, but, following an inspection of the hull by an Inspector of the RNLI, she was pronounced fit to put to sea in an emergency.

It was just before 06.00 hours that the lifeboat was called out into heavy seas and storm-force winds blowing at 50 miles per hour. It was while she was en route to the casualty that the lifeboat struck a glancing blow to a buoy just off Penlee Point. Coxswain Peter White was not deterred by the collision and continued his search for the *Kremsertor*. A Royal Air Force Shackleton joined the *Thomas Forehead and Mary Rowse* in the effort.

Communication was established between the lifeboat and the aircraft via an ultra-high-frequency link. This was the first occasion on which the lifeboat had used the UHF link in an emergency. The value of this technology was emphasised by Coxswain White who declared that, 'You would have thought you were sitting alongside the pilot of the aircraft.'

Upon locating the casualty the seas had moderated and it was established that the services of the lifeboat were not required. The lifeboat returned to her mooring after a 10½-hour spell at sea, the longest period of time that she had been engaged on a service for more than a decade. The crew were: Peter White, Fred Amos, Pat Marshall, T. Keane, M. Keane, R. Cottrell, J. Dare, J. Sheldon and F. Fowler.

The Hon. Secretary of the Plymouth Lifeboat Station subsequently received the following letter:

SCHLÜSSEL REEDEREI

28 Bremen, April 6, 1966

The Hon. Secretary
The Royal National Life-boat Institution
Plymouth
Devon
England

Dear Sir,

MV "KREMSERTOR"

After the loss of MV "KREMSERTOR" end of January off Falmouth we asked our agents Messrs. G. C. Fox & Co. to convey to you our sincere thanks for the assistance you and the crew of your life-boat gave to the crew of our ship. Although the crew of the "KREMSERTOR" was brought to safety without the help of your life-boat we appreciate the fact that the crew of you life-boat assisted the rescue work and spent many hours at sea. It was good to know for our Captain and his crew that your boat was at sea and heading for them.

Yours faithfully
SCHLÜSSEL REEDEREI

A Search and Rescue helicopter was scrambled, and the Plymouth lifeboat was launched, to go to the assistance of a craft that had experienced engine failure on Saturday 18 June 1966. The craft was two-and-a-half miles off Rame Head, and proved to be an aqua-glider, an experimental air-propelled craft, built at Falmouth, on the principle of a hovercraft. The crew of the aqua-glider, Mr Steve Law and Mr D. Graham, of Bath, were taking the craft on a proving run from Brixham to Falmouth, when

Reserve lifeboat Lloyds, ON 754, *at Sutton Harbour Regatta, 1968.*

Above: *The crew of 1967–68. Left to right, back: John Sheldon, Danny Biscombe, Albert Holmes (Bowman); front: Fred Fowler, Bill Rogers (Mechanic), Peter White (Coxswain), John Dare (Second Coxswain), Tom Keane (Second Mechanic).*

The relief fleet's Barnett Class lifeboat Lloyds, *at Plymouth, c.1967.*

This image: *Coxswain Peter White takes* Thomas Forehead and Mary Rowse *out for service to the Teignmouth crabber,* Sunlit Waters, *on 16 February 1967.*

The crew of 1969. Left to right: *M. Keane, D. Biscombe, P. Marshall (reserve), J. Dare (Second Coxswain), T. Keane (Second Mechanic), P. White (Coxswain), J. Sheldon;* kneeling: *C. Alcock (Mechanic), R. Jago (reserve).*

the engine failed. As the craft was not equipped with distress flares, the two men waved their yellow life-jackets in order to attract attention. Local people acknowledged the signal by waving a large sheet in return.

Mrs Holman, of the Freathy Café, Whitsands, raised the alarm with the Rame Head Coastguard at 17.11 hours, and within nine minutes the *Thomas Forehead and Mary Rowse* was launched. The helicopter, from RAF Chivenor, captained by Flight-Lieutenant Bob Jones, with Flight-Lieutenant Smyth as navigator, was the first emergency unit to arrive on the scene. The helicopter's winch-man, Sergeant Keith Davis, was lowered to the aqua-glider and remained on board the vessel until the lifeboat arrived.

In a strong south-westerly wind and a heavy swell, the crew of the aqua-glider were taken aboard the lifeboat and a tow-line was attached to the craft. The tow, however, proved exceptionally difficult and when rounding Penlee Point, a particularly heavy sea carried away items of equipment that were loosely stored on the glider. The lifeboat recovered the majority of the equipment and continued the tow into Millbay Docks, regaining her mooring at 21.20 hours.

At 07.37 hours on Tuesday 29 July 1969, Brixham Coastguard raised the alarm with the Plymouth Lifeboat Station, reporting that a dismasted yacht was burning distress flares and drifting rapidly, one mile south-south-west of the Eddystone Lighthouse. The Plymouth lifeboat cast off her mooring at 07.50 hours and set out for the casualty, in a north-westerly gale force 8 and rough sea. At 09.52 hours the lifeboat came up with the casualty, the 55-foot auxiliary schooner, *Morwenna* of Shoreham, which had six persons on board, including two children. At this

time the schooner's position was approximately three-and-a-half miles south-south-east of the Eddystone. Coxswain Peter White manoeuvred the lifeboat alongside the *Morwenna* but found that the schooner's mainmast was lying over her starboard quarter, hampering the rescue operation. A line was attached to the schooner's mast and, with the motor vessel *Ben Arkle* providing a lee in the heavy seas, an attempt was made to recover the mast aboard the *Morwenna*. The recovery attempt was unsuccessful. The lifeboat again approached the casualty and by perfectly matching the rise and fall of the two vessels, the six persons were taken off the schooner onto the lifeboat. Two lifeboat men were then placed aboard the schooner and a tow-line was established. At 10.25 hours, in gale-force winds and turbulent seas, the difficult operation of towing the vessel to port commenced. It was not until 16.15 hours that a safe anchorage was reached, at Cremyll. The *Thomas Forehead and Mary Rowse* regained her mooring at 17.20 hours.

Following this service, the Hon. Secretary of the Plymouth Lifeboat Station received the following letter from the Headquarters of the RNLI:

> *17 April 1970*
>
> *The Coxswain and Crew,*
> *Plymouth Life-boat Station.*
>
> *Gentlemen:*
>
> *I have read a report which has been received from the Inspector of Life-boats on the service by the Plymouth life-boat 'Thomas Forehead and Mary Rowse' on 29th July last when the auxiliary schooner "Morwenna" was saved and the six persons on board, including two children, were rescued after the schooner had become dismasted in gale force winds and was drifting three-and-a-half miles south-south-east of the Eddystone lighthouse.*
>
> *This long and arduous service was carried out exceptionally well, and I send to each of you the Institution's and my own warm appreciative thanks for your excellent service on this occasion.*
>
> *Yours sincerely,*
> *Nigel Dixon.*
> *Secretary.*

Both the *Western Morning News* and the *Western Evening Herald* carried similar headlines on Friday 17 April 1970: 'LIFEBOAT GETS £5 DONATION AFTER 33 MISSIONS' and 'FOR 33 LIFEBOAT TRIPS £5 AND ONE "THANK YOU."' The headlines were commenting upon the Annual Report of the Plymouth branch of the

The 1967 crew of the Thomas Forehead and Mary Rowse. *Left to right, back:
R. Cotterel (reserve), F. Fowler, P. White (Coxswain), A. Holmes (Bowman), J. Sheldon
(reserve), J. Dare; front: M. Keane (reserve), D. Biscombe, F. Amos (Second Coxswain),
W. Rogers (Mechanic), T. Keane (Second Mechanic), A. Hicks (Hon. Sec).*

Overshadowed by the cranes of Devonport Dockyard, the Thomas Forehead and Mary
Rowse *undergoing trials after an extensive refit and new engines, 1972.*

RNLI, released that day by the Hon. Secretary, Mr R.H.E. Sainsbury. The report stated that demand upon the Plymouth lifeboat continued to increase steadily, 33 launches being undertaken in the years 1968–69. For those 33 launches the station had received one donation of £5, and one letter of thanks. Mr Sainsbury commented: 'We are not looking for either, but it is a point not without interest.' Mr Sainsbury also reported the following statistics:

On the Plymouth station, the average number of calls, per year, from 1928–1949 was 2.2. The average from 1950–1969 was 6.5 and for the last decade, 13. The inshore boat answered 19 calls during the year, compared with 15 the previous year. The lifeboat and her crew rescued 15 people during the year, while the inshore rescue boat saved 16.

In the spring of 1972 the *Thomas Forehead and Mary Rowse* underwent a major refit and was fitted with two new 78hp Thornycroft diesel engines. A service was held for the boat at the Princess Royal Pier, Millbay Docks. This was con-ducted by the Revd Philip Withers, of the Mutley Baptist Church, 'for the re-dedication, intercession and thanksgiving for the lifeboat, her coxswain and crew, and those who man the inshore boat.' At the service the 'Pilots' Psalm', an adaptation of the 23rd Psalm, written for seafarers, by a captain in the Merchant Navy, was sung.

During the extensive six-month refit and general overhaul, the lifeboat was fitted with radar. The Hon. Secretary of the Port of Plymouth Branch of the RNLI, Mr Ray Sainsbury, said that the radar would be a great aid to future rescues.

During 1971 Coxswain Peter White left the service to take up a government position in the Gilbert Islands; and in August the then Second Coxswain, John Dare, took his place at the helm.

Winds in excess of 64 knots, which officially designates hurricane force 12, and heavy, pounding seas, relentlessly battered the South Devon coast on Wednesday 16 January 1974, culminating in the front-page headline that appeared in the *Western Morning News* the following day: 'CAPTAIN'S WIFE AND SON AMONG SEVEN DEAD AS SHIP SINKS OFF S. DEVON.'

Left: *Mechanic Bill Rogers and the Station Hon. Secretary Mr Hicks are introduced to the new 'Tannoy' system.*

Below: *The reserve fleet lifeboat, the City of Edinburgh, ON 802, on station 1971–72, during the refit of the Plymouth lifeboat.*

The dedication of new engines for Thomas Forehead and Mary Rowse, *1972.*

A service to celebrate the Harvest of the Sea.

It was at 14.17 hours on that fateful Wednesday that Coxswain John Dare and his crew launched the *Thomas Forehead and Mary Rowse* into the exceptionally violent seas, their mission being to assist the crew of a Danish coaster. The casualty was the 781-ton *Merc Enterprise*, which had left Liverpool the previous day with a crew of 14. It was just before 12.00 hours that the order had been given to 'abandon ship' some 23 miles south of the Plymouth break-water. Conditions at the scene were horrendous, the vessel being assaulted by 70-foot waves and winds that, at their worst, reached 100 miles per hour. Literally minutes after the crew took to the sea in two of the ship's lifeboats, and two inflat-able dinghies, the coaster sank. The ship's mas-ter, 25-year-old Captain Jens Peter Feddersen, who was on his last command of the *Merc Enterprise* before joining a new ship, was among the survivors, but his wife, who was on board for the first time, and their seven-year-old son were among those who were lost.

A request was made for the launch of the Salcombe lifeboat, but the Station's Hon. Secretary, Mr Bill Budgett and the Salcombe harbour-master, Captain J.J. Blazeby, were of the opinion that conditions were far too hazardous to attempt to take the lifeboat out over the notori-ous Salcombe Bar. Notwithstanding these truly appalling conditions, the Plymouth lifeboat con-tinued on her errand of mercy. The lifeboat was frequently swamped, from stem to stern, her crew finding themselves up to their waists in water. John Dare ordered his crew into the shelter of the after-cabin whilst he remained at the wheel, assisted solely by Motor Mechanic Cyril Alcock. Both men later commented that they had never experienced weather and sea conditions as they did on that day, albeit, when contacted by radio and asked if he thought the conditions too severe to continue the service, Coxswain John Dare replied, 'Negative – we are continuing.'

By this time a massive sea-and-air rescue operation was under way, a British trawler had responded to the MAYDAY, as had the Russian trawler, the *Leningrad*. Both British and German helicopters had been scrambled from RNAS Culdrose but by the time they had reached the scene of the disaster all the lifeboats and inflatable dinghies from the *Merc Enterprise* had overturned, spilling the survivors into the turbulent seas. The first vessel to reach the scene of the disaster was the *Leningrad*, which, with 50-foot waves crashing over her deck, successfully located and rescued four survivors. Through an interpreter her skipper, Captain Gyemnady Beljaev, related to the press the role that his ship had played in the rescue:

I received the SOS at 12.55 p.m. and headed straight for the ship's position. We arrived in the area in 40 minutes. We were first on the scene.

Right in front of my eyes the ship turned upside-down and I saw members of the crew in the water. Two life rafts were over-turned, but there was no-one hanging on to them.

All the crew members were in water up to their chests. We lowered our own men down the side of the ship and into the water. They tied ropes around the waists of the Danes and we hauled them aboard.

My own sailors jumped into the water to save the others. The whole operation took three hours.

Asked if he had ever encountered such sea conditions, Captain Beljaev replied, 'Thank goodness this was my first time.'

As the *Thomas Forehead and Mary Rowse* drove on through the merciless seas, John Dare was informed that the *Merc Enterprise* had cap-sized. He was made aware that four survivors had been taken on board the *Leningrad* with a further seven survivors having been picked up by the Search and Rescue helicopters. Above all he was informed that the helicopter pilots had reported that conditions at the scene were so appalling that they advised the immediate recall of the lifeboat. The fact that seven lives remained unaccounted for only served to increase the deter-mination and resolve of the lifeboat's crew, and the *Thomas Forehead and Mary Rowse*, which was now only four miles from the scene, carried on. Coxswain Dare later explained his action, and those of his crew, by saying: 'We knew there were still seven men missing. Our job is life saving and that is why we went out.'

When the lifeboat reached the scene she continued to be assailed by the raging seas, topped by white, blinding spray. Battling with these conditions, the safety of those missing being uppermost in their minds, the lifeboat crew maintained the search for survivors until 16.45 hours, when Rame Head Coastguard informed Coxswain Dare that the helicopter search was being called off. Being unable to locate survivors, John Dare set the *Thomas Forehead and Mary Rowse* on a course for Plymouth. On her return

Above: *Commander in Chief, Plymouth, being welcomed aboard the lifeboat by Coxswain Carter. Left to right, on the foredeck: J. Sheldon, F. Fowler, J. Dare; in the line-up: N. Carter (Coxswain), F. Amos (Second Coxswain), A. Holmes (Bowman), W. Rogers (Mechanic); ashore: Admiral Sir Charles Madden, A. Hicks (Hon. Sec.).*

Left: *The Thomas Forehead and Mary Rowse on her last journey to Mashford's Yard before being reallocated to another station. Crew: John Dare and Cyril Alcock.*

Below: *The Thomas Forehead and Mary Rowse greets her successor, the Thomas Forehead and Mary Rowse II.*

Above: *Coxswain John Dare, the BBC's Joe Pengelly, and another member of the broadcasting crew on board the Thomas Forehead and Mary Rowse for 'Good Morning Devon'.*

journey, at a position four miles south of Penlee, the *Thomas Forehead and Mary Rowse* came up with the Russian trawler, the *Leningrad*, and escorted her into West Wharf, Plymouth.

In paying tribute to the courage, skill and determination shown by the crew of the Plymouth lifeboat in carrying out a truly outstanding service, one must also acknowledge the bravery of the crews of the Search and Rescue helicopters, Lieutenant-Commander David Blythe, senior pilot of 700 Squadron, RNAS Culdrose, and his winch-man Petty Officer David Fowles, together with Lieutenant Fred Hatton, and Petty Office David Jackson, who with others flew and operated their aircraft in conditions which took them to the very edge of their operational limits. The lifeboat crew were: John Dare, Cyril Alcock, Pat Marshall, Michael Keane, David Dinham, Frank Parker and Douglas Jago.

John Dare received the following letter, in June 1974, from RNLI Headquarters, Poole, Dorset:

Dear Coxswain Dare,

At a meeting of the Committee of Management held in London on the 12th June 1974, a report was considered on the service launch by the Plymouth life-boat "Thomas Forehead and Mary Rowse" on the 16th January 1974, when the Danish coaster "Merc Enterprise" was in serious difficulties 23 miles south of the Plymouth Breakwater.

The Committee were impressed by the determination and excellent seamanship displayed by you on this occasion, so ably supported by your crew and decided to award you the Bronze Medal of the Institution. You will also receive a vellum recording the award and your crew will each receive a certificate to commemorate their participation in this service launch. Your Honorary Secretary will let you know the arrangements for the presentation of the awards in due course.

I should like to take this opportunity to send you my personal congratulations of your well deserved award and to express my admiration for your fine seamanship on this occasion.

Yours sincerely,
Nigel Dixon
Director and Secretary.

Members of the Plymouth crew take to the former Whitby pulling lifeboat, during the Plymouth Lord Mayor's Parade, 25 May 1974. From bow: John Sheldon, ?, A. Kendrick, Dave Dinham, Gerry MacManus, Ivor Lovering, Fred Fowler, Sid Harris, Tom Keane.

At 12.00 hours on Sunday 3 March 1974, maroons were fired and flags hoisted at the 252 lifeboat stations throughout the UK, to celebrate the 150th anniversary of the founding of the RNLI. Locally, a simple service of thanksgiving was held outside Longroom Signal Station, the service being attended by Revd Philip Withers, Chaplain of the Port of Plymouth Branch of the Royal National Lifeboat Institution; Captain Tom Hornsby, Chairman; Ray Sainsbury, Hon. Secretary; Plymouth lifeboat crew members John Dare (Coxswain), Frank Jago (Second Coxswain) and Cyril Alcock (Mechanic), together with Commander Peter Sturdee and Lieutenant-Commander Richard Little.

At a service held at the Mutley Baptist Church, Plymouth, on Sunday 5 May 1974, the Revd Philip Withers presented Coxswain John Dare with a Bible, which was to be carried on board Plymouth's new lifeboat, the *Thomas Forehead and Mary Rowse II*. Among those who attended the service was the Earl of Mount Edgcumbe, the President of the Port of Plymouth Branch of the RNLI, who read the lesson from the 50th Psalm. Each member of the lifeboat crew received a Modern English copy of the New Testament. At the time of this service, the new lifeboat was undergoing sea trials off the Isle of Wight.

Left: *Coxswain John Dare is presented to HRH The Duchess of Kent at the naming and dedication ceremony of the* Thomas Forehead and Mary Rowse II. Also in the party, left to right: *Mrs Pat Jago, Frederick Jago, Mrs Joan Dare, Ray Sainsbury.*

Below: *HRH The Duchess of Kent receives a bouquet from Debbie MacManus at the naming and dedication ceremony of the* Thomas Forehead and Mary Rowse II, *17 June 1975.*

Above: *The* Thomas Forehead and Mary Rowse II, *dressed for her naming and dedication ceremony, 17 June 1975.* Left to right: *Pat Marshall, Cyril Alcock, John Dare (Coxswain), Frank Jago, Danny Biscombe.*

HRH The Duke and Duchess of Kent at the naming and dedication ceremony of the Thomas Forehead and Mary Rowse II, *escorted by Commander F.R.H. Swann, CBE, RNVR, Chairman of the RNLI, and Ray Sainsbury, Honorary Secretary of the Plymouth Lifeboat Station.*

13

*T*HOMAS *F*OREHEAD AND *M*ARY *R*OWSE *II*
22 *M*AY 1974–12 *M*AY 1987

Class: *Waveney* **Propulsion:** *2 x 260hp General Motors GM 8V-53 diesel engines*
Speed: *15 knots* **Crew:** *5* **Length:** *44' 10"* **Beam:** *12' 8"* **Draft:** *4' 2"*
Official number: *1028* **Fleet number:** *44-010*
Builder: *Groves & Guttridge, Cowes, 1974* **Service Launches:** *181* **Lives Saved:** *91*
Coxswain: *John Dare*
Mechanic: *Cyril Alcock (1974–87), Derek Studden (1987)*

The year 1974 was dubbed 'The Year of the Lifeboat' and in Plymouth the year reached its high point when, at 12.00 hours on Friday 19 July, HRH The Duke of Kent, President of the Institution, arrived at the Royal Western Yacht Club, on board Plymouth's new 44-foot Waveney Class lifeboat, to open the first ever International Lifeboat Exhibition. The Lord Mayor of Plymouth, Councillor F. Johnson, accompanied His Royal Highness at the opening ceremony. Earlier that day, at Millbay Docks, the Duke had been introduced to both British and overseas lifeboat officials and crew. Following formalities, the Duke boarded the *Thomas Forehead and Mary Rowse II* and was escorted into Plymouth Sound by a fleet of 11 visiting lifeboats, all dressed for the occasion. The Plymouth Lifeboat Station's 18-foot McLachlan and an Atlantic 21 were also in attendance.

The festival atmosphere that surrounded the exhibition could not be completely divorced from reality for, even as the Duke of Kent was embarking on the Plymouth lifeboat, an ILB was picking up a canoeist who was in trouble at the mouth of Millbay Docks. It also transpired that the Norwegian lifeboat, the *Ragni Berg*, had stood-by a Dutch yacht that was in trouble off the coast of Esbjerg, on passage from Norway to Plymouth.

At the opening ceremony, His Royal Highness presented the Institution's Bronze Medal for Gallantry to Coxswain John Dare for the service, in appalling weather, to the *Merc Enterprise* on Wednesday 16 January 1974. In declaring the exhibition open, the Duke said:

I hope the exhibition, which lasts for four weeks, and is accompanied by a great variety of other events mostly of a marine flavour, will be visited by many thousands of our own citizens, by people from overseas, by the young and by the old. Apart from the valuable revenue this will bring to the Institution, I think it is important that the achievements and capability of the lifeboat service should be known as widely as possible – particularly of course to anybody who uses the sea in any way, whether for business, sport or recreation. To all of them the exhibition will, I believe, convey a message of hope for humanity and belief in the highest ideals of selfless service to others.

After attending a reception and visiting many exhibits, His Royal Highness left the exhibition to fly to Cornwall, where he performed the

Right: *The German lifeboat* Arwed Emminghaus *visits Plymouth for the International Lifeboat Exhibition, 1974.*

The Norwegian lifeboat R.S. Platou *heads the visiting fleet as they enter Plymouth Sound for the exhibition.*

Left: *John Dare shares a joke with HRH The Duke of Kent at the exhibition.*

Right: *The Arun Class lifeboat 54-03,* Civil Service and Post Office No.37, *which was later to become the Torbay lifeboat, the* Edward Bridges, *arriving in Plymouth for the International Lifeboat Exhibition, 1974.*

Above left: *Badge of the United States Coast Guard cutter* Duane. JOHN DARE
This image: *The Rother Class 37-31,* J. Reginald Corah, *dressed for the exhibition.*

naming ceremony of the new Sennen Cove lifeboat, the *Diana White*.

On the Sunday prior to the exhibition, six foreign lifeboats, on passage to Plymouth, were welcomed at the new Headquarters of the RNLI, Poole. On the morning of Tuesday 16 July in moderate force 5–6 winds and turbulent seas, the lifeboats set a course for Torbay and, at a position two miles off the Shambles Light-vessel, the fleet took up a formation in two columns behind the flagship, the *City of Bristol*, ready to rendezvous at 13.00 hours with HMS *Ajax*. Breaking formation once more, with the Arun *54-03* and the German vessel the *Arwed Emminghaus* at their head, all boats reached Brixham by 19.00 hours.

The following morning, in a calm sea, the boats set forth on the final leg of their passage. All sailed at their own speed, meeting up at a position off Gara Point, where they again took up formation and rendezvoused with HMS *Walkerton* for the run into Plymouth. The Plymouth Lifeboat, the *Thomas Forehead and Mary Rowse II*, which, together with two ILBs, met this proud and graceful fleet and escorted the vessels to their moorings in Millbay Docks. Three US Coast Guard cutters, *Duane*, *Chase* and *Ingham*, later joined the fleet. These cutters were 300 feet in length and between them carried a crew of approximately 600.

The lifeboats attending the exhibition were:

Germany: the 26.6m rescue cruiser *Arwed Emminghaus*, with daughter boat, the *Alte Liebe*;

Poland: the 21.09m rescue cruiser, *Monson*;

Sweden: the 78-foot patrolling steel lifeboat, the *Sigurd Golje*;

France: the 15.5m 'all season' lifeboat, the *Patron Emil Guyot*;

Norway: the 80-foot cruiser-type lifeboat, *R.S. Platou*, and the 45-foot patrol boat, the *Ragni Berg*.

The RNLI's own fleet was represented by four of their newest lifeboats, all being on trials prior to being placed on station. The fleet comprised:

City of Bristol: the 70-foot Clyde Class, trawler-type lifeboat, ON 1030, which was to be stationed at Clovelly;

Rotary Service: ON 1031, a prototype of the 50-foot Thames Class lifeboats;

Augustine Courtauld: the Waveney Class 44-011, ON 1029, which was to be stationed at Poole;

54-03 Civil Service and Post Office Fund No.37: ON 1037, the third 54-foot, wooden hull, Arun Class with rounded transom (later to become the Torbay lifeboat, the *Edward Bridges*);

37-31 J. Reginald Corah: the 37' 6" Rother Class lifeboat, ON 1023, which had not joined the main fleet for the passage to Plymouth.

The exhibition proper was held at West Hoe Park, Plymouth. The former Whitby boat, the *Robert and Ellen Robson*, built in 1918, and one of the two pulling lifeboats still in existence, was on display. The 'Liverpool' type lifeboat, the *Elliott Gill*, was displayed on her own carriage, whilst younger visitors showed great interest in a launch tractor. An Atlantic 21 and a 16-foot inflatable craft represented the Inshore Lifeboats.

The first rescue demonstration, which was scheduled for the morning of Saturday 20 July, had to be cancelled because, just as it was starting, the maroons sounded to launch the Plymouth lifeboat, a helicopter and an Atlantic 21 that was in Plymouth to take part in the rescue demonstrations. This service was to search for two boys overdue from a fishing expedition.

The last formal event of the exhibition was an open-air interdenominational service of thanksgiving and dedication for the work of the RNLI, and for the lifeboat services of all nations, which took place at the Princess Royal Pier, Millbay Docks, on Sunday morning. The Revd Philip Withers of the Mutley Baptist Church conducted the service, whilst Father Michael Cole, the Roman Catholic Port Chaplain, led the prayers. The Coxswain of the Plymouth Lifeboat, John Dare, read the well-known passage 'those who go down to the sea in ships', from the 107th Psalm. At the conclusion of the service, the lifeboats set out to sea for a short wreath-laying ceremony. Numerous yachts and small craft followed the flotilla, line astern, and whilst not all of the service could be clearly heard, some parts carried across the water. A Royal Marine bugler, standing on the bow of the 70-foot Clyde Class lifeboat, the *City of Bristol*, sounded the Last Post and Reveille. As Commander F.R.H. Swann, CBE, RNVR, and Chairman of the Committee of Management, laid the wreath from the flagship, ensigns were lowered in salute to the memory of all lost lifeboat men. The highly successful exhibition ran from Friday 19 July to Saturday 17 August 1974.

Coxswain John Dare welcomes the Lord Mayor and Lady Mayoress of Plymouth, Mr and Mrs F. Johnson, on board the Thomas Forehead and Mary Rowse II, *1974. Crew members left to right:* John Dare, Pat Marshall, Fred Jago, Mike Keane, John Sheldon.

Plymouth Lifeboat's Ladies Guild, 1978.

The Duke and Duchess of Kent are shown over the Thomas Forehead and Mary Rowse II *by John Dare and Danny Biscombe, 17 June 1975.*

44-010 plays host to the Port Admiral and Flag Officer, Plymouth, and their wives. Crew, left to right: 'Tiny' Parker, Cyril Alcock, Phil Reed with Coxswain John Dare at the helm.

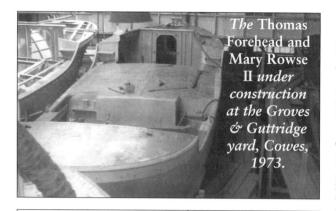

The Thomas Forehead and Mary Rowse II *under construction at the Groves & Guttridge yard, Cowes, 1973.*

The Plymouth lifeboat towing in British Oxygen, skippered by Robin Knox-Johnston, after completing the Round Britain Race, 24 July 1974.

HRH The Duchess of Kent returned to the Plymouth Lifeboat Station, at 11.40 hours, on Tuesday 17 June 1975, accompanied by HRH The Duke of Kent, President of the RNLI, for a dedication and naming service. Following the Royal Salute and formal introductions, Debbie MacManus, daughter of the Inshore Lifeboat crew member, G. MacManus, presented a bouquet of flowers to the Duchess. Souvenir programmes were presented to the Duke and Duchess by Adrian Sainsbury, aged six, and Christopher Sainsbury, aged eight, sons of R.H.E. Sainsbury Esq., the Hon. Secretary of the Plymouth Station. Commander F.R.H. Swann, CBE, RNVR, Chairman of the RNLI Committee of Management, delivered the lifeboat into the care of the Port of Plymouth Lifeboat Station. The lifeboat was received by R.H.E. Sainsbury, Esq., on behalf of the station.

The dedication was conducted by the Revd Philip W. Withers, BD, Honorary Chaplain to the Port of Plymouth Lifeboat Station. Lifeboat man John Sheldon read the lesson 'They that go down to the sea in ships; and occupy their business in great waters.' The Duchess of Kent then performed the naming ceremony. In naming the lifeboat, the Duchess commented that the city, with its seafaring traditions and combination of new and old, resembled the RNLI; both were forward-looking. Three maroons were fired and the lifeboat launched. Music was provided by the Flag Officer, Plymouth, Band of Her Majesty's Royal Marines; the director of music was Lieutenant R.J.P. Kempton, LRAM, RM.

The *Thomas Forehead and Mary Rowse II* cost approximately £100,000, the expense being defrayed by the legacy of Mr T. Field. At the naming ceremony the lifeboat was described thus:

Her machinery comprises twin General Motors 8v – 53 marine diesel engines with Twin Disc reverse and reduction gear boxes. These give her a maximum speed of 16 knots and a radius of action of 87 miles.

She is fitted with radar, echo sounder and two radio installations for communication with ship/shore stations and aircraft.

Her full crew is five and she can carry 25 survivors under cover. All seats are fitted with safety belts to ensure the safety of crew and survivors in heavy weather. For the same reason the cabins are lined with foam rubber which has the added advantages of sound insulation and prevention of condensation.

Plymouth's new 44-foot Waveney Class lifeboat was of a design pioneered by the American Coastguard. She was of steel construction, the hull being divided into seven watertight compartments. The aluminium structure was fitted with watertight doors to enclose the cabins and provide additional buoyancy, which, when combined with the hull design, enabled the boat to self-right in five seconds. The Waveney Class was named after the river at Lowestoft, where the first RNLI version of the boat was built.

The new lifeboat arrived in Plymouth on Friday 17 May 1974, following an extended passage from the Isle of Wight to Plymouth, via St Peter Port in the Channel Islands. The delivery crew were John Dare (Coxswain), Cyril Alcock (Mechanic), Fleet Mechanic Ian Jones, crew member Mike Keane and Lieutenant-Commander Roy Portchester, District Inspector of Lifeboats.

The new lifeboat was fitted with navigation lights, costing over £100, paid for by the Plymouth Round Table. The Plymouth Lions also provided funds towards a new lifeboat house and amenities.

The crowds and VIPs were intrigued by the fact that when the royal visitors left by helicopter, they took with them a long parcel, carefully wrapped in tin foil. The Lord Mayor of Plymouth, Mr W. Ivor Thompson, later revealed the secrets of the parcel – it had contained a salmon, which had been presented to the royal couple on the lifeboat earlier that morning. 'This is the kind of reception Plymouth tries to give its guests,' said the Lord Mayor, 'nothing too stuffy'.

It was at about 10.45 hours on Wednesday 15 February 1978 that Rame Coastguard contacted Second Coxswain Patrick Marshall by telephone and informed him that the maroons had been fired in response to a distress call received from a fishing trawler that was sinking ten miles south-west of Rame Head. He was also informed that a frigate, HMS *Sirius*, was steaming to the assistance of the stricken vessel. Two reserve crewmen, Ivor Lovering and Michael Foster, met Pat Marshall at the boat-house. They assembled ahead of the mechanic, but being himself the

former assistant mechanic, Marshall started the engines and the lifeboat slipped her mooring. The *Thomas Forehead and Mary Rowse II* made her way to Trinity Pier where the mechanic, Cyril Alcock, was taken on board and a course was set through the Bridges Channel and on towards Penlee Point. On reaching Penlee Point, Rame Coastguard advised a course of 238°(T). The course was followed for approximately five miles, whereupon a warship was sighted and identified by signal lamp as HMS *Sirius*. The warship was standing-by the casualty. The wind at this time was blowing from the south-east, at force 4, and was increasing in strength. The lifeboat passed to the stern of the frigate and took up station on the trawler's port quarter, at a distance of about 150 feet. It immediately became apparent that the trawler, the *Elly Gerda*, was awash amidships and had a list to port of 10–15°.

The skipper of the trawler informed the lifeboat by VHF radio of his intention to make for Looe. Second Coxswain Marshall advised the skipper that this would be an unwise move as, in a south-easterly wind, which was forecast to increase to force 7–8, the Looe Roads would offer a poor holding ground. It was also pointed

Plymouth Lifeboat House, Princes Royal Pier, Millbay Docks, which was built in 1976 with monies raised by Plymouth Lions and crew functions.

Duncan Godefroy (branch Chairman), Frances Zessimedes (Ladies Guild) and John Dare celebrate the 175ᵗʰ anniversary of the Plymouth Lifeboat Station, 1978.

Relief lifeboat Arthur and Blanch Harris at Plymouth, 1978.

Crew members with Miss Plymouth Lifeboat, 1978. Left to right, back: *Barry Blewett, Gerald MacManus, Mike Foster;* front: *Ivor Lovering, John Dare, Cyril Alcock.*

out that, because of her deep draught, the *Elly Gerda* would have to wait until 22.30 hours before she could enter Looe Harbour. As the trawler's intended anchorage was open to the south-easterly wind and entering the harbour at Looe meant crossing a very dangerous bar, the *Thomas Forehead and Mary Rowse II* offered to escort the *Elly Gerda* downwind to Fowey, which was accessible during all tides and weather conditions. The trawler skipper rejected this offer and continued to make for Looe, at a speed of 2–3 knots.

By the time that the trawler and her escort reached the Looe Roads, weather conditions had deteriorated considerably. The wind had backed to south-east by east, increased to 30 knots and was accompanied by steep seas. The depth of water was approximately 30 feet and there was two hours of ebb tide. The skipper of the *Elly Gerda* gave notice of his intention to anchor but had no chain readily available. At 14.00 hours he laid his anchor in a position that had been indicated to him by local fishermen, who had been summoned to Looe Coastguard lookout, at Hannafore Point. The vessel then dropped back close to Looe Island, having let out 90 fathoms of

his trawling warp. The lifeboat checked that the trawler was secure and laid its own anchor to the east of the trawler, at a distance of about 100 feet. The lifeboat's anchor was unable to find purchase and after letting out 40 fathoms of warp without success, the lifeboat had to recover the anchor. The Rame Coastguard confirmed that, at this time, the wind had increased in velocity to a steady 40 knots. The seas were now very steep and there was driving rain. The *Thomas Forehead and Mary Rowse II* was in 16 feet of water and the mechanic, Cyril Alcock, who was on the bow in very poor conditions working the winch, was being constantly drenched by the waves, which together with the spray and driving rain made the operation extremely difficult and hazardous. It was also extremely cold with the sea temperature at 44°F. Second Coxswain Marshall subsequently reported:

After stowing the anchor we asked the Coastguard at Looe if a buoy between the trawler and Looe Island would be able to take our weight. This was confirmed and we moved around the trawler's stern and made fast to the mooring buoy. This put us 150 feet west of the trawler and in a good position to render any assistance. An anchor watch was set and bearings taken on shore marks and by radar. The crew were sent below for shelter and the wheel-house cover was put on to contain the heat from the engines which were shut down. I took the first watch and was relieved after an hour by the mechanic. We moored at approximately 15.00.

After two hours at the mooring it was found, by bearings, that the mooring was dragging. This was slipped and we requested permission from the trawler to moor on his stern if he thought his anchor, on which he had let out more wire, would hold us both. He agreed and our tow-rope was passed and secured with a coir fender secured in the middle to provide a spring. Bearings were again taken. The time was 17.00, there was a very heavy sea running and the wind was east-south-east, 40–50 knots.

Low water had been reached and the tide, which ran down between the mainland and Looe Island, had stopped flowing. As both vessels had now started a slow drag, Second Coxswain Marshall slipped the mooring and moved the lifeboat to the east of the trawler.

Immediately the two vessels parted, having checked his position by DECCA, the trawler skipper reported that he had stopped dragging, although he expressed concern about entering Looe Harbour and stated that he was considering staying the night at anchor. Second Coxswain Marshall records:

By now visibility was extremely poor with very heavy snow. I requested the Looe Coastguard to contact the Island and ask if a light on one of the two cottages could be kept lit all night, this being the only reference point I could use to stay clear of the Rennie Reef which runs away south-east by east from Looe Island. They replied that it would be kept on all night. After one hour Mr. Lovering became unwell (he became colder and wetter than the other crew members and showed signs and symptoms of exposure) and I suggested to him to go below. Mr. Alcock then asked if I wished him to steer and I stood watch whilst we moved up and down between the Rennie Reef and Hannafore Point. It took about twenty minutes to do the half mile leg and between 4–5 minutes to return. This was done at very slow

revs. After the mechanic took the wheel I went on deck and, as darkness had already fallen, with Mr. Foster holding my legs I removed the searchlight cover.

Because of the movement of the boat, we had not been able to make hot drinks below and all three of us on deck were very cold. There was a high wind and very heavy snow. The forecast from Rame was wind steady at 50 knots, gusting 60, east-south-east, and no change in the next four hours.

The lifeboat had been steaming around for two and a half hours when Second Coxswain Marshall relieved Mechanic Alcock at the wheel. At about 19.45 hours, the lights on the trawler were seen to alter. The skipper of the trawler was contacted by radio and reported that, as his anchor had renewed its drag, he intended to steam south-east and relay it. Pat Marshall warned the skipper that the reef lay ahead and not to steer too far south-east; this he acknowledged but continued to steam ahead. He was then advised by Marshall to stop his engines:

I closed to within 200 feet of his port quarter and we entered the foam and broken water that was coming over the reef. There was a very confused sea. Our compass heading was south-west and we held station on the trawler's quarter. He was still steaming ahead. We then received the following message from the trawler "Plymouth lifeboat, I've got a lot of trouble here, will you come in and help me?" The trawler had struck the Rennie (Ranney) Reef and was aground. Seas were breaking over the reef and falling on his foredeck and waves were washing in over his port side. His stern was north-east and bow south-west and all his deck lights were on. The only approach I could make was on the weather side, due to the anchor wire which was running out along his starboard quarter.

As Second Coxswain Marshall took the *Thomas Forehead and Mary Rowse II* in for his first approach, Cyril Alcock and Michael Foster were on the starboard foredeck. The bow of the lifeboat struck the *Elly Gerda's* trawling gallows and set the lifeboat on the trawler's quarter. The lifeboat was above the trawler's stern and, as she fell on a wave, the flare of her bow caught on the bulwark. As the sea was pushing the stern of the lifeboat around the stern of the trawler, she was in danger of fouling the *Elly Gerda's* anchor wire. Pat Marshall avoided this danger by the skilful manipulation of his engines, holding the port engine half ahead, the starboard engine slow astern, and with starboard wheel on. By increasing power on the port engine, he could hold station on the trawler's port quarter. The lifeboat continued to hit the gallows and Second Coxswain Marshall was unable to estimate how much water he had ahead of him or, with the trawler aground, what rock formation lay before the lifeboat. Pat Marshall later casually remarked, 'If I had allowed her to move ahead I would have placed the gallows level with the wheel-house, which could have been very expensive.'

As the lifeboat was held in position, Mechanic Cyril Alcock succeeded in grabbing hold of one of the trawler's crew by the hair,

Mechnic Cyril Alcock carries out maintenance to the relief lifeboat Arthur and Blanche Harris, *1978.*

and dragged him to the safety of the *Thomas Forehead and Mary Rowse II*. As this operation took place, Michael Foster was just forward to the lifeboat's wheel-house, trying to keep the fenders in place, whilst Pat Marshall, who remained at the helm, could see nothing of the stern of the trawler due to the large illuminated after-deck lights and the vast amount of spray that was drenching the wheel-house windows.

A particularly large sea knocked the bow of the lifeboat to port, causing the stern of the boat to close too close to the wire. Pat Marshall went astern and after repositioning the lifeboat made a second approach and again placed the bow of the lifeboat against the gallows. Cyril Alcock, who was in an extremely dangerous position on the bow of *Thomas Forehead and Mary Rowse II*, with the gallows passing very close to him each time the boats rose and fell, held on with one hand as he hauled a second fisherman onto the lifeboat. With no other person being in view on the after-deck of the *Elly Gerda*, and the lifeboat continuing to be severely buffeted, the Second Coxswain pulled astern, repositioned his boat, and commenced his third approach. As Michael Foster was helping the second fisherman aft, he informed the lifeboat crew that the trawler's skipper had been lost overboard. The lifeboat once

more approached the stern of the trawler, and Cyril Alcock fired two parachute flares to illuminate the scene. The missing man could not be seen although it became evident that the bows of the trawler were up against a vertical rock face. As further flares were prepared, the *Elly Gerda's* skipper came on the VHF radio; he was in the trawler's wheel-house and unharmed. He stated his intention to remain with his vessel as the heavy seas, which were now on his bow, were swinging the trawler and he anticipated that she would soon refloat. After a few minutes she did float clear of the reef; her skipper restarted the trawler's engines and started to steam eastwards, under the direction of Second Coxswain Marshall. At this time the *Elly Gerda* was still towing her anchor. The trawler skipper reported that his vessel did not appear to be holed and that he would steam around until 22.00 hours when, if he could haul in his anchor that now had a knot in the wire, he would attempt to cross the Looe Bar. The lifeboat stayed close to the port quarter of the trawler as she steamed north-easterly, clear of the reef. The vessels were still in only 30 feet of water and were tossed around by the heavy seas, at times losing sight of each other.

At 21.30 hours the Coastguard reported that they had men above the harbour and on the pier to talk the trawler in. The lifeboat was asked to manoeuvre onto the Bar and pump oil onto the sea, Pat Marshall refused to comply with this request as, should the trawler have broached, the lifeboat would have been unable to turn safely in the entrance of the harbour to effect a rescue; also the lifeboat could have been stranded in a drying harbour. Having recovered her anchor, the *Elly Gerda*, guided by the Coastguard on the cliffs above, made for the Bar. The lifeboat had pumped oil before the trawler started off, thus giving all help possible. It stayed close to the vessel's starboard quarter in order to clear the chimney rock on the port side of the harbour approach. The lifeboat stood-by as the trawler crossed over the Bar before also entering the harbour. At 23.15 hours the *Thomas Forehead and Mary Rowse II* left Looe and returned to

Plymouth, once again encountering heavy seas, particularly when crossing the Looe Bar and at Rame Head. Following refuelling, she was back on her mooring, fully serviceable, by 01.20 hours.

As a direct result of the rescue both Mechanic Cyril Alcock and lifeboat man Michael Foster received injuries, each severely straining arm muscles, but neither required hospitalisation. The *Thomas Forehead and Mary Rowse II* received minimal damage during the rescue operation, which could not have been reduced by fendering.

The rescue of the crew of the *Elly Gerda* and the subsequent saving of the vessel was a truly memorable and demanding service, putting both the skill of the lifeboat's crew and the durability of the lifeboat to the extreme test.

Second Coxswain Marshall commented in his Service Report:

During this service the crew were a constant source of confidence, although only Mr. Alcock and myself had any real experience of lifeboat work. Mr. Foster did everything at once and in a very seamanlike way and to everyone's satisfaction. Mr. Alcock was at all times giving me his wealth of knowledge and experience and did about three jobs that day. To stand on the foredeck so close to the gallows and pull men

aboard is, in my opinion, one of the best things I have seen.

Mr. Lovering looked after both men in the cabin and tended them. It was most uncomfortable below and at no time did he let his personal discomfort affect the efficiency of the boat.

In acknowledgement of this outstanding service, which was carried out in atrocious conditions, the RNLI awarded Bronze Medals to Second Coxswain Patrick Marshall and Mechanic Cyril Alcock. Vellum Service Certificates were presented to lifeboat men Ivor Lovering and Michael Foster in acknowledgement of their respective roles in this rescue.

On Sunday 30 April 1978 distinguished guests accompanied the officers, Coxswain and crew of Plymouth Lifeboat Station, in a service to mark the 175th anniversary of the Plymouth lifeboat.

It was reported in the *Church Magazine* at the time that:

It will be a service of thanksgiving to God for the devotion of generations of crews, including those of the small, very fast inshore lifeboat, stationed at Plymouth since 1967.

Also for the patience of their families and the work of the officials and supporters during

Cyril Alcock accepts a firkin of real ale from Nick Boyd (left) and Stuart Fearnley, of Halls Brewery, Plympton, for the crew's Christmas party.

The BBC's 'Spotlight' weatherman, Craig Rich, is winched from the lifeboat by a RN Wessex during a display off Looe.

The Duke of Kent presents the RNLI Bronze Medal to Cyril Alcock for his part in the service to the Elly Gerda, *15 February 1978.*

Crew night out. Left to right: Duncan Godefroy (branch Chair.), Tom Keane, Ivor Lovering, Cyril Alcock, John Dare, Frank Parker, Chrispen Gill, Doctor Beaton, Dave Fowler, Danny Biscombe.

Left: *Skipper Jean-Claude Cardron* (centre) *and fellow survivors of the* St Simeon, *with a member of the Coastguard, 15 February 1985.*

Below: *Proud holders of RNLI awards following the service to the St Simeon. Left to right: John Dare, F. Parker, A. Roberts, C. Alcock, F. Jackson, I. Lovering, R. Jago, M. Smaldon, K. Rimmer, P. Marshall.*

Below: *Vice-Admiral Sir Robert Gerken with Coxswain John Dare, Mechanic Cyril Alcock, Raymond Jago and Keith Rimmer.*

Below: *The RNLI contingent of the Armistice Service held at the Plymouth Guildhall, November 1982. The flag-bearer is R. Jago. Left to right, back: I. MacDonald, G. Parker; front: Coxswain John Dare, Mechanic Cyril Alcock.*

Right: *Back from another successful 'shout', Coxswain John Dare.*

the 175 years there has been a lifeboat in Plymouth.

The Revd Philip Withers conducted the service at the Mutley Baptist Church.

A major aid was added to the Plymouth lifeboat's launch facilities in 1979, when on Thursday 12 July a new mooring pontoon was officially inaugurated. The pontoon, which was placed alongside the Princess Royal Pier, Millbay, drastically reduced the launch time as the crew could access the lifeboat from the pier by steps directly onto the pontoon and without a boarding boat. The inshore lifeboat was also moored on the pontoon.

Rear-Admiral Wilfred Graham, director-designate of the Royal National Lifeboat Institution, officially opened the pontoon. Rear-Admiral Graham, a former captain of the aircraft carrier, HMS *Ark Royal*, cut red, white and blue tapes at the top of the steps leading to the pontoon.

Janet Foulkes, MP, with Mechanic Cyril Alcock on the bridge of Thomas Forehead and Mary Rowse II.

The pontoon was paid for by Plymouth businessman Mr Ralph Allen and his wife, Yvonne, and was installed on special piles at a cost of approximately £10,000. Funds to meet the installation costs were raised by Coxswain John Dare, members of the lifeboat crew, and many individuals and supporters in the Plymouth area.

The Plymouth lifeboat crew and the *Thomas Forehead and Mary Rowse* II were once again to perform a remarkable service, on the evening of Friday 16 February 1985. It was at 15.04 hours that Brixham Coastguard received a signal from the Marine Rescue Coordinating Centre (MRCC), Falmouth, stating that the Falmouth Arun Class lifeboat, *52-11 Elizabeth Ann*, ON 1058, commanded by Coxswain Vivian Pentecost, had been launched to assist a French trawler, south-east of the Lizard Lighthouse. The Frenchman was the 22.5metre FV *St Simeon*; her crew were Jean Claude Caerdron (skipper), Jean Jacques Focret (engineer), Arnoard Joignant, Hearvele Vourch and Marcel Le Paule. The trawler was enduring easterly winds, approaching hurricane force, which were whipping up savage, mountainous seas. The wind was officially recorded as 'violent storm – force 11' giving a wind speed of 56–63 knots, with

exceptionally violent gusts. The MRCC, Falmouth, was, at this time, controlling the incident. The Brixham Coastguard station was subsequently informed that the *St Simeon* was leaking in two places but that a pump had been placed on board by a lifeboat and appeared to be coping. Information was also received that the Penlee Arun Class lifeboat, *52-24 Mabel Alice*, ON 1085, commanded by Coxswain Kenneth Thomas, had relieved the *Elizabeth Ann* and was escorting the casualty towards Plymouth, at a speed of about six knots.

At 15.37 hours, the position of the casualty was 23 miles east of the Lizard. As the French trawler, *La Gardere*, left Plymouth to rendezvous with the *St Simeon* and relieve the Penlee lifeboat, the Hon. Secretary of the Plymouth Lifeboat Station was made aware of the incident. The DSO (Deputy Station Officer) MHQ Mount Wise stated that there were no warships in the area. By 16.30 hours the casualty and her escort had reached a position 19 miles off Pendennis Point, on a bearing of 122° (T), and by 17.50 hours a position 13.5 miles from the Eddystone Light on a bearing of 240°(T).

The crew of the trawler could not speak English so, as a precaution in the event that Falmouth should lose contact with the *St Simeon*, French interpreters, Mr and Mrs Foster, were requested to attend the Marine Rescue Sub Centre (MRSC), Brixham. With the interpreters in position, at 18.09 hours incident control was transferred to Brixham. *La Gardere* had been expected to RV with the *St Simeon* at about 17.40 hours but neither vessel responded to radio calls from the Brixham Coastguard.

After continuous efforts to establish radio contact, at the request of the MRSC (Marine Rescue Sub Centre), the Cross Joberg station at Cherbourg also attempted to establish radio contact. This was finally achieved at 18.48 hours, when the *St Simeon* reported 'Pump failed but do not need lifeboat assistance.' *La Gardere* was now in attendance and maintained radio contact with Brixham throughout the incident. Brixham MRSC monitored the progress of the vessel, recording VHF direction-finding bearings via the Rame Head aerial.

Left: *Vice-Admiral Sir Robert Gerken presents a service certificate to Keith Rimmer.*

Above: *The Plymouth lifeboat crew of 1985. Left to right, back: Fred Jackson, Mike Smaldon, Archie Roberts, Franklin Parker, Ray Jago, Brian Bellamy, Keith Rimmer; seated: Pat Marshall (Second Coxswain), John Dare (Coxswain), Cyril Alcock (Mechanic).*

Right: *Landing survivors from the* St Simeon, *15 February 1985.*

An exhausted crew following the service to the St Simeon.
Left to right: *Ray Jago, Ian Watson, Cyril Alcock, Keith Rimmer and Coxswain John Dare.*

Plymouth lifeboat crew and reserves of 1980. Left to right, back: *K. Rimmer (reserve), R. Jago, C. Alcock (Mechanic), B. Blewitt (ILB), M. Foster (Asst Mechanic); front: P. Marshall (Second Coxswain), J. Dare (Coxswain), B. Bellamy (reserve).*

The *St Simeon* continued to take in water and at 19.01 hours requested the assistance of a lifeboat with a replacement pump. At 19.04 hours a request was made to the Search and Rescue Control Centre for a pump to be airlifted to the trawler by helicopter. MRSC was informed that it would take about two hours for a pump to be located. The skipper of *La Gardere* confirmed that, should the *St Simeon* be lost, he could take off her crew, at the same time requesting the launch of the Plymouth lifeboat with a replacement pump. At 19.19 hours RNAS Culdrose placed a Sea King helicopter on immediate alert, and it was agreed that the Sea King would be flown to Plymouth's Roborough Airport, for life-saving purposes only. At 19.20 hours the Plymouth lifeboat was launched. The *St Simeon* supplied a DECCA fix, but a direction-finding bearing indicated an error. The lifeboat was given a course to make good the error from Penlee Point, her ETA to rendezvous with the trawler being 23.30 hours.

On this launch, the lifeboat, the *Thomas Forehead and Mary Rowse II*, was under the command of Coxswain John Dare, and his crew comprised Cyril Alcock (Mechanic), Raymond Jago, Ian Watson and Keith Rimmer. The *Thomas Forehead and Mary Rowse II*

immediately encountered horrendous weather conditions with severe gale-force-9 winds blowing from the east-south-east. The lifeboat had to battle through 50-foot waves, and snow squalls, whipped up by 47-knot winds. Thus commenced a seven-hour rescue mission during which time the Plymouth lifeboat would be working close to her operational limits.

As the lifeboat made her way to assist the trawler she was struck by a series of heavy seas, one of which washed the handle of the replacement pump over the side. Coxswain Dare tried to determine if the pump on the *St Simeon* had a handle, or if another pump was available. It was quickly established that the pump on board the *St Simeon* had a lanyard start. At 20.00 hours the trawler skipper was asked to consider transferring some of his crew to *La Gardere*; he replied that he did not consider the situation to be bad enough for this action. The lifeboat was still 30 minutes away.

It was at 20.06 hours, when the *St Simeon* was at a point on a bearing 219°(T) from Rame Head, that the helicopter was scrambled with a request to proceed to the trawler's position and hover over the scene. The Brixham Coastguard informed the casualty that the lifeboat was an estimated five miles from her position and requested the trawler to switch on her searchlight; this she did and the lifeboat sighted the vessel at 20.18 hours.

The weather at the scene was now south-easterly, force 7–8, with a 20-foot swell and a very rough sea, although visibility was good. Following further attempts to locate a pump, the *St Simeon* was advised that none was available. The skipper was asked if she could make Plymouth under escort by the *Thomas Forehead and Mary Rowse II* and the Sea King helicopter. His reply was described as 'not helpful'.

The lifeboat reported that the *St Simeon* had stopped, at 20.35 hours, and was rolling badly in heavy seas that were breaking over her. Longroom, the Royal Navy Signals Station, Plymouth, reported that HMS *Amazon* was due in Plymouth but the DSO, who again stated that no warships were in the area, contradicted this report. Controversially, at 20.50 hours the DSO reported HMS *Amazon* to be in Plymouth Sound and agreed to enquire into the possible loan of a pump. The skipper of the *St Simeon* reported that his vessel was now manoeuvrable but did not wish to get under way as movement caused a surge in the ingress of water. He also stated, for an unknown reason, that the vessel could not be towed. The helicopter, 'Rescue 91', which had developed VHF radio problems, was informed that a pump was available but required collection from the flight deck of HMS *Amazon*, which was now in the Hamoaze.

Both SRCC (Search and Rescue Coordinating Centre) and the pilot of the Royal Navy Sea King, Lieutenant David Duthie, believed such a transfer to be too dangerous. The *St Simeon* was now in 58 metres of water and the crew were observed, by *La Gardere*, preparing the anchor. The SRCC were becoming more and more anxious about the situation and once again urged Caerdron to consider leaving his vessel; again he insisted that a pump be found. The skipper was repeatedly informed that a pump was not available and at 21.45 hours Cardron agreed to call his owners. The Cross Joburg station was requested, via MRCC Falmouth, to impress upon both the owners and the skipper of the trawler the seriousness of the situation. Following a radio link-call, at 22.17 hours Cardron stated the he and his crew would leave their vessel. Following a quick interchange between Brixham MRSC, 'Rescue 91' and Coxswain John Dare, the *St Simeon*'s skipper agreed that his crew would leave their vessel on a life-raft, from which they would be recovered by the lifeboat, with the helicopter standing-by in

case of an accident. Cardron stated that his crew would be ready in 15 minutes; it was in fact 25 minutes later, at 22.42 hours, that the trawler crew launched their life-raft. With the crew of the *St Simeon* assembled in their life-raft, Mechanic Cyril Alcock threw a line to them, but no attempt was made to catch it. Coxswain John Dare manoeuvred the *Thomas Forehead and Mary Rowse II* clear just as a heavy sea broke over the top of the trawler. On four occasions Cyril Alcock threw a line before it was caught and secured to the life-raft. In the pounding seas the fishermen were encouraged to cut the line that secured them to the trawler, and the raft was hauled through the churning waves to the lifeboat. The *St Simeon*'s crew of five were taken on board the lifeboat at 22.59 hours, and Coxswain John Dare set a course for Plymouth, as did the Frenchman, *La Gardere*. 'Rescue 91' commenced her 30-minute flight to RNAS Culdrose.

The homeward journey for the *Thomas Forehead and Mary Rowse II* was not without incident. Initially John Dare was able to maintain a good speed, despite encountering heavy seas, but as the lifeboat crested one particularly large wave, her propellers were left clear of the water and she crashed violently into the trough below. The impact was such that damage was caused to the lifeboat's radar, which became inoperable. John Dare reduced speed and reached Millbay Docks at 01.22 hours. Interpreters and members of the Shipwrecked Mariners Society greeted the French crewmen at Plymouth. The five fishermen were taken to the Royal Fleet Club, Devonport, from where the skipper of the *St Simeon*, Captain Jean-Claude Cardron, paid tribute to the lifeboat crew, summing up the gratitude of the crew with the words: 'The rescue was perfect – they were superb.'

Later commenting on the rescue to a local newspaper, the pilot of the Royal Navy Sea King, 'Rescue 91', Lieutenant David Duthie, described Coxswain John Dare's seamanship as 'the best I have ever seen'. Coxswain John Dare told the *Western Evening Herald*:

It was a difficult job. But it was one of those things, you are there to save lives and you do what you can. The crew were first class. When we got those Frenchmen on board it was better than winning the pools.

The conditions were really atrocious and the seas were terrific. We were 50 yards from the trawler but a lot of the time we couldn't see it.

On 18 February, the Hon. Secretary of the Plymouth Lifeboat Station received the following message, relayed via the Falmouth and Brixham Coastguard Stations:

From Marine Cherbourg
Subject: Rescue carried out of crew of trawler Saint Simeon.'
Congratulate you and thank you very warmly for the efficiency with which you have been able to save the crew of the trawler 'Saint Simeon', in spite of very difficult sea conditions.
Signed Vice-Admiral Fuzeau.

For their respective roles in this difficult and pro-tracted service, the RNLI awarded their Thanks on Vellum to Coxswain Vivian Pentecost of the Falmouth lifeboat, the *Elizabeth Ann*, also to Coxswain Kenneth Thomas of the Penlee lifeboat, the *Mabel Alice*, and to Coxswain John Dare of the Plymouth Lifeboat, the *Thomas Forehead and Mary Rowse II*. Vellum Service Certificates were presented to all members of the lifeboat crews who took part in the service.

Saturday 31 May 1986 was to be a light-hearted day for Coxswain John Dare and the crew of the *Thomas Forehead and Mary Rowse II*, as they were to be engaged in a fund-raising event at Cawsand. The day also marked the 67th anniversary of the first Trans-Atlantic air crossing by a flying boat, and the 75th anniversary of US Naval Aviation. To mark the anniversary, two Catalina flying boats, both of which were veterans of the Second World War, having crossed the Atlantic, flew in to 'land' in Plymouth Sound. From their position off Drake's Island, the crew of the lifeboat had a grandstand view as the aircraft made their final approach to the Sound.

The first Catalina made her approach and executed a perfect touchdown in the channel that had been specially cleared for the landing. Along with hundreds of onlookers, both on the sea and the shore, the lifeboat's crew watched the final approach run of the second Catalina, *The Spirit of US Naval Aviation*. Horror spread throughout the crowd as, on making contact with the water the seaplane slewed, its left wingtip crashing into the main channel buoy. The impact of the colli-sion was such that the tip of the wing, and float, were torn from the aircraft. The Catalina settled by the nose and immediately began to rapidly take in water. An eyewitness told a reporter from the *Western Evening Herald*:

The US Naval Catalina flying boat, The Spirit of US Naval Aviation, *'crash landed' in Plymouth Sound, 31 May 1986.* PLYMOUTH CITY LIBRARY

Brian Bellamy, Mike Foster and Ray Jago on board the Thomas Forehead and Mary Rowse II.

The Thomas Forehead and Mary Rowse II.

Revd Withers, Ray Jago, Fred Fowler, Peter White and Tom Keane admiring a model of the lifeboat at the Mutley Baptist Church.

The **Thomas Forehead and Mary Rowse II** *alongside the* Waxoyl, *formerly the 47-foot Watson Class lifeboat,* Mabel E. Holland, *of the Isle of Wight, Bembridge Station, upon skipper Peter Cowper's return from his round-the-world voyage.*

Left: *'Rupert' does his bit for fund-raising, Plymouth Lifeboat Station, 1981.*

Opposite: Left to right, includes: *F. Jackson, K. Rimmer, R. Jago, P. Marshall, J. Dare, C. Alcock, A. Roberts, M. Smaldon. In front of the wheel-house are F. Parker and D. Staddon.*

The **Waveney Class 44-011** Augustine Courtauld *greets the* **Arun Class 52-40** City of Plymouth, *17 January 1988.*

The second Catalina seemed to make a clean touchdown on the water then suddenly it seemed to veer right as though the pilot tried to open the throttle to clear the starboard permanent buoy.

Then the aircraft's port wingtip struck the buoy and ripped off about 12ft of wing, which included the float.

There was a lot of spray, the aircraft spun round and the engines were cut.

Longroom immediately broadcast a signal requesting the assistance of all vessels in the area. The Plymouth lifeboat responded at once and was quickly alongside the stricken aircraft. Coxswain John Dare put one of his crew on board the Catalina and a line was passed to the aircraft. Within minutes the suction end of the lifeboat's fire pump had also been passed across and the pump proved able to counter the ingress of water into the hull of the flying boat and prevented it from sinking.

Commander Howard Wheeler, the editor of the *American Naval Aviation News* and publicity liaison officer for the flight, joined *The Spirit of US Naval Aviation* at the Azores to fly the last leg into Plymouth. The Commander was injured in the crash landing, sustaining a gash to his thigh. He was taken off the aircraft by a Royal Marines craft, landed at the Barbican, and conveyed by ambulance to the Royal Naval Hospital, Stonehouse.

Having stabilised the seaplane, John Dare had to undertake the tricky tow, across the Sound, to the slipway of RAF Mount Batten. In order to balance the aircraft and to keep her on as even a keel as possible, members of the crew climbed onto the wing of the aircraft in an attempt to compensate for the lost wingtip and float. The *Thomas Forehead and Mary Rowse II* successfully completed the tow to the Mount Batten slipway, where the Catalina sank, in about eight feet of water.

The two flying boats had set out from Rockaway, New Jersey, earlier in May and had completed a 4,000-mile flight to Plymouth. Following a civic reception, presided over by Plymouth's Lord Mayor, Bill Glanville and Vice-Admiral Robert Schoultz, Deputy Commander-in-Chief, US Naval Forces, Europe, the aircraft

were due to fly on to the Royal Naval Air Base at Yeovilton. They were to have been escorted by two Second World War Royal Naval aircraft, namely a Swordfish and a Firefly.

The Plymouth lifeboat rescued two brothers, Raymond and Malcolm Murphy, on Thursday 20 November 1986, when their yacht was washed onto Plymouth's breakwater. The 27-foot yacht *Kathleen* had run aground when her skipper had been temporarily blinded by a sail, which had struck him in the eye. The *Thomas Forehead and Mary Rowse II* left her mooring at 18.05 hours and, upon reaching the casualty, found that the rough seas had lifted the vessel on top of the breakwater. Using all his skills, Coxswain John Dare manoeuvred the lifeboat up to the breakwater's landing stage and placed crewmen Pat Marshall and Frank Parker onto the structure. In a strong wind and heavy, breaking seas, the lifeboat men made their way to the stranded yacht. Pat Marshall recalled: 'It was a bit wet out there and we were knocked over a couple of times while we were trying to reach the yacht.'

Although the £30,000-yacht was completely on top of the Breakwater, there was a real danger that the vessel would slide back into the sea, on the Plymouth side. Pat commented 'There was a chance of getting run down on the breakwater by a boat.'

Having reached the casualty, the lifeboat men set up life-lines, in case they were washed from the breakwater, and set about their task of rescuing the two-man crew. The four men roped together for safety and set out back along the breakwater to regain the safety of the lifeboat.

The *Thomas Forehead and Mary Rowse II*, after caring for the yachtsmen, remained with the *Kathleen* for one hour, until high water, when Coxswain Dare attempted to refloat the vessel. As the attempt failed, the lifeboat returned to Millbay Docks at 20.20 hours. The *Kathleen*, which had been holed above the waterline, was recovered the following day and towed into the Mayflower Marina.

The ferry company, Compagnie Maritime Belge and Aseco UK, had been operating their Anglo-Spanish service for only three months when fire broke out in the engine-room of the 9,000-ton roll-on, roll-off ferry, the MV *Kaprifol*, as she battled with heavy seas and severe gale-force-9 winds off Rame Head, on Saturday 13 December 1986. From initial reports, a decision was quickly made to evacuate the ship.

Setting out in what was described at being 'one of the worst gales of the winter', Falmouth Coastguard recording gusts of force 10, the *Thomas Forehead and Mary Rowse II* made her way to the stricken vessel. Upon reaching the *Kaprifol*, Coxswain John Dare sought the lee of the vessel and skilfully manoeuvred the lifeboat up to the ferry to take off the passengers and crew. Holding the lifeboat steady on the rising and falling waves, the first man was taken off safely but as a second man climbed down a ladder into the lifeboat, he was washed into the turbulent sea. Coxswain Dare explained:

We had got one man off safely when a second lorry driver started climbing down the side of the ship. We were rising and falling 10–15 feet with the waves. The man just jumped at the wrong time and he was washed into the sea, but we quickly picked him up and he was alright. The skipper then told us the fire was under control so we didn't take off any more.

Eight other lorry drivers, and the crew of 22, remained on board the ferry.

The MV *Kaprifol*, which had recently returned to service following an annual overhaul in dry dock at Copenhagen, restarted her engines and returned to Millbay under her own power. She had been at the centre of a local seamen's dispute, as her twice-weekly sailings, from Plymouth to Bilbao competed with Brittany Ferries'

Plymouth–Santander crossings. The two men landed by the lifeboat recovered from their ordeal at the Royal Fleet Club, Devonport.

On 12 May 1987, the *Thomas Forehead and Mary Rowse II* was taken to Mashford's Boatyard for a survey and did not return to the Plymouth station. After 13 years of service, *44-010* was subsequently reallocated to the RNLI station at Fowey, the rededication ceremony taking place at the Town Quay, Fowey, on 26 April 1988.

In the Queen's Birthday Honour List, 1987, Her Majesty Queen Elizabeth II honoured Plymouth's Motor Mechanic Cyril Alcock by graciously awarding him the British Empire Medal.

Cyril had joined the Service in 1954 and initially served at the RNLI's Spurn Head Lifeboat Station, on the Humber. He became the station's Assistant Mechanic. In 1962 Cyril was transferred to New Brighton, as Motor Mechanic, subsequently joining the Plymouth crew in May 1967. In September 1987, Cyril Alcock, BEM, retired as Motor Mechanic of the Plymouth Station, having completed 33 years' service with the RNLI.

The relief fleet Waveney Class lifeboat, the *44-004 Faithful Forester*, ON 1003, initially replaced the *Thomas Forehead and Mary Rowse II*. On Saturday 31 October 1987, the Waveney Class lifeboat, *44-011 Augustine Courtauld*, ON 1029, formerly of Poole, replaced the *Faithful Forester*. The *Augustine Courtauld* remained on station until January 1988, when Plymouth received one of the new breed of fast lifeboats, the Arun Class *52-40 City of Plymouth*.

When she was eventually discharged from the RNLI fleet, the *Thomas Forehead and Mary Rowse II*, renamed the *Westgate*, served as the Coastguard/Lifeboat at New Plymouth, Taranaki, North Island, New Zealand.

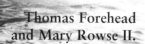

Thomas Forehead and Mary Rowse II.

14

THE *CITY OF PLYMOUTH*

26 JANUARY 1988–21 NOVEMBER 2002

Class: Arun   *Propulsion: 2 x 485hp Caterpillar diesel engines*   *Crew: 7*

Length: 51' 9"   *Beam: 17' 9"*   *Displacement: 31^T*   *Draft: 4' 7"*

Official number: 1136   *Fleet number: 52-40*   *Builder: Souters, Cowes, 1987*

Service Launches: 579   *Lives Saved: 115*

Coxswain: John Dare (1988–90), Pat Marshall (1990–2001), Keith Rimmer (2001–)
Mechanics: Derek Studden (1988–2002), Sean O'Kane (2000–03)

Plymouth's new Arun Class lifeboat arrived in the port on Sunday 17 January 1988 and, following crew familiarisation, was officially placed on station, nine days later, on Tuesday 26 January. The boat was built at a cost of £529,478, and was provided by the citizens of Plymouth, together with the help of bequests from George Wilfred Glass, Phyllis Maud Lyneham, Margaret Scott, Dorothy Janet Gertrude Singleton and other gifts and legacies. The lifeboat was of GRP construction and was powered by two 485hp 'Caterpillar' 3408TA diesel engines. She was fitted with the very latest life-saving equipment, including radar, DECCA navigation, VHF and MF radio, auto direction-finding and echo-sounding equipment.

The first launch of the new lifeboat, the *City of Plymouth*, took place on the evening of the very day that she was placed on station. It was truly a bitter-sweet experience for her crew! She slipped her mooring at 23.40 hours on Tuesday 26 January, in response to a call from a Looe fishing vessel which was drifting without power in heavy seas five miles off Rame Head. In deteriorating weather conditions, and with an imminent gale forecast, it was decided to take the vessel, with its crew of two, under immediate tow to Sutton Harbour. The vessels arrived safely at 04.00 hours.

The *City of Plymouth* had performed and handled perfectly to the delight of the Coxswain and crew, one crew member commenting: 'It was a lot quicker than the old one, and we knocked about 15 minutes off the usual journey.'

It was as the crew came ashore that a shadow was cast over their euphoria for, as they returned to the Millbay boat-house, it became apparent that vandals had looted and damaged their cars. Quite rightly, the crew hit out at the mindless wreckers who had taken advantage of their absence, whilst they were risking their lives for the benefit of others. Assistant Mechanic Fred Jackson summed up the feeling of the crew:

Pat Marshall had expensive camera equipment stolen from his car. I discovered my car had also been rifled. About £60 in cash had gone – along with my chequebook and card.

Everything had been scattered around – they even searched the boot and looked under the bonnet. The windscreen wiper and indicator arms had been bent and the rear-view mirror ripped off.

We couldn't believe they would deliberately wait until we were called out on a rescue and then go through our cars.

Who the hell has that sort of mentality?

The *City of Plymouth* slipped from her mooring at 19.34 hours on Monday 21 March 1988, following a report from the Coastguard that a number of people were stranded, having been cut off by the tide in Bigbury Bay. The lifeboat was quickly on the scene and the Arun's 'Y' boat,

Royal National
Lifeboat
Institution

Royal National Lifeboat Institution
Supported entirely by voluntary contributions
Registered charity number 209603

Handing Over Ceremony
and Service of Dedication

of the

Port of Plymouth
'Arun' Class Lifeboat

at THE PARADE, SUTTON HARBOUR

on

FRIDAY, 15th APRIL, 1988, at 6.00 p.m.

*The cost of this Lifeboat was provided by the Citizens of Plymouth together
with the bequests of George Wilfrid Glass, Phyllis Maud Lineham, Margaret
Scott, Dorothy Janet Gertrude Singleton and other gifts and legacies.*

The future 52-40 City of Plymouth, undergoing a self-righting test at Souters, Cowes, 29 September 1987.

manned by two crewmen, was launched into the heavy surf that was surging onto the beach. Upon reaching the shore the lifeboat men found the stranded party, which comprised two men, a mother-to-be and a four-year-old boy, sheltering in a cave. The lifeboat men offered reassurance and comforted the party, as preparations for their rescue were made. The Coastguard launched a large-scale rescue operation, and lowered blankets and sleeping bags to the casualties when it became clear that the procedure would take some time. As it became apparent that the sea conditions were too hazardous for the casualties to be taken off by the lifeboat, after five hours the *City of Plymouth* received instructions to stand-down. Leaving the casualties in the care of the Coastguard, the crew of the 'Y'-boat attempted to return to the Arun but the boat overturned, on several occasions, in the raging surf. Eventually they got off the beach and returned safely to the lifeboat. The *City of Plymouth* regained her mooring at 00.05 hours.

The handing-over ceremony and service of dedication of Plymouth's new Arun Class lifeboat took place in a thick swirling sea mist at The Parade, Sutton Harbour, at 18.00 hours on Friday 15 April 1988. The proceedings were opened by Mr Duncan Godefroy, JP, the Chairman of the Plymouth Station branch, in the presence of the Lord Mayor and Lady Mayoress of Plymouth. A bouquet of flowers was presented to the Lady Mayoress by Catherine Marshall, and souvenir programmes to both the Lord Mayor and Lady Mayoress by Paul Jago, both Catherine and Paul being children of lifeboat crew members.

The Lord Mayor of Plymouth, Councillor Tony Parish, patron of the City of Plymouth Lifeboat Appeal, handed the lifeboat into the keeping of the RNLI. Mr Raymond Cory, CBE, Deputy Chairman of the RNLI, accepted the lifeboat on behalf of the Institution and delivered her into the care of the Plymouth Station branch. Major Philip Reed, the branch Honorary Secretary, accepted the boat.

The service of dedication was conducted by the Revd Dr Derek J. Tidball, BA, BD, Station Honorary Chaplain. A brief service of dedication was followed by the congregation singing the traditional hymn, 'Eternal Father, strong to save', and the blessing. Salvation Army bands provided musical accompaniment. At the invitation of Vice-Admiral Sir Robert Gerken, KCB, CBE, President of the Plymouth Station branch and Chairman of the City of Plymouth Lifeboat

Appeal, the Lady Mayoress, Mrs Jeanne Parish, named the lifeboat the *City of Plymouth*.

Three brass plaques carried by the *City of Plymouth* subsequently commemorated the support given to the lifeboat by the citizens of Plymouth; they read:

RNLB City of Plymouth
*named in Sutton Harbour
on 15th April, 1988
by
Mrs Jeanne Parish
Lady Mayoress of Plymouth.*

*The cost of this lifeboat
was provided by the citizens of
Plymouth together with the
bequests of George Wilfred Glass,
Phyllis Maud Lyneham.
Margaret Scott,
Dorothy Janet Gertrude Singleton
and other gifts and legacies.*

*The cost of the portable VHF
radio aboard RNLB* City of
Plymouth *was met by
donations from family
and friends in memory of
John Stallard.*

In heavy seas and a strong easterly wind, the Plymouth lifeboat crew had one of their busiest days on Sunday 22 May 1988. In the Sound the inclement conditions brought the Plymouth International Multihull Grand Prix to a premature close when a 26-foot catamaran with a crew of three pitch-poled. Race rescue boats rescued the crew. The *City of Plymouth*'s first call came at 10.40 hours, while she was at sea on exercise. The service was to a yacht that was in distress off Penlee. The lifeboat found that the yacht, the *Candace*, had foundered on rocks, and that all of her crew had reached the safety of the shore. The yacht was taken in tow and berthed at Sutton Pool at 11.35 hours.

Coxswain John Dare later told a local reporter:

By then we realised there might be a few problems about so we decided to cruise around the Sound and see if anyone else was in trouble. It has never been so busy.

Having been tasked by Longroom, the lifeboat then rendered assistance to a catamaran, which had encountered difficulties to the east of Drake's Island. As the fishing vessel, the *Metan*, had secured a tow, the lifeboat escorted both vessels into Sutton Harbour. Whilst heading for Sutton Harbour, the lifeboat was tasked to the mouth of the River Yealm where a dinghy was

Main: *The Arun Class lifeboat, 52-40 City of Plymouth, ON 1136, which served as the Plymouth lifeboat from 1988–2003.*
Left: *Fred Jackson and Mike Kitt enjoy a fund-raising trip on board the Arun Class lifeboat* City of Plymouth, *1991.*

Above left: *A 'casualty' is recovered into the Arun's 'Y'-boat.*

Above right: *Fred Jackson and Mike Kitt with an RNLI inspector, on board the* City of Plymouth.

reported to be in trouble. The lifeboat was recalled, at 11.50 hours, the dinghy and its occupants having been reported safe.

At the request of the Coastguard, the *City of Plymouth* remained on stand-by and at 12.15 hours Coxswain Dare took up a position off Drake's Island.

The next service took place a little after 13.00 hours, the lifeboat having intercepted a call for assistance from a dive-boat, which had reportedly taken an inflatable craft in tow, off Rame Head. The lifeboat reached the dive-boat at 13.20 hours and relieved her of the tow. Seven divers were recovered and the lifeboat headed towards the diving centre at Fort Bovisand. On their way, Coxswain Dare and his crew were tasked to the rocks below West Hoe, where a small powerboat was reported to have run ashore. On reaching this casualty at 13.45 hours, four persons from the powerboat, together with a windsurfer, were found to be on the rocks. The lifeboat crew secured a line to the small craft but, as she was towed off the rocks, the craft capsized, its occupants scrambling back onto the rocks, from where they clambered ashore. The powerboat was towed to Queen Anne's Battery by the lifeboat, which then completed its journey to Fort Bovisand. The divers were eventually landed at 15.12 hours. Other services provided that day included that to a catamaran off the River Yealm, and to a canoeist reported 'missing' in the Sound. In total on that day, the Plymouth lifeboat responded to 23 incidents, remaining at sea for a total of nine hours after the first call. The *City of Plymouth* returned to her station at 17.15 hours.

Due to the redevelopment of the Millbay site in 1989, the lifeboat station was moved, on a temporary basis, to a Portakabin at Sutton Harbour, where the lifeboat was to be moored.

The crew of the *City of Plymouth* watched in horror as the Arun's 'Y' boat was overturned by 20-foot waves, pitching crewmen Pat Marshall and Mike Kitt into turbulent and rock-strewn seas on the afternoon of Saturday 30 June 1990. The lifeboat had been launched to assist the 31-foot yacht, *Parbleu*, which was on her first major voyage – from the River Hamble, Southampton, to Plymouth's Mayflower Marina. Having suffered engine failure, the yacht's two-person crew hoisted sail and attempted to pass through the notoriously hazardous waters between the Great Mew Stone and Wembury. Fighting her way through the confused seas, the yacht stranded approximately 200 yards offshore at Wembury. Upon arriving at the scene, in heavy seas and a gale-force wind, Coxswain John Dare found conditions to be far too treacherous to attempt to reach the casualty with the all-weather boat. The decision was taken to launch the 'Y'-boat. The little inflatable was taken into the tumbling sea in an attempt to get a line aboard the *Parbleu*. In the terrible conditions, the 'Y'-boat soon began to ship water and became waterlogged but Pat and Mike remained resolute in their effort to secure a tow-line. As the 'Y'-boat was taken in to enable another attempt to be made, it was caught by a particularly heavy sea and capsized. Fortunately, a helicopter, which had initially been scrambled to the scene, quickly moved in and lifted the two lifeboat men from the water, placing them back on board the *City of Plymouth*. Coastguards hauled the crew of the *Parbleu* safely ashore. The *City of Plymouth* regained her mooring at 19.00 hours.

John Dare retired from the position of Coxswain on 9 November 1990 after 31 years of service at Plymouth, including five years as Second Coxswain and 19 years as Coxswain. During that time, the all-weather lifeboat launched on 465 occasions and saved 188 lives.

Upon John's retirement, Patrick Marshall was appointed Coxswain of the Plymouth lifeboat. Pat had followed an established family tradition when, in 1965, he joined his uncle, Tom Keane, and cousins Peter Plaice and Michael Keane, as a member of the crew of the Plymouth lifeboat, the *Thomas Forehead and Mary Rowse*. In an interview for the *Western Morning News* in 1999, Pat commented:

Back when I started, most of the crew was drawn from the area close to the lifeboat station. Most people didn't have their own cars, so whenever we got an emergency call-out we had to make our way on foot. You could always tell who the coxswain was because he had a moped.

With the majority of lifeboat stations drawing their crew from within the local community, it was almost a birthright, particularly in the smaller communities, for successive generations to carry on the tradition of crewing the boat. Pat explained: 'It was the natural thing for people to do. They grew up around the lifeboat and the sea. It was the way of life.'

Times and circumstances have changed and lifeboat crews are now drawn from further afield. However, the Marshall family continued their connection with the lifeboat when, in 1993, Pat's son Sean became a member of the Plymouth crew. In 1997 Pat's daughter Cath joined her father and brother, becoming the first female crew member of the Plymouth lifeboat. The RNLI has always been in their blood; in fact, as babies, both were christened aboard the lifeboat. Cath told the *Western Morning News*:

As children, we spent a lot of time around the lifeboat and learnt to respect the sea. I am treated the same way as everyone else. I'm just one of the lads at the end of the day. If I did something wrong I wouldn't be able to hide behind my father because he's the Coxswain.

The family christening tradition was followed with Sean's son Cameron also being christened on board the Plymouth lifeboat.

Coxswain John Dare at the helm of the Arun Class City of Plymouth*.*

The Plymouth and Salcombe lifeboats and a Search and a Rescue helicopter from RNAS Culdrose were scrambled at 19.02 hours on Friday 6 September 1991, following the receipt of a MAYDAY call from the Plymouth-based chartered fishing vessel, *Artilleryman III*, stating that she was taking on a great deal of water. The vessel, which was carrying a party of fishermen from East Anglia, was returning from a fishing trip to the Channel Islands when the boat became stranded three miles south of Bolt Tail, near Hope Cove. A pump was lowered onto the *Artilleryman III* from the helicopter, bringing great relief to the party of 12, who were bailing furiously with buckets, as water continued to gush into the vessel.

Upon the arrival of the *City of Plymouth* a second pump was put on board the fishing vessel and the situation was stabilised. *Artilleryman III* was taken in tow and beached in Sutton Harbour.

The skipper of the *Artilleryman III*, Geordie Dickson, who only four months earlier had lost his previous vessel, *Artilleryman II,* in a collision at sea, said that the cause of this incident appeared to have been a broken drive-shaft. The service that had started out as a race against time ended with the all parties being landed safely and the lifeboat returning to her mooring at 21.00 hours.

The lifeboat was launched at 14.10 hours on New Year's Day, Wednesday 1 January 1992, to go to the assistance of four persons who were seen clinging to the hull of their upturned speed-boat in Bovisand Bay. The alarm had been raised by Mrs Abbot, of Manor Bourne, Down Thomas, who had heard cries for help as she hung out her washing in the garden of her cliff-top home.

The casualty was reached within ten minutes and, in a strong south-westerly wind, Second Coxswain Keith Rimmer, accompanied by lifeboat men Fred Jago and Brian Bellamy, jumped into the sea and assisted the four persons to reach the lifeboat. The casualties, who had been clinging to the hull of their vessel for some 45 minutes, were extremely cold and near to being hypothermic; they were not wearing life-jackets.

The four had intended to travel to Newton Ferrers from Queen Anne's Battery, but turned back when they encountered heavy seas off the breakwater. Unfortunately, the speedboat was struck by a huge wave, which had caused the vessel to capsize. The lifeboat subsequently landed the casualties at Plymouth. Coxswain Pat Marshall said:

They could hardly move. They are very lucky people because within a few minutes I am sure they would have started sliding away from the boat. They were very cold and dressed the way they were I don't think they would have survived for a great deal longer.

A crew member from the speedboat later commented:

The Coastguards sent up a flare from their Landrover on shore so we knew it was only a matter of waiting for a lifeboat to come out. When they arrived to get us out they were wonderful, reassuring us, and very professional.

The crew of the *City of Plymouth* lifeboat gave a display in the waters off The Hoe, to celebrate the opening of their new £75,000 station, by the Lord Mayor of Plymouth, John Richards, on Tuesday 16 June 1993. A dilapidated old building, which had once been the Customs House at Millbay Docks, was transformed into the lifeboat station, thanks to a £3.5 million bequest from a Bristol woman, who had died earlier that year. The benefactor was Russian-born Eugene Baucher, who had fled from Penza on the south-eastern borders of old Russia in the 1920s.

The RNLI spent this generous bequest by rebuilding eight lifeboat centres throughout the country. These centres became affectionately known as *Penza* stations.

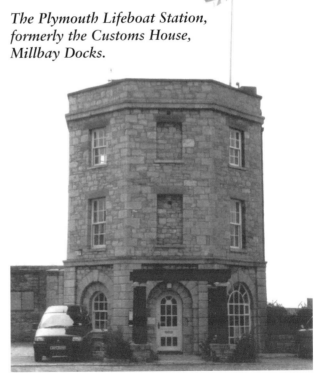

The Plymouth Lifeboat Station, formerly the Customs House, Millbay Docks.

At 15.27 hours on Saturday 8 January 1994, the Brixham Coastguard received a message from the PZ 622, FV *Silver Harvester*, reporting that her propeller had fouled. The position of the fishing vessel was given as 2.5nm south-west of Gara Point. At this time the message was for 'information only', the skipper stating that her crew would call back in ten minutes when he had assessed if his anchor was holding. At 15.32 hours the *Silver Harvester* reported that she was drifting in an east-north-easterly direction, at a speed of a little over a knot. At this time, at the location of the casualty, a force 6 wind was blowing from the south-west, visibility was poor and the sea was rough, with a 2-metre swell. In view of these conditions, and in case the situation deteriorated, the MRSC, Brixham, informed the *Silver Harvester* that a request would be made for the launch of the Plymouth lifeboat.

The *City of Plymouth* was launched at 15.45 hours and was immediately requested to proceed to a more serious incident at Picklecombe Point, as minutes earlier, at 15.42 hours, a 999 call had been received, reporting a fishing vessel aground with one man in the water. Simultaneously, a call had been received on Ch.16 from the YH 187, FV *Sarekei*, reporting that she was on rocks and that the two people on board were attempting to get a rope out.

The Rame Head Coastguard rescue team was alerted and, at 15.46 hours, the Search and Rescue helicopter, Rescue 193, was airborne from RNAS Culdrose. At 15.48 hours the *Sarekei* reported her engine-room flooded; luckily the lifeboat was only three minutes away.

The fishing vessel was aground, bow first, on the rocky shore and was being constantly swept by the heavy seas. In these conditions it was not possible to take the Arun in close to the casualty. The lifeboat crew prepared and launched the 'Y'-boat in order to take off the *Sarekei's* crew, but they refused to climb into the craft.

By 15.54 hours the *Silver Harvester* was only 1.5nm from shore and concern was growing regarding her position. With Coastguard agreement, the *City of Plymouth* left the *Sarekei*, instructing the crew of the 'Y'-boat to put her ashore but, if conditions prevented their landing, they were to rejoin the Arun at the location of the *Silver Harvester*. Rescue 193 was also diverted. The Coastguard took the crew of the Sarekei off their vessel from the shore. The 'Y'-boat returned to station, accompanied by a Ministry of Defence launch.

Sean Marshall and Jon West aboard the City of Plymouth.

The lifeboat approached the fishing vessel at 16.10 hours, having established radio contact with the vessel via Ch.67 and successfully connected a tow-line. At 16.23 the *City of Plymouth* commenced the tow to Millbay Docks. Due to the size of the 192-ton vessel, this was slow and difficult. When inside the breakwater, the lifeboat came alongside the *Silver Harvester* but, because of her size and draft, was unable to satisfactorily manoeuvre the vessel. Plans to berth the casualty at Millbay were abandoned, and she was left at anchor, her skipper making alternative arrangements for a larger vessel to assist her to a berth. The *City of Plymouth* regained her mooring at 18.50 hours.

The lifeboat was launched to the *Sarakei* for a second time at 00.05 hours on Sunday 9 January, when her crew returned to the vessel in order to carry out a salvage operation. There was concern, not only for the crew's safety but also for that of the crew of the salvage vessel, which was operating in the dark, on the surf line, amongst the rocks at the Hooe Lake Light, near Picklecombe. As a further precaution, helicopter Rescue 193 also returned to the scene.

At 23.23 hours, the tug *Persuasion* attended the scene and at 00.27 hours attempted to pull the fishing vessel off the rocks. Both the lifeboat, which had again launched the 'Y'-boat, and the helicopter illuminated the scene but after an hour the *Sarekei's* crew requested that they be taken off their vessel. The two men were airlifted to Roborough airport by Rescue 193. The *City of Plymouth* stood-by until it became apparent that the salvage attempt would not be successful. She then recovered the 'Y'-boat and returned to station. The crew were: P. Marshall (Coxswain), K. Rimmer (Second Coxswain), D. Studden

(Mechanic), A. Owen, P. Millet, D. Hole and D. Milford. (First launch only: M. Kitt. Second launch only: F. Jackson, S. Marshall.)

The *City of Plymouth* had a full crew of 11 on board as she undertook a special exercise in Plymouth Sound on Saturday 19 February 1994. There was a calm sea, with a 1-metre swell, as the lifeboat made her way across the Sound to return to station. At a point between Penlee and Pier Cellars, a member of the lifeboat crew spotted three people waving from a small fishing boat. Upon investigation, the vessel was found to be the PH 74, *Aquilla*, which had suffered fuel problems and subsequent gear failure. The fishermen were desperately holding on to a string of crab pots in an attempt to prevent their vessel from drifting onto the rocky shore, some 20–30 metres away.

Left to right: *Fred Jackson, Pete Berry, Ray Jago.*

Coxswain Marshall manoeuvred the lifeboat alongside the *Aquilla* and took off the crew, at the same time placing a member of his crew on board the fishing boat. A line was connected and the boat was towed to Mashford's Yard, where the fishermen were also landed. The crew were: P. Marshall, K. Rimmer, D. Studden, A. Owen, P. Millet, D. Hole, M. Kitt, D. Milford, M. Emden, F. Jackson and S. Marshall.

For many years the port of Plymouth has been the embarkation point for passengers travelling to the Continent. The *City of Plymouth* had only just returned to station, following the service rendered to the *Aquilla*, when she was launched to the 8,313-ton, 129-metre, Channel ferry *Quiberon*, of Morlaix, owned by Brittany Ferries. The *Quiberon* had left Plymouth earlier that day, bound for Roscoff. At 13.02 hours MRSC Brixham received a telephone call from MRCC Cross Corsen via MRCC Falmouth, informing them that a person had been reported missing, and believed lost overboard, during the passage. MRCC Cross Corsen had no knowledge of the time that the missing person was last seen but announced their intention to task an aircraft to search their sector. As more information was received, the incident was upgraded to a PAN situation and a PAN Relay broadcast initiated. Rescue 193, a Search and Rescue helicopter, was scrambled at RNAS Culdrose and proceeded to Plymouth. At 13.45 hours the *City of Plymouth* launched and commenced to search on a bearing of 175°(T), following the course followed by the *Quiberon*. Rescue 193 was also tasked to follow this search pattern.

Confirmation was received from the Coastguard at Cross Corsen that a male passenger was in fact missing from the ferry, and that it was known that he had embarked at Plymouth and was last seen reclining in a deck-chair. He had been travelling alone and his luggage remained on the ferry.

In a force 5–6 south-easterly wind, a rough sea and a 2-metre swell, the Plymouth lifeboat conducted her search to a position approximately midway between Plymouth and Roscoff before turning and retracing her course. MRCC Cross Corsen confirmed that the UK sector had been covered, and they no longer required the assistance of Rescue 193 and the lifeboat. At 16.09 hours the UK element of the search was abandoned.

Whilst returning from this search, at a position approximately 7nm east of the Eddystone Light, the lifeboat sighted a dismasted yacht. Upon reaching the casualty at 17.25 hours, the yacht was found to be the 20.42-metre yacht, *British Steel Challenge*. The yacht was carrying a crew of 11 who were engaged in cutting away and buoying the mast, rigging and sails. Sea conditions had deteriorated to a rough sea, with a 2-metre swell, aggravated by force 6 south-easterly winds. The skipper of the yacht declined assistance and motored in to Plymouth, under her own power, escorted by the lifeboat. The *City of Plymouth* finally arrived back on station at 20.30 hours. The crew were: P. Marshall, K. Rimmer, D. Studden, A. Owen, D. Hole, M. Kitt, D. Milford, S. Marshall.

'Crew fatigue and equipment failure' were the reasons for the launch of the *City of Plymouth* on Tuesday 17 May 1994, the vessel in distress being

Above: *The 'relief' Arun Class lifeboat, the* A.J.R. & L.G. Uridge.

Above: *Coxswain Pat Marshall at the radar set of the* City of Plymouth.

Left: *Motor Mechanic Derek Studden in the engine-room of the* City of Plymouth. WESTERN MORNING NEWS

the 'Fisher 30' motor cruiser, *Grace Louise*, of Southampton. The alarm was raised when, at 12.45 hours, the Brixham Coastguard monitored a call on Ch.67 from the vessel. The crew of the craft gave their position as being south of Plymouth, but their exact location was unknown to them. Direction Finding (D/F) bearings were requested from both Rame Head and Prawle Point stations from which the position of the vessel was estimated to be 32 miles south of the Plymouth breakwater.

The skipper of the *Grace Louise* reported that at the vessel's location the wind was north-easterly, force 4–5, the sea was moderate to choppy and was accompanied by a 2–3-metre swell. It was reported that the vessel had insufficient fuel to reach Plymouth, estimating sufficient for only eight hours' steaming. The skipper also reported that the crew was experiencing difficulty sailing the cruiser. The Coastguard instructed the vessel to maintain her course and to report her position hourly. The FV *Guyona*, which was fishing in the area, undertook to monitor the boat's progress.

D/F bearings taken at 14.13 hours placed the *Grace Louise* 29 miles south of Plymouth, maintaining her northerly course. Further reports indicated that she was making painfully slow progress and that the crew were now experiencing great difficulty in handling the vessel in the prevailing conditions. Having received further confirmation that the vessel could not reach Plymouth on her remaining fuel, the *City of Plymouth* was launched at 17.30 hours. The lifeboat came up with the motor cruiser at 18.45 hours, at a position 50°00.53'N 04°12.65'W, approximately 21 miles on 190°(T) from the Plymouth station. The vessel had been on passage to Plymouth, from Trebeurden, France, when the DECCA failed. The skipper had attempted to navigate by dead-reckoning, but with sea conditions, tacks and diversions to avoid shipping having thrown out their calculations during the previous night, they believed their position to have been only five miles south of Plymouth. It became immediately apparent to the lifeboat crew that the cruiser had suffered damage to her rigging and that she was making very heavy going into a head sea. An offer was made to take off the *Grace Louise's* crew of three, but they elected to stay on board and be towed to Plymouth. A drogue was passed to the cruiser, together with a tow-rope. The lifeboat commenced to tow the cruiser into a head sea,

at approximately 5.5 knots, the *Grace Louise* frequently burying her bow into the swell. Upon entering the Sound, at the request of the skipper, the lifeboat took off one crew member, landing him at Millbay. The drogue was recovered and the *Grace Louise* was cast off, allowing her to make her own way under motor to her mooring. The *City of Plymouth* regained her mooring at 22.55 hours. The crew were: P. Marshall, K. Rimmer, D. Studden, P. Millet, D. Milford and F. Jackson.

In a book such as this it is impossible to record in detail all services provided by a lifeboat station. The services provided by the crew of the Plymouth lifeboat on Sunday 7 August 1994 may be summarised as follows:

At 03.59 hours the *City of Plymouth* was launched following the report of a person in the water off The Hoe. On arrival at the scene, it was established that the casualty had regained the shore and was receiving medical attention. The lifeboat was back on station by 04.25 hours.

The lifeboat was again launched at 09.56 hours, to assist the French sloop, *Avocette II*, which had been dismasted 5nm south-east of Looe. Upon meeting up with the distressed vessel, the lifeboat found her to be in tow of the FV *Rebecca Elaine*. The vessel was dragging her rig over the side. The 'Y'-boat was launched and three lifeboat men were placed aboard the sloop. The three male persons on board were found to be well but the four female crew members were suffering from seasickness. The lifeboat men took control of the situation and under their leadership the top of the mast was hauled back on board, the cockpit closed, and the roller-reefing was disconnected. This clearance operation took over an hour. The *Avocette II* was then towed to Queen Anne's Battery, Plymouth, where the seven crew members were landed. Further assistance was then given to remove the sails, rigging and spars.

Whilst returning to her station at 14.04 hours the *City of Plymouth* was diverted to a position, 1.5nm south-west of Rame Head, from where the sloop, *Islay Mist*, had reported a fire on board, at the same time requesting medical attention. As the lifeboat approached the scene, they became aware of the occupants of a small cabin cruiser, waving frantically. As they were in no immediate danger, the lifeboat continued on its original service. When the lifeboat reached the scene, at 15.03 hours, the yacht, *Star of Jura*, had the sloop in tow. The vessel's skipper confirmed that the fire had been extinguished and that he had suffered only minor burns. Being released from the *Islay Mist* incident, the *City of Plymouth* moved on to the small cabin cruiser that had suffered steering failure. The occupants of the vessel had rigged a 'jury rudder' but found it ineffectual in the sea conditions. Having secured a tow, the lifeboat headed back for Plymouth but, finding the vessel to be riding poorly, brought the cruiser alongside, took off the crew and replaced them with a lifeboat man. The tow to the Mayflower Marina was successful and whilst returning to her station, at 16.30 hours, the lifeboat was tasked to the *Lady Llamedos*.

The *Lady Llamedos* was off Ramscliff Point when she contacted MRSC Brixham, by VHF radio, requesting that an ambulance meet her at Queen Anne's Battery Marina, as the skipper's son had received a blow to the head and appeared to be verging on unconsciousness. The *City of Plymouth* came up to the *Lady Llamedos* at 16.39 hours in Jennycliffe Bay; the boy was transferred to the lifeboat and conveyed directly to the marina and a waiting ambulance.

The lifeboat regained her mooring at 17.45 hours but, at 17.54 hours, whilst still on board, Mechanic Derek Studden monitored a frantic VHF call reporting that a vessel was in imminent danger of going onto the rocks at Penlee. Derek responded that the lifeboat would attend. The fast cabin cruiser, *Amie*, was located 200 yards north of Penlee Point. The *Amie* was clear of Penlee Point, and under tow from the yacht *Vjat*; the MOD launch, *Juno*, was also in attendance. It transpired that the *Amie* had run out of fuel for her primary engine and was unable to make headway under auxiliary power. The *Vjat* slipped her tow, which was then taken up by the lifeboat, and the *Amie* was towed to the Mayflower Marina. The *City of Plymouth* finally regained her mooring at 18.55 hours.

Throughout the day the lifeboat crew had operated in a south-easterly wind, of force 4–5, a moderate sea and a 1–2-metre swell. In total the crew had assisted 21 people.

In the Return of Service for the *Amie*, the Hon. Secretary of the Plymouth Lifeboat Station recorded:

This concluded the sixth service of the day (the middle four all overlapping). For the majority of the crew their labour began at 03.50 and finished 15 hours later. Although none of the services was life threatening the skill and endurance of the crew were well tested and worthy of note.

The crew were: P. Marshall, K. Rimmer, D. Studden, P. Millet, D. Milford, F. Jackson, A. Hole and S. Marshall.

Plymouth's Arun Class lifeboat, the *City of Plymouth*, was launched into particularly bad weather conditions when she went to the assistance of the Dartmouth-registered yacht, *Blue Star*, on Tuesday 9 August 1994. Brixham Coastguard received a PAN PAN message from the yacht at 23.30 hours, stating that she was out of control with two very sick and tired people on board and requesting assistance to reach port. The vessel gave her position as 11nm, on 145°(T) from the Eddystone Lighthouse. The Brixham station immediately broadcast a PAN PAN Relay, which was acknowledged by the 6,000-ton coastal tanker *Anchorman* and the container ship *Bell Pioneer*, both of which proceeded to the location of the casualty to provide a lee until the arrival of the lifeboat. The lifeboat was launched and initially encountered a slight sea with a 1-metre swell. The wind was easterly, force 5–6. Upon reaching the casualty, the sea conditions were rough, with a very uncomfortable 3–4-metre swell. The easterly wind had increased in velocity to severe gale force 9.

Upon reaching the *Blue Star*, the two-man crew informed Coxswain Marshall that they were fearful that their yacht would broach in the heavy following seas. They declined the Coxswain's offer to take them off the yacht. Due to the atrocious weather conditions and the poor state of the yacht's crew, lifeboat men Dave Hole and Sean Marshall were asked to board the *Blue Star*. Coxswain Marshall instructed his men to carry out an assessment of both the vessel and crew and, if in their opinion, the state of either the men or the vessel was likely to deteriorate, to recommend evacuation. The other lifeboat men were also briefed regarding Coxswain Pat Marshall's plan of action for evacuation and coming alongside.

With both vessels rising and falling dramatically on the swell, Pat Marshall manoeuvred the lifeboat towards the yacht, bringing the Arun's starboard bow alongside the port quarter of the *Blue Star*. As the yacht continued to motor ahead, Coxswain Marshall instructed her skipper to heave to.

As Pat Marshall made a second approach to the yacht, both it and the lifeboat were outside the protection of the lee of the *Bell Pioneer*. Judging the rise and fall of the two vessels, Dave Hole and Sean Marshall chose their moment to leap aboard the casualty. The *City of Plymouth* immediately stood-off. The lifeboat men quickly and professionally assessed the situation and informed Coxswain Marshall that, although the crewmen were sick and exhausted, the vessel appeared sound and, in their judgement, a tow could be undertaken. In the exceedingly rough and difficult conditions, such a tow would leave just two men to work the deck of the lifeboat. For a third time Pat Marshall approached the *Blue Star* and a drogue was passed on board. Using all his skills of seamanship he took the Arun in for a fourth time and his crew successfully passed a tow-line to his men, it was secured and he slowly began the tow at 02.15 hours. Dave Hole and Sean Marshall tidied the decks of the *Blue Star* and then relieved the yacht's crew of all duties, allowing them to rest.

During the slow, uncomfortable tow, the speed of which at times, over the ground, was under two knots, the weather conditions deteriorated further. Even with the tow-rope weighted with a coir fender, the speed had to be frequently regulated to maintain a safe tow. For much of the passage the lifeboat was forced to steer a course of approximately 45° to achieve a northerly course.

Throughout the service the lifeboat monitored the wind speed, which did not drop below 40 knots, severe gale force 9, and frequently gusted well in excess of that speed. *The Blue Star* was successfully berthed at Sutton Harbour and, after a long, arduous night, the lifeboat arrived back on station at 07.35 hours. The crew were: P. Marshall, K. Rimmer, D. Studden, P. Millet, D. Hole, F. Jackson and S. Marshall.

At 07.40 hours on Friday 10 February 1995, Longroom Port Control reported that a MAYDAY had been received via MRSC Brixham from the coaster *Marianne Danica*, stating that she was taking in water and sinking 8nm south of Plymouth. A MAYDAY Relay was broadcast, to which vessels responded. Longroom reported that RMAS tugs and warships were proceeding to the scene. A helicopter was scrambled from RNAS Culdrose and, at 07.57 hours, the *City of Plymouth* was launched.

As the lifeboat made her way to the casualty, the 1,409-ton *Marianne Danica* of Copenhagen, with six crew on board, visibility was fair, although overcast, and heavy rain squalls were being experienced from time to time. The wind was blowing from the south, from strong wind, force 7, to severe gale, force 9. The sea was rough with a tremendous 6–7-metre swell.

En route, the lifeboat was made aware that the FV *Theo* had recovered members of the *Marianne Danica's* crew from a life-raft. The lifeboat took a VHF direction-finding reading of the *Theo* that indicated that the original position given for the casualty, 50°13.00'N 04°09.00'W, must have been incorrect. A position was obtained from the *Theo*, which tied in with the D/F bearing, and the revised longitude of 04°01.00'W was passed to the Brixham Coastguard, who relayed the corrected position to other vessels. This was five miles to the east of the original position given.

As the lifeboat reached the scene, at 08.35 hours, the Search and Rescue helicopter, Rescue 193, was already in attendance having arrived minutes earlier. The pilot had lowered his diver onto the Dutchman, the latter waving to the lifeboat to come alongside. The winch-man expressed his deep concern over the depth of water in the vessel and feared imminent capsize, and requested that both he, and the remaining members of the *Marianne Danica's* crew, be taken off immediately. Coxswain Marshall and his crew made no less than three separate approaches to the casualty, each time taking off one man. With each approach the *City of Plymouth* was thrown heavily against the hull of the *Marianne Danica* by the 6–7-metre swell. Additional fenders were rigged on the lifeboat's port side, with the lifeboat men physically holding fenders in place as the vessels crashed together. Despite these extra precautions, the lifeboat sustained crush damage on her forward port-side belting. HMS *Sheffield* and the RFA *Orangeleaf* had now joined the lifeboat at the scene.

Coxswain Marshall took the Arun into the lee side of the casualty. The rescue was impeded by a large, partially-inflated life-raft, with drogue streamed, which was tied to the ship. It was later established that the life-raft was in fact tied to the bottom of the pilot ladder. The ferocity of the swell, combined with the rolling of the vessels, worried Marshall greatly; for he feared that the life-raft would foul the lifeboat's port propeller. On her first approach, the *City of Plymouth* took off a crewman, on the second the ship's master, and on the third the Royal Navy diver.

Four other crewmen from the coaster were aboard the *Theo*, which had another life-raft alongside. As the fishing vessel had very limited cabin space, the crewmen were forced to remain in an exposed position on deck. Having considered the risks, Pat Marshall decided that it was in

Snooker star John Virgo pays a visit to the City of Plymouth. *Left to right:* Jeremy Greenaway, Chris Cook, Derek Studden, John Virgo. WESTERN MORNING NEWS

the interests of the crewmen to be transferred to the safety of the lifeboat. The Royal Navy vessel, the RFA *Orangeleaf*, deployed her crash boat and, using this RIB, the four crewmen were transferred from the *Theo* to the *City of Plymouth* in one operation. The RIB was working at its operational limit, so the RFA *Orangeleaf* recovered the craft. The *Theo* then returned to port with the life-raft.

At this time the RMAS tug, *Forceful*, was steaming for the scene. She later took up station close to the casualty, which, now abandoned, was drifting in the gale-force wind at approximately two knots towards the lee shore, which was some four miles off. HMS *Sheffield* had been designated 'on scene commander' and was stationed some distance to the south. Whilst HMS *Sheffield* was in communication with the master of the *Marianne Danica*, discussing salvage terms, the lifeboat crew noticed that the coaster's radar scanner had stopped working and the vessel's navigation light had been extinguished; it was assumed that this was due to rising water levels. The vessel was now visibly lower at the stern than it had been when the lifeboat first arrived on the scene. Brixham Coastguard reported that the builders of the vessel had advised that she would not sink if only the engine-room were flooded, but her master was more sceptical!

Coxswain Marshall proposed that Rescue 193 lift their diver, and lifeboat man Dave Hole, back onto the casualty to connect a tow-rope. Because of the prevailing weather conditions, the pilot requested the lifeboat to steam into the lee of RFA *Orangeleaf* to effect the transfer. However, the motion of the lifeboat proved too excessive and the transfer was aborted. The Arun closed further onto the *Orangeleaf*, and hove to, allowing for a successful transfer. Before Rescue 193 could, in turn, transfer the diver and lifeboat man onto the coaster, she was tasked by HMS *Sheffield* to return to Longroom and collect a Salvage Officer. Lifeboat man Hole was disembarked at Longroom.

Both Pat Marshall and the master of the tug, *Forceful*, had been made aware that the coaster was carrying a cargo of oil and were greatly concerned about the potential environmental disaster which threatened to ensue. The casualty had now drifted to within '2.4 miles of the shore' and the men agreed that lifeboat men should be put aboard the casualty and a tow established. Coxswain Marshall took the *City of Plymouth* into the casualty's lee side, placing the lifeboat's starboard side to the casualty's starboard quarter in an attempt to overcome the problem of the life-raft, which was still attached to the vessel. In extremely uncomfortable conditions, on the first approach Second Coxswain Keith Rimmer grabbed the pilot ladder and scrambled aboard. On the next approach lifeboat man Jackson leapt for the bulwark but unfortunately, as he jumped, the lifeboat dropped into a trough causing him to lose momentum and he was lucky to hold onto the ship's side. Fred Jackson was left clinging on for his life and, had it not been for the Coxswain's quick thinking and swift actions, he would have been crushed by the lifeboat. Pat Marshall immediately took the Arun astern and Keith Rimmer pulled Fred Jackson inboard.

The lifeboat men made their way to the ship's foredeck, where a line was passed to them from the *Forceful*. By now there was a steady 30–35 knots of wind and a 6–7-metre swell. The Plymouth Pilots, who had been on the scene, had left due to the weather conditions. Unfortunately, with the motion of the boats, the lifeboat men lost their grip on the wire hawser and it was pulled away, causing both men to lose their footing. Fred Jackson fell and, although he was wearing protective headgear, received an injury above his right eye and suffered concussion. Keith Rimmer moved Jackson to a safe position, and, having assessed his injury, offered reassurance. Keith Rimmer advised Pat Marshall of the injury and requested assistance. Coxswain Marshall informed HMS *Sheffield* of the situation and requested that Rescue 193 should be made available for a Medivac. The lifeboat approached the coaster once more and the lifeboat man Dave Milford clambered aboard the *Marianne Danica*. Seeing that the combined efforts of Rimmer and Milford could not pull the hawser aboard, the tug-master called for them to release the hawser and ropes saying that he would send a nylon tow across. The *Forceful* passed a line across, to which a nylon tow-rope was attached. This was successfully hauled in and secured by Rimmer and Milford. This operation had taken 35 minutes and radar showed the casualty to be only '1.47 miles from the shore'.

With the tow under way, and as the casualty no longer offered a lee, Rescue 193 was requested to lift off the lifeboat men. Initially it was intended to lift the party from the centre of the hatch covers. Second Coxswain Rimmer was unhappy with this arrangement for although Fred Jackson could walk with support, the covers were wet and slippery, with no safety rails. The men made their way down the side-deck, to midships and Rescue 193 lowered her diver onto the covers. The diver said that a recovery could not be

made from the side-deck position and that it was necessary to move onto the covers. The four-man party made their way across the hatches, with lifeboat man Jackson crawling on all fours, each man holding on to a colleague's harness for safety, until a clear area was reached. Whilst Jackson had remained conscious throughout, the SAR diver considered the possibility of him losing consciousness during the winching and decided that a stretcher lift was necessary. Keith Rimmer and Dave Milford were winched off first, followed by Fred Jackson in the stretcher and the SAR diver. During this operation wind gusts of 45 knots were recorded. The *City of Plymouth's* crew now comprised the Coxswain, Mechanic and Assistant Mechanic. As the rescued Dutch crewmen could speak English, and were dressed in survival suits, Coxswain Marshall thought it an unnecessary risk having Rimmer and Milford winched back aboard the lifeboat. The Search and Rescue helicopter flew directly to Roborough Airport, Plymouth, from where lifeboat man Jackson was transferred to Derriford Hospital to receive stitches to his wound.

A Lynx helicopter from HMS *Sheffield* subsequently transferred a salvage party to the *Marianne Danica*, and the lifeboat recovered the life-raft with the use of the 'A'-frame. The *City of Plymouth* escorted the *Forceful* and her tow into Plymouth Sound where the Plymouth Pilot boat placed lifeboat man Dave Hole and two other crew members back on board the lifeboat.

The lifeboat regained her station at 12.55 hours and was once more ready for service at 13.20 hours. The crew were: P. Marshall, K. Rimmer, D. Studden, A. Owen, D. Milford, D. Hole and F. Jackson. Also involved were: S. Marshall, A. Hole, P. Millett and M. Kitt.

On the evening of Friday 16 June 1995, Brixham MRSC copied a transmission, from the yacht *Halcyon* to the Falmouth MRCC, stating that the vessel had no navigation lights as they had suffered a total loss of electrics. Their only means of communication was by way of a hand-held VHF radio and their ability to fix a position was dubious. During the night the Brixham MRSC made several calls to the *Halcyon*, without acknowledgement. At 05.17 hours on Saturday 17 June 1995, Brixham MRSC monitored a call, on VHF Ch.16, from the yacht *Halcyon* to Falmouth MRCC, reporting that a crewman had sustained a head injury and requesting a Medivac. There were two crew on the vessel, which was on passage from Falmouth to Plymouth, and they stated that they believed their position to be half way between Rame Head and the Eddystone Light.

The RNAS Culdrose helicopter, Rescue 193, was tasked to a position 'west of Rame Head' as a second bearing to fix the casualty's position was not available. At 06.00 hours the *City of Plymouth* was launched to assist and helicopter in the Medivac, and to assist the remaining crewman in bringing the vessel into port.

Rescue 193 reached the yacht at 06.13 hours but due to the sea conditions had experienced great difficulty in placing his diver on board the yacht. The lifeboat came up with the casualty at 06.40 hours, at a position 1.5nm south of Downderry. The weather conditions at the scene were overcast with fair visibility. A force-6 wind was blowing from the south-south-west, the sea being moderate to rough with a 2-metre swell. With both vessels rising and falling on the waves, one lifeboat man was transferred to the yacht, but in order to facilitate the Medivac, both crewmen and the diver were transferred to the lifeboat. The lifeboat then stood-off as the casualty and diver were recovered to the helicopter.

After the evacuation had been completed, the lifeboat returned to the *Halcyon* and passed a drogue, a VHF radio and a tow-rope to the lifeboat man, who secured the line. The tow to Plymouth commenced but, during the passage, the *Halcyon's* tender became swamped and parted its tow-line. The tender was recovered and taken on board the lifeboat. When close to Torpoint Yacht Harbour the *Halcyon's* skipper, and the tender, were placed back aboard the yacht, and the lifeboat man recovered. The vessel then berthed under her own power. The *City of Plymouth* regained her mooring at 09.12 hours. The crew were: P. Marshall, K. Rimmer, A. Owen, P. Millett, D. Milford and F. Jackson.

The crew of the *City of Plymouth* were involved in an outstanding service on Wednesday 6 September 1995, which in exceedingly violent weather and mountainous seas, culminated in the saving of five lives.

It was at 15.43 hours that Coxswain Pat Marshall, who was monitoring his scanner, became aware of the fact that the 76-foot fishing vessel, the LT 266 *Senex Fidelis*, of Lowestoft, was experiencing major difficulties. The call that Pat monitored was from the *Senex Fidelis* to Brixham Coastguard, reporting that the vessel had blown an oil filter and was unable to use her engines. The vessel had five crew on board and

gave her position as '7 cables off Rame Head and drifting towards the shore.' The fishing vessel had dropped her anchor but it was not holding. A helicopter from the warship HMS *York* was tasked to keep the fishing vessel under observation. HMS *Orwell* and the MOD police launch, *Juno*, also proceeded to the scene. The warship HMS *Liverpool* acknowledged a PAN PAN but, as she was 14nm away, was stood down.

The *City of Plymouth* slipped her mooring at 15.50 hours in calm waters and a moderate south-easterly wind. Conditions were to change dramatically at the location of the casualty, east of Rame Head. As it was nearing high water, the Arun Class lifeboat was able to take the shortest possible route to the casualty, passing through the narrow passage inside Drake's Island. Coxswain Marshall continued to take the shortest route by passing inside the buoy that marked the off-lying rock of Penlee Point. Throughout the journey, and with the 12-foot seas just forward of the beam, the *City of Plymouth* held her top speed.

At 16.04 hours the *Senex Fidelis* reported that her anchor warp had parted and that she was now within 3.2 cables of the shore. The lifeboat reached the casualty at 16.05 hours in conditions that had deteriorated drastically. Visibility remained fair beneath cloud-covered skies, but the south-easterly wind had increased from severe gale-force-9 to storm force 10, 41–58 knots of wind. The sea state had worsened to very rough, with a 4-metre swell. These conditions were set to test the seamanship of the Coxswain and the skill, professionalism and bravery of every member of the crew.

It was close to high water (16.24 hours) and the *Senex Fidelis* was now no more than 300 yards from the shore. Waves 12 feet high were crashing against the foot of the high cliffs that dominate the shoreline, bouncing back only to make the sea even more confused. The casualty was now perilously close to a small cove to the east of Rame Head, she was almost head to wind and her skipper had lowered his trawl beams in an attempt to steady the vessel. Coxswain Marshall established VHF contact with the skipper of the *Senex Fidelis* and asked the Coastguard to minimise communication with the vessel. Keeping the *Senex Fidelis'* skipper fully aware of his intended movements, Pat Marshall manoeuvred the Arun around the stern of the vessel, taking the lifeboat so close to the shore that Coastguards on the cliff top lost her from view. Negotiating his way around the trawl beam, he came alongside the starboard side of the trawler. The *City of Plymouth* was violently thrown about by the seas that were continuously breaking and rebounding from the cliffs; the lifeboat also shipped water. Nevertheless, fortune shone on the lifeboat crew for, at the first attempt, a line was passed to the trawler. In what *Lifeboat Magazine* described as 'perhaps the understatement of the year', Pat Marshall said later, 'It was a good pick-up. Everything went well.'

Being fearful that the tow-rope might part, given the ferocity of the movement of the vessels, and the weather conditions, the lifeboat commenced the tow at a very slow speed. Playing out the tow-warp behind her, she gradually took the strain and pulled the *Senex Fidelis* into the teeth of the gale to gain sea room. With spare warps ready, a mile offshore, Coxswain Marshall increased speed and turned for Plymouth.

For a time during the rescue operation, the Severn Class lifeboat, *17-03 Albert Brown*, ON 1202, which was on sea trials in the area, stood-by and offered her services, should they have been required.

On the return journey, as the *City of Plymouth* entered the Sound, the *Senex Fidelis* was brought alongside the lifeboat for the final stages of the tow, on this occasion the lifeboat passing outside Drake's Island. Despite using all the fenders, in the exceedingly heavy swell, the lifeboat sustained burst fenders, a broken quarter block and two set bitts loosened. The crew of the trawler remained aboard their vessel until it was berthed at Victoria Wharf.

Thankfully no one was hurt during this service and damage to the vessels was minimal, but the skills of the Coxswain and his crew were tested to the utmost. In his official report, Leslie Vipond, the RNLI's Divisional Inspector of Lifeboats (South), said:

Without the timely assistance of Plymouth lifeboat there can be no doubt that the vessel would have been stranded below Rame Head, with the probable loss of her crew. The Coxswain considered taking them off, but feared that they would be injured during the transfer. He had enough confidence in his lifeboat to carry out a deft piece of manoeuvring, to pass a tow-line, and then to draw the casualty into deep water before she could touch the bottom. Coxswain Marshall conducted himself in a thoroughly seamanlike manner. His command of the situation, his

boldness in approaching the casualty which was in the most precarious position, and then exercising patience and good seamanship on towing her into a safe harbour, was in the best traditions of the RNLI.

In further recognition of the skills and courage shown that day, Wednesday 26 June 1996, the Committee of Management of the Institution awarded its Thanks on Vellum to Coxswain Pat Marshall, with Vellum Service Certificates being deservedly awarded to each member of his crew. The crew were: Pat Marshall, Keith Rimmer, Derek Studden, Dave Milford, Paul Millett, Dave Hole and Martin Emden.

The relief fleet lifeboat *52-46 Duke of Atholl*, ON 1160, was on station when the Plymouth crew undertook a particularly difficult service on Monday 25 March 1996. Throughout the evening the Brixham Coastguard had been monitoring communications between the Macwester 8-metre yacht *Gemini*, and the RFA *Sir Tristram*. The exact nature of the difficulty being experienced by the yacht was initially unknown, but the *Sir Tristram* undertook to keep a watch on the vessel throughout the night. The *Gemini* gave her position as ten miles south-west of Plymouth.

The yacht, with two persons on board, reported to the Brixham Coastguard at 23.42 hours that one of her crew was seasick. She had taken down her sails and was attempting to motor into Plymouth but, owing to the wind and tide she was unable to make headway. Her skipper requested a tow, if one could be arranged. The *Sir Tristram* proceeded to the scene but stated that the difference in size of the vessels would place limitations on the assistance that she could offer. The *Sir Tristram* was requested to provide a lee for the *Gemini*.

It became apparent that the situation was deteriorating quickly and the lifeboat, the Arun Class *Duke of Atholl*, slipped her mooring at 23.59 hours. At this time the position of the *Gemini* was 50°15.18'N 04°24.42'W. Visibility at the scene was poor and an easterly wind of severe gale force 9 was gusting to storm force 10. The sea was very rough and there was a 3.5–4-metre swell. As the lifeboat crossed Plymouth Sound, there was no moon and heavy rain.

Coxswain Marshall monitored a VHF transmission from the *Sir Tristram* to the *Gemini*, indicating her intention to attempt to pass a tow-line. Pat Marshall raised the *Sir Tristram* and notified her that the lifeboat's estimated time of arrival at the scene was 45 minutes. In view of the prevailing weather conditions and the size of the vessel, an attempt to pass a line was not to be made unless the situation became critical. Such an operation would preferably have been undertaken by the lifeboat, which had far superior manoeuvrability. The *Sir Tristram* acknowledged and concurred with this advice, she also stated that scrambling nets and lifelines had been rigged should it become necessary for the casualties to abandon their vessel. The *Sir Tristram* estimated the swell to be 4 metres and agreed to stand-off and provide a lee pending the arrival of the lifeboat.

The *Duke of Atholl* arrived on scene at 00.52 hours when contact was made with the female crew member of the *Gemini* who reported that they were cold, wet and exhausted. Coxswain Marshall explained that, in the existing weather conditions, he considered it too hazardous to attempt to take the crew off the yacht.

He outlined his intentions of coming alongside the yacht and passing a drogue, which the crew were to deploy once the lifeboat had pulled clear. At this point the *Sir Tristram* was 400 yards to the east of the casualty and providing little or no lee. Marshall requested the warship to pull clear in order to allow the lifeboat maximum room for manoeuvring. The lifeboat was taken in on the yacht's starboard quarter, but the yacht pulled away. On the second run the yacht ran under the Arun's bow. A third attempt was made, the lifeboat approached the stern of the *Gemini* and the drogue was successfully passed. At this point Pat Marshall became aware that the yacht remained under motor and pulled clear. By radio link the crew of the yacht were instructed on how to deploy the drogue and informed that, when they were ready, the lifeboat would come along-side and pass the tow-rope. The crew were also instructed to cut their engine and lash the tiller amidships. After some time they radioed their readiness to accept the tow.

Both the *Gemini* and the *Duke of Atholl* were rising and falling alarmingly on the heavy swell and Coxswain Marshall deemed the vessel's motion too violent to attempt to put a lifeboat man aboard the yacht. Having secured the tow-rope, the yacht's crew went below decks, as it was considered safer for them to remain there rather than to attempt their transfer to the lifeboat. With the man and woman safe, the lifeboat commenced the arduous five-hour tow to Plymouth. The yacht was greatly stabilized by the drogue that had been deployed, but the lifeboat encountered extreme difficulty in steering at a very slow speed. At one point the Coastguard queried the lifeboat's position as her reports indicated that her speed was down to one knot. For the full duration of the tow, Pat Marshall steered the boat from the open steering position; he was accompanied throughout by lifeboat man Fred Jackson, who kept the casualty floodlit at all times.

Upon their safe arrival in Plymouth, the skipper of the *Gemini* informed Pat Marshall that before their rescue by the lifeboat he had made less than one mile in four hours and, but for the fear of having a following sea, had considered turning about for Fowey. The yacht had lost her Avon dinghy and in an attempt to recover it he had lowered his sail. The yacht immediately lost the steadying effect of the sails, which he was then unable to hoist as the halyards had become tangled around the mast.

In his Return of Service, Coxswain Marshall paid tribute to this crew saying: 'The crew were as complete a team as any coxswain could wish.' He particularly brought to the attention of the Hon. Secretary the efforts of Fred Jackson, who had manned the searchlight for nearly five hours, in extremely cold and wet conditions. The crew were: P. Marshall, K. Rimmer, D. Studden, A. Owen, P. Millett, D. Milford and F. Jackson.

A chain of circumstances led to the Arun Class lifeboat, the *Duke of Atholl*, putting to sea on Sunday 19 May 1996 with a crew of only three. The service was in answer to a MAYDAY call, which was received by Longroom, at 10.12 hours, and relayed to the Brixham MRSC. The vessel in distress was the garbage barge *Skippy*, which, with two persons and a dog aboard, was taking in water just off Plymouth Breakwater. Longroom informed MRSC that the MOD police launch, *Juno*, an inflatable from HMS *Boxer* and the RNAS tug *Faithful* were proceeding to the scene. At 10.16 hours a MAYDAY relay was broadcast and acknowledged by the dive-boat *Maureen of Dart*, which was also tasked to assist. The lifeboat assembly signal was made at 10.18 hours and the lifeboat launched at 10.30 hours under the command of the Deputy Second Coxswain, Dave Milford.

The lifeboat set out into a very rough sea and a 2-metre swell. Visibility was fair with a wind of force 6–7 blowing from the west. The *Duke of Atholl* took only seven minutes to reach the casualty, at a position 0.5nm west of the

Plymouth breakwater lighthouse, 50°20.00'N 04°10.20'W, and could clearly see that the barge was lying heavy by the bows. In an attempt to slow down the ingress of water, the vessel, which was still under power and navigating stern first, was escorted by the lifeboat into the calmer waters of Cawsand Bay. There Mechanic Derek Studden and lifeboat man Jon West boarded the barge, taking with them a portable pump. After pumping a quantity of water from the vessel, an operation that took approximately ten minutes, Derek Studden returned to the lifeboat, and the *Juno*, *Maureen of Dart* and the inflatable from HMS *Boxer* were stood down. At 10.55 hours the *Skippy* reported to Longroom that she had stopped the ingress of water and, escorted by the *Duke of Atholl* and the *Faithful*, was making her way slowly across the Sound. When off the Mount Batten breakwater, the *Faithful* was stood down and the lifeboat escorted the *Skippy* on to her berth at the Cattewater, where lifeboat man Jon West and the pump were recovered.

The shortage of crew that day was due to the fact that the Coxswain, Assistant Mechanic and three crew members were on passage from Falmouth to Plymouth with the station boat, the *City of Plymouth*, following her refit. The Second Coxswain was on leave and one crew member had car problems! Every cloud has a silver lining and this chain of events gave Deputy Second Coxswain Dave Milford his first operational service in command of the Plymouth lifeboat. The crew were: D. Milford, D. Studden and J. West.

The *City of Plymouth* launched into a south-westerly wind and moderate sea on Friday 5 July 1996, when she went to the assistance of the dive-boat, *Cee King* of Plymouth. The position of the casualty, 50°18.60'N 04°12.63'W, was approximately 800 yards east of Rame Head.

Divers from the *Cee King*, which had a total of nine crew on board, had been diving on the wreck of the *James Eagan Layne* in Whitsand Bay, when a diver got into difficulty. The diver, who had just undertaken his first dive to a depth of 22 metres, for 30 minutes, had completed a normal ascent but, upon reaching the surface, immediately gave the recognised distress signal to the dive-boat. At 12.06 hours the Coastguard received a PAN PAN Medico from the *Cee King*, stating that the diver was having convulsions and was vomiting blood. At this time the dive-boat was unable to make for Plymouth as she still had divers in the water. At 12.19 hours the Search and Rescue helicopter, Rescue 193, was

scrambled from RNAS Culdrose, and the lifeboat was launched at 12.25 hours, both units having a similar ETA.

As the lifeboat approached Penlee Point, the *Cee King* indicated that the diver had stopped breathing and that two other divers were rendering first aid. The *City of Plymouth* reached the casualty at 12.42 hours and immediately transferred Deputy Second Coxswain Dave Milford and lifeboat man Mike West onto the dive-boat. The lifeboat men carried further first-aid equipment and oxygen apparatus with them. The face, hands and ears of the casualty were deep-purple in colour and he was extremely cold. Dave Milford successfully fitted the oxygen mask to the diver's face but his efforts to find a pulse were unsuccessful. Rescue 193 arrived on the scene within two–three minutes, and both a Royal Navy diver and a doctor were lowered to the *Cee King*. The latter immediately took over the resuscitation attempt. A stretcher was lowered and the casualty was airlifted directly to Derriford Hospital, Plymouth. Unfortunately, the casualty was pronounced 'dead on arrival'.

As the *Cee King* made her way into Plymouth, Dave Milford became increasingly concerned for the welfare of the remaining members of the dive team, who were showing signs of shock. The lifeboat passed 'space blankets' to the dive-boat, and trainee crew member Catherine Marshall transferred to the boat to give comfort to the group. Two divers were giving particular cause for concern, as was the skipper of the *Cee King*. Dave Milford took command of the dive-boat and requested that they be met by an ambulance at the Queen Anne's Battery Marina where the eight members of the party were placed in the care of ambulance personnel.

The crew for the dive-boat incident were: P. Marshall, D. Studden, A. Owen, P. Millett, D. Milford, M. Emden, ? Stevens, C. Marshall and M. West.

One of the mass-produced Liberty ships built to bolster Allied merchant shipping during the Second World War, the *James Eagan Layne* was torpedoed on Thursday 15 March 1945. An attempt was made to beach her, but water slowly overcame the ship's pumps and she sank, about a mile from shore in Whitsand Bay *(see page 65)*. She now lies upright in approximately 26 metres of water.

The *City of Plymouth* was launched on Thursday 22 August 1996, following the report of a 'man overboard'. It was at 14.14 hours that the Brixham Coastguard received a call for help from a 13-year-old boy aboard the 25'6" Folkboat, the *Timoneer*, reporting that his father had been washed overboard. The youth, quite understandably, was unsure of his position. D/F bearings were obtained from Rame Head and MRCC Falmouth, on their Pendennis aerial, giving a position of '50°14'N 04°29'W; 6.3 miles south-west of Looe Island'. A MAYDAY relay broadcast was initiated. MRCC Falmouth was requested to scramble Rescue 193 from RNAS Culdrose, and both the Plymouth and Falmouth lifeboats were asked to launch. The *City of Plymouth* launched at 14.25 hours, in the knowledge that the warship, HMS *Roebuck* was also proceeding to the scene, and made her way to an amended location five miles on 245°(T) from Rame Head, 50°17.5'N 04°20.0'W. The lifeboat crew were able to hear the *Timoneer* on VHF, and were able to D/F and run down the bearing. Whilst proceeding, the position was further amended by the Coastguard, to '193°T, 6.3 miles from Looe Island', and 11.4nm from Rame Head. This position was derived from D/F bearings obtained by the helicopter.

By 14.45 hours Rescue 193 had established radio communication with the *Timoneer,* and the yacht *Louteen*, with a doctor on board, was within one mile of the position given for the vessel. At 14.55 hours, when about two miles from the casualty, the Plymouth lifeboat was in communication with the Fowey lifeboat, her coxswain reporting that they were at the scene. Upon coming up with the Fowey lifeboat, it was established that the young boy had woken from sleep to realise his father was missing. It was believed that the man could have been missing for up to two hours. It was further established that the casualty was not wearing a life-jacket, but that he was wearing a red sailing jacket. At 15.07 hours a second helicopter, Rescue 169, was also tasked from RNAS Culdrose to the scene, her ETA being 25 minutes.

Conditions in which the lifeboats and helicopters commenced a sector search for the lost crewman were far from ideal; a full southerly gale was blowing although visibility was fair. The sea conditions were very rough with a 3–4-metre swell. The *City of Plymouth* commenced to search to the west, the casualty believed to have been sailing from Falmouth to Plymouth. At 15.30 hours HMS *Roebuck* reported that she was launching her sea-boat to an object sighted in the water. Rescue 193 immediately requested the *Roebuck*

to stand clear as they had also had visual contact with a person, floating face-down in the water, approximately ten yards from a red-coloured jacket. Although immediately airlifted to Derriford Hospital, the man could not be revived.

The youth remained on the yacht with members of the Fowey lifeboat crew as the vessel was towed back to Fowey. The *City of Plymouth* regained her mooring at 17.35 hours. The crew were: P. Marshall, K. Rimmer, D. Studden, D. Milford, P. Millett, M. Emden and S. Marshall.

A call was received from Brixham Coastguard at 15.20 hours on Thursday 3 April 1997, reporting two youths to be stranded, and possibly injured, having fallen from cliffs near Wembury. The *City of Plymouth* launched at 15.30 hours into a north-westerly wind, force 4, and a calm sea. On reaching a point off HMS *Cambridge*, Coxswain Pat Marshall launched the Arun's 'Y'-boat so that it could proceed inside the Mew Stone, whilst the lifeboat proceeded outside of the Mew Stone. The lifeboat went towards Season Point whilst the 'Y'-boat went to the east of Blackstone Ledge; the vessels then searched the cliffs on a converging course. At this location the wind was north-westerly, force 7–8, the sea moderate, with a half-metre swell.

When the youths were spotted from the lifeboat, the 'Y'-boat was directed into a cove where a lifeboat man was put ashore. The crewman reached the casualty, who was found to be stranded ten metres up a near-vertical cliff face, whilst the second youth was taken out to the lifeboat by the 'Y'-boat. On climbing to a position adjacent to the casualty, the lifeboat man was able to determine that the injuries were not serious. The 'Y'-boat then returned, with an additional crewman, and was directed to an alternative landing-place from which the casualty could be reached via an easier route. The lifeboat man scrambled up the steep incline and assisted the casualty down to the 'Y'-boat by means of which he was taken out to the lifeboat. The 'Y'-boat then collected the two lifeboat men from the shore, transferring them back to the *City of Plymouth*. Both boats then made their way to Wembury Beach, in anticipation of being met by an ambulance. Upon being informed that the ambulance was in fact waiting at Bovisand, Coxswain Marshall temporarily recovered the 'Y'-boat and proceeded to a point off Bovisand, there re-launching the 'Y'-boat, which took the casualties ashore. The 'Y'-boat was then recovered and the lifeboat returned to her station at

17.04 hours. The crew were: P. Marshall, K. Rimmer, D. Studden, A. Owen, D. Milford, Sean Marshall, Mike West and Carl Baccus.

A MAYDAY call to the Brixham Coastguard from the Brixham fishing vessel the BM 367, *Bon Accord*, prompted the launch of the *City of Plymouth* on Friday 18 April 1997. The 20.26-ton vessel was off the eastern end of the Plymouth breakwater when she reported that her prop-shaft had broken and slipped backwards, causing her to take in water. The alarm was raised at 12.45 hours, the lifeboat slipping her mooring at 12.58 hours.

The weather conditions were good and the lifeboat reached the casualty within seven minutes of her launch, only to find that another fishing vessel was already alongside the *Bon Accord*. Lifeboat men Dave Milford and Tony Owen were placed on board the fishing vessel with a portable pump and, having checked below with the *Bon Accord's* skipper, Matthew Dodd, Dave Milford was reasonably satisfied that the vessel's own pumps were coping with the intake of sea water. At this time it also became evident that the fishing vessel's rudder had jammed hard over and was apparently being held in place by the shaft and propeller. Following consultation with the skipper, it was decided to take the casualty to Mashford's Yard.

As the *Bon Accord* was without steering, Coxswain Marshall came alongside the vessel and secured her to the lifeboat. The short passage was slow and not without steering difficulties, but thanks to the skilful manoeuvring of the lifeboat, the *Bon Accord* was successfully berthed at Mashford's Yard. The crew were: P. Marshall, K. Rimmer, D. Studden, A. Owen, M. Kitt, D. Milford, W. Stephens, M. West and D. Ellis.

Wednesday 21 May 1997 saw the crew of the *City of Plymouth* carry out two services back-to-back, the first being to a large powerboat and the second to a small fishing vessel.

It was at 08.16 hours that the lifeboat was launched in response to a call from the 6.5-metre powerboat *Dolphin,* which had lost its propeller at a position '0.6 nautical miles', on 072°(T), from the Eddystone Lighthouse. No other vessels in the area responded to Brixham Coastguard's general broadcast. The lifeboat, which was launched into a calm sea, light winds and good visibility, reached the casualty at 08.55 hours. The lifeboat came up to the *Dolphin,* which had anchored, and passed a drogue. As the three adults on board the powerboat were quite happy

to remain there, the lifeboat established at tow-line, the powerboat recovered her anchor and by 09.02 hours the *City of Plymouth*, with the *Dolphin* in tow, had set a course for home.

The tow was well under way when, at 09.38 hours, the lifeboat monitored a call for assistance from the FV *Metan*, which was in the area of the West Rutts, four-and-a-quarter miles east-north-east of the lifeboat's current position. As no other vessel responded to the call, Coxswain Marshall, being satisfied that the conditions would permit towing both vessels, set out for the *Metan* with the *Dolphin* still in tow. The lifeboat reached the *Metan* at 10.29 hours and found that the fishing vessel had lost all drive. At the *Metan's* position, the *Dolphin* was instructed to recover the drogue, and the tow was then short-ened and passed to the *Metan*. Under instruction, the *Dolphin* reset the drogue and the *City of Plymouth* then headed for Sutton Harbour with the *Dolphin* astern the *Metan*.

Off Mount Batten breakwater, the *Dolphin* once again recovered the drogue and the vessels were brought either side of the lifeboat to contin-ue the tow into Sutton Channel, where the *Metan* was passed over to the Sutton Harbour dory. The *Dolphin* was towed to Mutton Cove, where she was berthed with the assistance of the 'Y'-boat. The *City of Plymouth* was back on station at 13.00 hours. The crew were: P. Marshall, K. Rimmer, D. Studden, A. Owen, D. Milford and D. Ellis.

The two-person crew of the 15-ton fishing vessel, PH 587 *Belle Etoile*, radioed the Brixham Coastguard at 15.51 hours on Thursday 17 July 1997, requesting urgent assistance as their vessel was taking in water, 9nm on 163°T from the Great Mew Stone. Sea conditions at the scene were rough with a north-north-westerly force 6–7 wind, gusting to gale force 8–9. Upon the lifeboat being launched at 15.58 hours, Coxswain Pat Marshall was made aware that two warships, fishing vessels and a rescue helicopter were also making their way towards the casualty. The first vessel to reach the casualty was the FV *Franjo A*, which arrived at about the same time as the rescue helicopter, the warships joining them shortly afterwards. The helicopter landed its diver and a pump on the stricken vessel, although it was some time before the pump became operational. A running commentary of events was established between the *Franjo A* and the *City of Plymouth*.

The lifeboat arrived on the scene some 15

minutes later, when Coxswain Marshall put two of the lifeboat's crew and an additional pump aboard the casualty. With both auxiliary pumps now operational, the *City of Plymouth* went alongside the *Belle Etoile* and recovered the diver, who was then winched off the lifeboat, the rescue helicopter having been re-tasked to assist a wind-surfer near Penlee. The lifeboat returned to the casualty and, having established that the situation had been stabilised, set up a tow-rope and, in a rough sea with a 2-metre swell, began a slow tow back to Plymouth. For the first hour or so of the tow both pumps were kept running, but by this time water could be seen coming up the rudder-post. The post was quickly packed with grease, which reduced the rate of flow. Being satisfied that the *Bell Etoile* was not now going to sink, the tow continued and the fishing vessel was finally berthed at Sutton Harbour. The crew were: P. Marshall, K. Rimmer, D. Studden, D, Milford, S. Marshall, W. Stephens, M. West, R. Anderson and D. Ellis.

When the *City of Plymouth* slipped her moorings on Thursday 28 August 1997, she put out into a slight sea state, negative swell and a westerly wind of force 5–6. The launch was purely to undertake a PR visit for the Royal Marines at Turnchapel. Whilst committed on this PR engagement, the lifeboat was diverted to locate and assist a catamaran that was reported dismasted one mile south of the Mew Stone. Due to the dismasting, VHF communication could not be established with the casualty but the Brixham Coastguard, via a mobile-phone system, had established communication.

The position of the casualty, the 3.5-ton sailing multihull *Myros*, which carried a crew of three, was given as Bigbury Bay, search area 50°16.06'N 04°00.44'W, but initially the vessel could not be located. Contact was made by phone, and the *Myros* was requested to fire a flare in order that her position could be verified. The flare was not sighted. This request was made on a further three occasions but again flares were not sighted. The Coastguard relayed a new position for the casualty to the lifeboat and shortly afterwards the catamaran was sighted; it was reached at 15.50 hours.

At the location of the casualty the lifeboat crew encountered very rough seas and a 4-metre swell, the wind was now blowing from the west at 48–58 knots; storm force 10. In extremely trying conditions, Coxswain Marshall placed the *City of Plymouth* alongside the *Myros* and

lifeboat men Mike Kitt and Dave Milford were transferred to the vessel. In driving rain, the lifeboat came alongside for a second time and took off the female member of the crew, leaving one adult male and one juvenile male aboard the casualty. The lifeboat stood-off for a second time as attempts were made to secure the broken mast and rigging. Eventually a drogue and a hand-held VHF radio were passed to the vessel, the drogue was deployed, and a tow-line was passed and secured. At 16.30 hours, the long, dangerous tow was commenced. During the tow, some structural damage to the *Myros* was noticed, including a large crack that appeared between the two hulls. The adult male crew member was very cold, hypothermic and suffering from seasick-ness. He was confined to his bunk and kept under strict observation by the lifeboat crew.

After what started out as a simple PR exercise, the *City of Plymouth* eventually berthed the *Myros*, at Mayflower Marina, four-and-a-half hours after arriving at the scene of the incident. The crew were: P. Marshall, D. Studden, D. Milford, A. Owen, M. Kitt, S. Marshall and R. Anderson.

Not all lifeboat services result in the saving of property or lives; on many occasions the lifeboat crews have the unenviable task of recovering a body; this was the case on the evening of Monday 22 September 1997. The lifeboat launched at 21.26 hours, following the receipt of a call reporting a person in the water in Firestone Bay, between Millbay Docks and Western Kings. The person was reportedly clinging to a yellow buoy and shouting. The night was calm, with a glassy sea; visibility was good, in light airs, and there was little or no tidal movement.

The vicinity of the yellow-coloured swimming area marker buoy, off Third Beach and the bay, was searched whilst preparations were made to launch the Arun's inflatable 'Y'-boat. Lifeboat men Dave Milford and Sean Marshall manned the 'Y'-boat and, under direction passed via VHF radio by the lifeboat's Coxswain, searched various areas of Firestone Bay. The *City of Plymouth*, acting as the on-scene command post, was assisted in the search by the Coastguard's 'general-purpose' boat. A request for further assistance was made, via Longroom, and the Ministry of Defence police boat *Juno* and a RIB joined the search. Whilst directing the four search craft, including the 'Y'-boat, the lifeboat continued her search using the facilities of night-vision equipment, flares and searchlights. Longroom confirmed that the shoreline was being searched using infra-red cameras.

A Search and Rescue helicopter had been scrambled and, upon arriving at the scene, was instructed to commence a second search of the area already covered. The surface vessels formed a line abreast, roughly east to west, or down the approximate line of the bay, and proceeded to search in a southerly direction, across the main shipping channel, towards Drake's Island. As the waters off the island became shallower, the Arun stood off, allowing the inflatable to search closer to the shoreline.

The 'Y'-boat found the casualty, a male person, in the shallow waters near Drake's Island. He was wholly submerged in the sea. Sean Marshall entered the water and the casualty was recovered to the 'Y'-boat, the man's eyes were fully dilated and the lifeboat men were unable to distinguish a pulse. The casualty was taken back to the *City of Plymouth* where he was again checked for the vital signs of life; none were found. Preparations were immediately made for the casualty to be airlifted to hospital by helicopter. Unfortunately, the casualty was pronounced to be 'dead on arrival' at Plymouth's Derriford Hospital.

Having recovered the 'Y'-boat, the lifeboat returned to her station at 22.42 hours. The crew were: P. Marshall, K. Rimmer, D. Studden, A. Owen, D. Milford, J. West, S. Marshall and R. Anderson.

Not all maritime disasters or rescues carried out by the lifeboats of the Royal National Lifeboat Institution take place in hurricane-force winds, with coxswains and crews having to face waves of 'mountainous proportions', as was demonstrated in the case of the *Koningin Der Engelen* on Saturday 21 February 1998. A MAYDAY call from the vessel had been monitored by the Brixham Coastguard, and at 08.00 hours the *City of Plymouth* launched into a smooth sea, with a slight swell, a westerly wind of force 3–5 and good visibility, to go to the assistance of the 78-ton Belgian fishing vessel at the search area coordinates 49°55.14'N 04°00.34'W. The search area was 26.7nm, on 167°(T), from the Plymouth Lifeboat Station. The 27-metre, steel-hulled *Koningin Der Engelen* of Ostende was reportedly taking in water from a pipe in the engine-room and sinking. Other vessels responded to the distress call and a Search and Rescue helicopter was scrambled to the scene from RNAS Culdrose. During the journey to the casualty, Coxswain Marshall was informed that the

helicopter had reached the trawler and taken off her crew of four. The lifeboat also received information that a tanker, *British Tamar*, was on the scene and had both the casualty and a life-raft in sight. Coxswain Marshall was requested to attempt to save the vessel, or to guard the position until she sank.

The *City of Plymouth* was within five miles of the casualty when the *British Tamar* informed her that the *Koningin Der Engelen* was slipping under. As the lifeboat closed on the scene, in what was now a rough sea, with a 3-metre swell, and winds that had increased to force 6–7, the crew could see the bow of the Belgian trawler sticking up out of the water. At 09.38 hours she sank completely. The lifeboat recovered the life-raft and then spent the next one-and-a-half hours recovering flotsam, in the shape of dozens of fish baskets and boxes, together with assorted loose gear. The *City of Plymouth* returned to her station at 12.35 hours.

The Brixham Coastguard later reported that the *Koningin Der Engelen* had started to take in water whilst in the Bristol Channel and that the vessel had been attempting to reach her home port in Belgium. The crew were: P. Marshall, K. Rimmer, D. Studden, A. Owen, S. Marshall and R. Anderson.

When the *City of Plymouth* was launched on Saturday 23 May 1998 she was under the command of Second Coxswain Keith Rimmer. The lifeboat was launched, at the request of the Brixham Coastguard, to search for a skin diver from the dive-boat *Sea Urchin*, who had failed to surface. The diver had been diving on the wreck of the liner, *Afric*, at a chart depth of 55 metres. The search location of 50°01.27'N 04°32.90'W was 23.25nm from the Plymouth station. The lifeboat slipped her mooring at 14.42 hours and in a northerly wind of force 5–7, a moderate sea with a 1-metre swell, made for the search area. The Brixham Coastguard requested that, upon her arrival at the scene, the *City of Plymouth* should assume the role of 'on scene commander'. As the Plymouth lifeboat approached Penlee, and the position of the casualty became clear, Coxswain Keith Rimmer requested the launch of the Fowey lifeboat; it was also suggested that the latter should adopt the role of OSC as she would reach the scene before the Plymouth boat.

As the *City of Plymouth* approached the scene, at 16.15 hours, a small fleet of vessels, which included the *Sea Urchin*, a Customs boat, the Fowey lifeboat plus a Search and Rescue helicopter, were already engaged in the search for the missing diver. Various search patterns were established, as determined by the Brixham Coastguard. The search patterns allocated to the various vessels crossed over each other, providing a good coverage of the area. The crew of the *Sea Urchin* were all too fully aware of the estimated survival time for the diver and at 19.30 hours the search coordinator, Brixham Coastguard, recommended the termination of the search. Following communication between the Coxswains of the Plymouth and Fowey lifeboats, Brixham Coastguard agreed to the search continuing until dark. At 21.25 hours, as darkness fell, and with both coxswains being satisfied that the area had been thoroughly searched, the lifeboats left the scene and returned to their respective stations. After eight hours at sea the *City of Plymouth* arrived back in Plymouth at 22.38 hours.

The missing diver was not found. The crew were: K. Rimmer, Derek Studden, Tony Owen, Dave Milford, Mike Kitt, Jon West and Sean Marshall.

The distressed vessel requiring assistance on Monday 24 August 1998 was the 2,223-ton Danish gas tanker, *Linda Kosan* of Kobenhavn. The tanker, carrying 320 tonnes of propane and 640 tonnes of butane gas, reported that she had been on fire but that the fire had been extinguished. The *Linda Kosan's* position was given as 9.5nm south-south-east of the Eddystone. At that location visibility was good, the wind westerly force 3–5 and the sea moderate with a 1.5-metre swell. Coxswain Pat Marshall slipped the *City of Plymouth* from her mooring at 10.22 hours and commenced the one-hour journey to reach the casualty. It soon became apparent that the tanker was continuing to steam to the west, and the appropriate intercept course was set. The Search and Rescue helicopter, Rescue 193, had been scrambled from RNAS Culdrose and was making her way to the scene, carrying a fire-fighting crew from Falmouth.

Some time later Coxswain Marshall requested the captain of the *Linda Kosan* to alter course to the north, providing this caused no danger to his ship. This manoeuvre would alter the wind direction over the tanker's deck. The captain complied with this request. The lifeboat intercepted the casualty 6.8nm south-south-west of the Eddystone, 50°05.02'N 04°20.66'W, at 11.25 hours. Due to the fear of static from Rescue 193, the master of the tanker refused to allow the fire crew to be winched down to his vessel. An

initial team of two firemen were winched aboard the *City of Plymouth* from where they were transferred onto the *Linda Kosan*. The assessment carried out by the firemen proved that the fire was out; however, the ship's engineer had cut himself badly and required medical assistance. A medic on board the helicopter was winched onto the lifeboat and then transferred to the tanker. The lifeboat stood off until such time that the firemen and medic were in a position to leave the tanker, at which time Coxswain Marshall came alongside the casualty, took off the rescue team and the injured seaman, and held steady as they were winched back on board the helicopter. The seaman was transported to hospital by Rescue 193.

The *City of Plymouth* was requested to escort the *Linda Kosan* west until the Falmouth lifeboat could relieve her. After 30 minutes, at 12.34 hours, the lifeboat was stood down and permitted to return to her station. The crew were: P. Marshall, K. Rimmer, D. Studden, D. Milford, S. Marshall, D. Ellis and S. O'Kane.

It was the relief Arun Class lifeboat, the *52-25 A.J.R. & L.G. Uridge* (ON 1086) which slipped her mooring at Plymouth at 12.49 hours on Saturday 24 April 1999 to go to the assistance of a 10-metre yacht. The crew were aboard the lifeboat following an exercise, when a VHF call was received from the Brixham Coastguard, requesting the boat to stand-by as they were in the process of taking a 999 call. Coxswain Marshall slipped the moorings and moved the lifeboat to the entrance of the Millbay Docks. The lifeboat was tasked to a yacht with a collapsed person on board, which was between Mount Batten Breakwater and Fishers Nose, Cattewater. The identity of the yacht was unknown and the only means of contact with the casualty was via a mobile phone. At the entrance to Sutton Channel, the lifeboat crew observed a yacht behaving erratically. On the foredeck of the vessel they saw a female kneeling beside a body that was jammed between the coach-roof and the rails. A male person was seen to be at the tiller of the yacht, that person seeming to possess little or no boat-handling skills.

Coxswain Marshall laid the Arun alongside the moving yacht, the *Satsula*, and two lifeboat men were transferred aboard. A medical assessment was made of the male casualty and Sean Marshall immediately commenced mouth-to-mouth resuscitation and external chest compressions. The yacht was taken into the marina, the lifeboat crew continuing the resuscitation until the casualty was handed into the care of a paramedic ambulance crew. The resuscitation attempts were unsuccessful and ceased after 20 minutes. The crew were: P. Marshall, D. Studden, T. Owen, S. Marshall and trainees C. Cook and C. Hall.

The *A.J.R. & L.G. Uridge* was launched into a south-south-westerly wind, of force 6–7, and a rough sea, with a 2–3-metre swell, at 13.45 hours on Monday 10 May 1999, to assist a small power craft, with cabin, that was in extreme difficulty near Bovisand Harbour. The sea conditions at the scene were rough, with a 2–3-metre swell, accompanied by a south-south-westerly wind of force 6–7. On reaching the location, the lifeboat crew found a 4.5-metre craft, the *Dignity*, secured amidships to a mooring buoy near Fort Bovisand. The boat, which was secured by a weed-covered rope, was almost broadside-on to the weather and was being battered by heavy seas. The small craft had some protection provided to her by the Bovisand sea wall, over which waves were breaking. The Arun had to stay outside the lee of the wall, due to the lack of depth of water, and to allow for sea room. Initially it was thought that no one was on board the craft and conditions were too bad to permit the launch of the 'Y'-boat to investigate. At that point a male person emerged from the cabin and the crew realised that a rescue had to be made. Without the option of the 'Y'-boat, Coxswain Marshall considered the alternative of anchoring the lifeboat and veering down to the casualty. In the prevailing weather conditions, this option was also dismissed. The remaining option was to physically pass a line to the occupant of the cabin cruiser. A second mooring buoy, close to that to which the *Dignity* was secured, made manoeuvring the lifeboat difficult but the *A.J.R. & L.G. Uridge* was skilfully placed into a position from which Keith Rimmer could pass a line to the casualty. It took several minutes of encouragement before the lone occupant of the *Dignity* could be coaxed onto his vessel's foredeck to receive the lifeboat's line. It took the occupant, Mr Wright, who seemed totally confused, three attempts to secure the line. The lifeboat then pulled the small craft, which was still attached to the buoy, clear before Mr Wright succeeded in releasing the fastening he had made to the buoy.

As Second Coxswain Rimmer expressed concern over the man's condition, the *Dignity* was brought alongside the lifeboat. The casualty had to be lifted bodily aboard the lifeboat by Keith Rimmer and Dave Milford. Mr Wright was cold, exhausted and confused but it was established that the vessel, which had been towing the *Dignity*, had capsized in the heavy weather; he mentioned that a man and a dog had been in the water, but thought that they were safe. Enquiries were made with the Coastguard's Plymouth Mobile Unit, who quickly confirmed that the 'first informant' of the *Dignity*'s distress was, in fact, the occupant of the tow craft who had scrambled his way ashore. A lifeboat man was placed on board the *Dignity* and the vessel was taken, in tow, to Millbay Marina.

Speaking to the press after the incident, Keith Rimmer said:

He had set out from Ernesettle on the River Tamar in the boat in the morning and was being towed by a friend to Bridgend on the River Yealm when the towing craft ran out of fuel. The cabin cruiser itself had only a small outboard motor, and that didn't have any fuel. The chap drifted a bit apparently, but managed to pick up the mooring buoy just off the diving centre at Bovisand, but the waves had knocked the boat against the quay several times and he was in a very shaky state.

Coxswain Pat Marshall added:

It was a very close call. We were just in time. Although the cabin cruiser was just in the lee of the breakwater at Bovisand, the lifeboat itself was in heavy breaking seas – it was quite nasty.

The crew were: P. Marshall, K. Rimmer, A. Owen, D. Milford, D. Ellis, S. O'Kane and trainees A. Thompson and C. Cook.

'Concern for welfare' is the reason often given when requesting the assistance of the emergency services, particularly in the case of the RNLI lifeboats, when individuals making a sea passage are reported as 'overdue'. Such was the reason for the launch of Plymouth's relief lifeboat, the *A.J.R. & L.G. Uridge*, on the afternoon of Friday 9 July 1999. On this occasion the concern for welfare was for an elderly gentleman, who was two or three hours overdue in returning from a sail in a Laser dinghy from the Joint Services Sailing Club at the Camber.

Brixham Coastguard was first informed of this situation at 13.36 hours and immediately tasked the Plymouth lifeboat, which was launched at 13.54 hours. The designated search area was the

Plymouth Port limits, rivers and estuaries. The lifeboat was tasked as on scene commander, and was ordered to liaise with the Camber Rescue Boats and the MOD police vessels, which had apparently been searching the area for some time prior to the lifeboat being tasked. Via Longroom, Ch.0 was designated as the communications channel for this search. Coxswain Marshall announced his search plan but the other rescue vessels failed to acknowledge Ch.0. The announced search plan included the fact that the lifeboat would search the area of Cawsand, but the MOD police RIB made an independent decision to search that area; this being the case the lifeboat proceeded to Penlee, down to Rame Head, searching the shoreline and then a little more offshore. A line was then taken back to the Mew Stone. The 'Y'-boat had been deployed to search the areas of Millbrook Lake, St Johns Lake and Torpoint. As the lifeboat did not receive a response from the MOD vessels, it was assumed that they had withdrawn from the search. On reaching the Mew Stone, Pat Marshall headed the *A.J.R. & L.G. Uridge* into a position where, with the use of binoculars, a search was made of the mouth of the River Yealm, and then proceeded down the eastern side of the Sound to Queen Anne's Battery. Having arrived on the scene, the Search and Rescue helicopter, Rescue 193, was directed to initially search Whitsand Bay, following which, at the direction of the Coastguard, the aircraft moved on to the upper reaches of St John's Lake.

When, at a point just to the east of Drake's Island, the lifeboat crew spotted a dory, with a laser dinghy inboard, travelling at speed across the Sound and making towards the Camber. Coxswain Marshall approached the Camber and established that the laser was indeed that used by the missing person, who was now at the Camber. It would appear that, although having his sailing waters defined as those within the Plymouth breakwater, the sailor had made his way out of the Sound and up the River Yealm.

The crew of the Arun recovered her 'Y'-boat and regained her mooring at 15.50 hours.

On this occasion the service achieved the required result, with the sailor being found safe and well.

However, the requirement for such services highlights the irresponsible actions of some people when going to sea, and the unnecessary burden they place upon the emergency services and in particular the men and women of the RNLI. The crew were: P. Marshall, K. Rimmer, A. Owen, S. O'Kane, and trainees A. Thompson and C. Hall.

At 12.29 hours on Saturday 2 October 1999, the Brixham Coastguard Station received a signal from the 11,209-ton liner, the *Black Prince*, on passage from Dover to the Mediterranean, that she was diverting into Plymouth with an injured man on board, and required a Medivac. As weather conditions at the time were not ideal, a strong to gale-force wind was blowing from the west-south-west, and the sea was moderate with a 15-metre swell, Cawsand Bay was readily identified as potentially giving the best shelter for the undertaking of a Medivac.

At 14.34 hours the *A.J.R. & L.G. Uridge*s left her mooring and rendezvoused with the *Black Prince* at 14.48 hours. To facilitate the Medivac, the *Black Prince* deployed a steel platform, just above her waterline. The platform had vertical steel girders, which served as fenders and ended at a level corresponding with that of the gunwales of the lifeboat.

As Coxswain Marshall took the lifeboat alongside the *Black Prince* to put Second Coxswain Keith Rimmer aboard, both vessels were rolling in the heavy swell.

The vertical steel girders of the liner's platform lodged beneath the lifeboat's starboard rubber fending and, as the vessel lifted, a section of the fending was torn away. The lifeboat stood off whilst Keith Rimmer assessed the casualty's condition and planned his transfer to the lifeboat. The casualty had received medical attention on board the *Black Prince*, having been sedated and placed in a Neil Robertson stretcher, awaiting transfer. The lifeboat came alongside the liner to complete the transfer but at that crucial moment the *Black Prince* engaged its propellers, throwing the lifeboat against the steel platform, causing damage to the lifeboat's hull, including the gel coat and guard-rails. The transfer of the casualty was completed quickly and professionally and, at 15.00 hours, the slow passage back to Millbay commenced. The casualty's condition was monitored throughout the journey and until he was placed into the hands of an ambulance crew. The crew were: P. Marshall, K. Rimmer, D. Studden, A. Owen, S. Marshall, S. O'Kane and trainee C. Cook.

Friday 29 October 1999 saw the return to station, after refit, of Plymouth's own Arun Class lifeboat, *52-40 City of Plymouth*. The very next day, Saturday 30 October 1999, she was called into action to assist the 9-metre, Westerly 30 sailing yacht, the *Kishmul*.

It was at 20.51 hours that information was received from the Brixham Coastguard that the yacht, with a crew of five, had reported to be striking rocks at the eastern entrance to Plymouth; the crew were abandoning the vessel and taking to a life-raft. There was initially some confusion as to the exact location of the incident, the breakwater being a possibility. The *City of Plymouth* launched at 21.01 hours and whilst crossing the Sound was informed by Longroom Port Control that the duty harbour launch and the MOD police patrol boat, *Excalibur*, had both gone to the eastern entrance to the port, only to return inside the Sound as conditions were beyond the operational limits of both vessels. However, the coxswains of these vessels expressed their opinions that the casualty was more than likely further to the south, in the vicinity of the Renney Rocks.

As the lifeboat proceeded across the Sound, the lifeboat crew readied the 'Y'-boat for launch but it became evident that conditions were also well beyond her operational limits. Wind speeds reached 34–63 knots – gale force 8, gusting violent storm force 11, and the sea state was very rough with a 3–4-metre swell.

The lifeboat arrived on scene at 21.15 hours and as she neared the Renney Rocks, at 50°19.01'N 04°07.10'W, from the north-west, Coxswain Pat Marshall, using the night sight, spotted a small light, close to the cliffs at Renney Point, to the east of the Renney Rocks. Parachute flares were fired from the lifeboat and in the

turbulent sea, amongst deep troughs created by the swell, the mast of a yacht could be made out. The hull of the vessel could not be made out in the surf, and no crew could be seen. At the time of sighting, the yacht was approximately 150 metres from the lifeboat but, with the mechanic reporting that the lifeboat's depth alarms were ringing at 6 feet, no course could be found to the casualty. From the lifeboat's position to the north of Renney Rocks, the small light could not be located, even with the night sight; neither was there any sign of a life-raft. In atrocious conditions, Coxswain Marshall took the *City of Plymouth* to the south of the Renney Rocks in the hope that the small light originally sighted had been that of the life-raft, which might have drifted into Heybrook Bay.

Throughout the search, on a rising tide, which had now reached its zenith, the swell had continued to build. Mechanic Derek Studden reported that, due to the presence of sea clutter, the lifeboat's radar was of little use. With the sea breaking onto the Renney Rocks, Pat Marshall had great difficulty in distinguishing their whereabouts, he therefore requested Derek Studden to constantly update the lifeboat's position by using the satellite GPS. Whilst the lifeboat was being manoeuvred stern-first towards Renney Point, the GPS lost its signal connection, which was not regained.

The lifeboat constantly fired para-flares over the last known position of the yacht, but it could not be located. Unknown to the lifeboat crew, during their passage to the opposite side of the rocks, the mast had fallen, as a result of the

52-40 City of Plymouth. LIFEBOAT MAGAZINE

constant battering to which the yacht was being subjected. Again there was no sight of the life-raft or survivors. Once again Coxswain Marshall found himself in shallow water and in the heavy breaking surface could not progress further without endangering the lifeboat and his crew.

It was apparent that, given the wind, tide and manner in which the sea was running, it was likely that a life-raft, or any person in the sea, would be taken ashore; the lifeboat therefore requested MRSC, Brixham, to ensure that the maximum number of Coast-guard units possible conducted a search of the shoreline. Confirmation was also sought that a Search and Rescue helicopter had been tasked to the scene. This was confirmed. The spirits of the

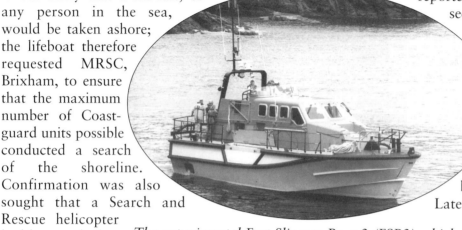

The experimental Fast Slipway Boat 2 (FSB2) which was developed at DML, Devonport, and launched on 31 August 2000. WESTERN MORNING NEWS

lifeboat men were raised when, once again, from time to time, the small light was sighted. The light appeared to remain in the original position, 150 metres from the lifeboat. At this time the first shore units arrived and VHF contact was established with the Plymouth Coastguard.

The lifeboat continued to illuminate the scene with flares and searchlights and the helicopter found a person in the water, in the area illumi-nated by the lifeboat. A Coastguard shore unit located two more persons on the rocks; they were also winched to safety by the helicopter. The three casualties were conveyed to HMS *Cambridge*. The helicopter then flew to Plymouth to refuel before rejoining the search. The helicopter crew later became fatigued and requested that they be relieved. The lifeboat was then informed by the Plymouth Coastguard, via MRSC Brixham, that one casualty had made it safely to shore; four of the five casualties were now accounted for.

The *City of Plymouth* returned inside the breakwater in order that hot drinks could be made for the crew, and to renew her supply of para-flares, which were supplied by a police boat. After six hours of searching in truly atrocious and demanding conditions, and with several of her crew suffering from the wet and cold, the *City of*

Plymouth was released from the search in order to rest her crew. With only one crew change, due to work commitments, shortly after first light, the lifeboat returned to the search area. By now con-ditions had moderated and the wreck of the yacht could be seen some 50 metres offshore; the lifeboat spent some time searching as close to the wreck as possible. Coastguard units reported that they were unable to see anyone close by.

After the lifeboat had been on scene for about one-and-a-half hours, a replacement heli-copter arrived and the search pattern was extended to allow for possible backwash and drift. Later, Brixham Coast-guard reported an EPIRB about 19 miles from the search area; the helicopter was tasked to investigate, but nothing was found. There were several 'false alarms' as items of flotsam and wreckage were mistaken for the missing casualty. Whilst the helicopter was away from the scene, a Coastguard shore unit reported an object worthy of investigation. The sighting was in a rocky area which it was impossible for the lifeboat to reach. With the return of the helicopter imminent, it was thought unwise to launch the 'Y'-boat. The heli-copter hovered over the area indicated for several minutes before a diver was lowered into the water. As he worked amongst the wreckage, he was tossed about by the still confused sea, and, on several occasions, was totally engulfed by the breaking waves. Eventually the diver was recovered to the helicopter with the body of the missing casualty.

To a man, the lifeboat crew were very impressed by the ability, professionalism and courage shown by the diver in carrying out such work in horrendous conditions.

After this recovery was completed, the *City of Plymouth* and her exhausted crew set a course for home. The lifeboat was once more ready for serv-ice at 10.53 hours on Sunday 31 October 1999. The crew were: P. Marshall, K. Rimmer, D. Studden, A. Owen, D. Milford, S. Marshall, J. West, A. Thompson and trainee P. Jago.

The *City of Plymouth* was launched at 23.40 hours on Monday 29 May 2000, in answer to a MAYDAY from the trimaran, the *Spirit of Belgium*, which had reported 'running ashore at the entrance to Plymouth'. Her exact position was unknown. The vessel was sighted by a MOD police launch, aground on the south side of the breakwater, approximately 200 yards to the east of the breakwater lighthouse. Upon arriving at the scene, inside the breakwater, Coxswain Pat Marshall ordered the launch of the Arun's 'Y'-Class inflatable in order to place two lifeboat men, Sean Marshall and Jon West, onto the breakwater. Having landed the men, the 'Y'-boat was recovered. The MOD police RIB cleared spectator vessels from the scene to allow the lifeboat to manoeuvre to the south of the breakwater, all subsequent lifeboat work then taking place on the seaward side of the structure.

Coxswain Dave Milford, Coxswain of the Plymouth lifeboat in 2003.

Following discussion with the trimaran's skipper, Patric de Radigues, of Monaco, it was decided that the lifeboat would attempt to pull the *Spirit of Belgium* from the breakwater. The skipper was made aware of the fact that further damage might be caused to the trimaran, but agreed that the attempt should be made. The *Spirit of Belgium's* crew were evacuated and taken ashore by the MOD launches. As lifeboat men West and Marshall sought shelter in a blockhouse on the breakwater, the lifeboat fired a rocket-line across the trimaran and a tow-rope was established. Throughout this operation, a 2-metre swell that was being stirred up by a force 6, westerly wind, continuously swept the trimaran some 15–20 feet up and down the south slope of the breakwater. The lifeboat men were constantly being hit by the swell, frequently having to seek shelter as they found themselves waist-deep in water.

As West and Marshall were taken off the northern side of the breakwater by a police launch, the lifeboat took the strain and slowly but surely pulled the trimaran clear of the breakwater. The police launch returned the lifeboat men to the trimaran to check for leaks; the water level appeared steady and Pat Marshall commenced to tow the casualty to Mount Batten,

where it was grounded on a slipway. An examination of the trimaran revealed numerous large holes in the hull and floats. The vessel had remained afloat purely due to watertight compartments, which held.

It subsequently transpired that the *Spirit of Belgium* had been in-bound for Plymouth to compete in the Trans-Atlantic Race. At the time that the vessel struck the breakwater, her skipper had been on the telephone to his wife! This was the second service in 48 hours in which the Plymouth lifeboat assisted a yacht in-bound for the Trans-At.

Pat Marshall retired as Coxswain of the Plymouth lifeboat in November 2000, his duties being taken over by Second Coxswain Keith Rimmer.

Throughout its long history, the Royal National Lifeboat Institution has constantly reviewed its requirements and working practices, which have seen the fleet develop, from the earliest pulling boats to the modern-day Severn Class vessels. However, fleet development does not rest here and the sights of the Institution are firmly fixed on the future. To this end, Plymouth has played its part in the development of the lifeboats of tomorrow, with the construction, at DML Devonport, of the experimental Fast Slipway Boat 2 (FSB2), which first took to the water on Thursday 31 August 2000. This new breed of lifeboat, designated the Tamar Class, will eventually replace the tried and trusted Tyne Class lifeboats.

In July 2001 Dave Milford was appointed Coxswain of the Plymouth lifeboat.

All RNLI stations regularly receive calls reporting 'persons cut off by the tide' or 'persons in danger of drowning', the latter being the cause of service to which the *City of Plymouth* responded on Thursday 18 October 2001. The alarm was raised via the Brixham Coastguard at 18.34 hours, indicating the position of the casualty to be 50°20.20'N 04°07.25'W, 0.5 cables south of Bovisand Beach. The lifeboat launched at 18.45 hours and was on scene in six minutes. A Search and Rescue helicopter had also been scrambled. At the scene of the incident visibility was good, the wind was a south-south-easterly force 5, the

The Plymouth lifeboat crew of 2002 with the Arun Class lifeboat, City of Plymouth. *Left to right:* Chris Hall, Valerie Brett, Tony Giblett, Sid Lawrence, Tom Russell, Sean O'Kane (Mechanic), Andrew Leigh, Andrew Thompson, Tony Owen, Derek Studden, Dave Milford (Coxswain), Andrew Redwood (Second Mechanic), Chris Cook, Jon West, Dave Ellis, Sean Marshall (Second Coxswain).

Above: *Severn Class 17-35 Sybil Mullen Glover arriving at Plymouth, Tuesday 11 February 2003.*
DEVON AND CORNWALL POLICE, AIR OPERATIONS UNIT

Left: *The Arun* Newsbuoy *and the* Sybil Mullen Glover, *11 February 2003.*

sea state was rough with a 4-metre swell. On arriving at the scene, the exact location of the female casualty was obtained, from the informant via a mobile telephone. It was established that the casualty and a friend had been swimming when the female got into difficulty and was swept into a gully. It was also learned that the casualty was wearing a wetsuit, which would provide added buoyancy and protection from the cold, but when located she was floating face down in the water. A MOD police RIB, which was in the vicinity, reported to the lifeboat that due to the raging, breaking surf, he had been unable to effect a rescue.

Coxswain Milford requested the ETA of the helicopter but was informed that it was unknown. Coxswain Dave Milford and Second Coxswain Sean Marshall reviewed the situation and realised that the only option for rescue available to them was to launch the Arun's 'Y'-boat. Both men knew that to launch the 'Y'-boat in the prevailing conditions would mean taking the craft to its operational limits. Coxswain Milford explained:

We knew it would be dangerous but then life-boating is dangerous. Whilst there was still a chance of saving a life we had to take it, it's the nature of the animal.

Sean Marshall agreed to helm the 'Y'-Class, with Jonathan West as crew, as close inshore as possible in order to make a thorough assessment of the conditions in the immediate vicinity of the casualty. With the scene illuminated by para-flares, the 'Y' was eased to within 30–40 yards of the casualty, maintaining its position in the surf, which was breaking heavily. As the 'Y' held her position, Jon West shouted to warn Sean Marshall of a particularly heavy sea that was approaching. The small craft was turned to south-west (seaward), in an attempt to negotiate the sea at a point where it was not breaking. Both Jon West and Sean Marshall positioned their weight as far forward as possible to meet the wave.

As the 'Y'-boat was powering up and through the wave Jon West was washed overboard and to the stern of the craft. The craft filled with water but by drawing on all his boating skills, Sean Marshall kept the boat upright and, after making a quick and professional assessment of the situation, was able to manoeuvre the boat and recover Jon West.

Having established that Jon was uninjured, the 'Y' was drained of water and returned to the task of rescuing the casualty. Sean Marshall gallantly made eight further attempts to reach the gully containing the casualty before deciding that the rescue could not be made by boat. This decision was not taken lightly but was based on a professional assessment of the sea state/height, the height of the tide (high-water springs) and the fact that had the 'Y'-boat been overwhelmed in the gully where the casualty was known to be the rescue of the crew would have been extremely difficult. As this decision was conveyed to Coxswain Milford aboard the *City of Plymouth*, it was learned that the ETA for the helicopter was seven minutes. The 'Y'-boat was taken clear of the surf and the helicopter's operating area, and stood-by as the casualty was recovered by the helicopter. The 'Y'-boat was then recovered to the ALB. During the flight to Roborough Airport the helicopter crew performed resuscitation procedures on the casualty, until relieved by an ambulance crew. Unfortunately their efforts were in vain. The crew were: Dave Milford, Sean Marshall, Derek Studden, Jon West, Sean O'Kane, Chris Cook, Valerie Brett and Tony Owen.

South-south-easterly winds, of severe gale force 9, and a very rough sea state prevailed, as the *City of Plymouth* was launched to assist the yacht *Headstrong*, at 18.12 hours on 21 May 2002. Initial information suggested that the yacht had fouled her propeller off the Great Mew Stone but, as the lifeboat cleared the breakwater, it became apparent that there was doubt regarding the position of the casualty, and communications were poor. As Coxswain Dave

The Arun Class City of Plymouth, *provided, in part, by the citizens of Plymouth.*

Milford kept the Arun at full speed, 18 knots, on more than one occasion the Arun became totally airborne as she left the crest of the waves and crashed into the trough and face of the next wave. A series of D/F bearings were taken and the casualty was located at 50°17.3'N 04°02.8'W, much further inshore than was originally indicated. Upon reaching the *Headstrong*, at 18.46 hours, she was found to be only two cables south of Hilsea Point. The lifeboat crew could clearly see that the casualty was lying with her stern to the weather and breaking seas, pitching and rolling heavily. The vessel was tangled in fishing gear. Coxswain Milford made a professional assessment of the situation, his initial intentions being to pass a tow to the casualty and tow her seaward. As the lifeboat closed to within hailing distance to inform the crew of their intentions, the four crew members could be seen in the cockpit of the yacht and it immediately became apparent that they were cold, wet and suffering from seasickness. Even though the yacht was snagged in fishing equipment, with waves breaking over her, the craft was rolling and pitching violently and continuing too close the shore. The situation was further complicated by the sea state deteriorating in the shallower waters. In these perilous conditions, the only option available to Dave Milford was to place a lifeboat man aboard the stricken yacht.

Without hesitation Second Coxswain Sean Marshall volunteered to try to board the casualty. All available fendering having been rigged on the starboard shoulder of the Arun, Coxswain Milford eased the *City of Plymouth* onto the bow of the casualty, instructing his Second Coxswain to jump at his own discretion. Timing his jump to perfection, Sean leapt onto the yacht. A VHF set and drogue were transferred to the casualty. Second Coxswain Marshall made an immediate assessment of the vessel and her crew, and advised the crew to go below, due to their physical condition. It was ascertained that two of the four had never sailed before, and they received reassurance; their two colleagues were lethargic and struggled to respond to Sean's questioning.

Second Coxswain Marshall attempted to free the yacht from the fishing gear, but, in the prevailing sea conditions, his attempt failed. With the cockpit of the yacht becoming swamped by the waves that continuously broke over her, the *Headstrong's* distance from the shore became critical. Dave Milford made the decision to pass

a tow-rope and, when secured, cut free the gear in which the yacht was tangled. The tow was passed at the first attempt and secured. Slowly the *City of Plymouth* eased the casualty seawards. An attempt was made to deploy the drogue but it fouled the fishing gear. At the second attempt it was successfully deployed. Dave Milford found steering to be restricted, due to the residue of the fishing gear carried by the *Headstrong*. The situation was exacerbated by the fact that the yacht's wheel had become detached and a temporary repair had to be made. Slowly but surely, the lifeboat eased the casualty from the beckoning shore until sufficient searoom had been made. With a final safety check at 19.07 hours, the lifeboat set her course for Plymouth. The lifeboat kept in constant communication with Sean Marshall, via the VHF, making regular safety checks. At one point during the tow, a particularly large sea broke over the stern of the casualty, causing her to broach. Although the *Headstrong* rolled onto her beamends, no damage was caused or injuries sustained. Throughout the tow, Sean Marshall constantly provided reassurance to the yacht's crew and monitored the safety of the vessel.

Having gained the relative shelter of the Sound, arrangements were made for the lifeboat to be relieved of the tow by a motor launch from the Jupiter Point Sailing Club.

After a truly demanding service, the *City of Plymouth* returned to her station at 21.10 hours and was once more ready for service at 21.40 hours. The crew were: Dave Milford, Sean Marshall, Sean O'Keane, Jon West, Dave Ellis, Andrew Thompson and Chris Cook.

For this outstanding and demanding service, the RNLI awarded Second Coxswain Sean Marshall the Institution's Bronze Medal. Coxswain Dave Milford was awarded the Thanks of the Institution on Vellum and the crew were each awarded Medal Service Certificates.

On Tuesday 30 July 2002, the *City of Plymouth* sailed from her berth for a refit in Falmouth. As the proud lifeboat left her station she was under the command of Coxswain Dave Milford, with two of her former coxswains, Pat Marshall and Keith Rimmer together with Derek Studden, her former mechanic, as crew. This proved to be her final voyage from Plymouth as the Plymouth lifeboat for, on Thursday 21 November 2002, the Plymouth Lifeboat Station was informed that the RNLI had reassigned the *City of Plymouth* to the relief fleet.

Far left: *Second Coxswain Sean Marshall.*

Left: *The RNLI's Bronze Medal, award-ed to Sean Marshall and presented by the Duke of Kent, in London, on Thursday 22 May 2003 for the service to the* Headstrong, *21 May 2002. (The station's previous medal had been awarded to Sean's father, Pat Marshall, in 1978.)*

The Arun Class relief fleet lifeboat, the *52-31 Newsbuoy,* ON 1103, replaced the *City of Plymouth.*

The launch undertaken by the Plymouth lifeboat on Friday 25 October 2002 saw her crew engaged on service for some 14 hours, during which the lifeboat covered in excess of 130 miles.

It was at 21.50 hours that the Brixham Coastguard contacted the Plymouth station requesting that the lifeboat be launched, having received a MAYDAY from the 6,395-ton Cypriot registered freighter, the *Bothnia Stone,* which had suffered engine failure. At this time the freighter, which was laden with timber, was nearly 50 miles south-south-east of Plymouth, listing heavily in storm-force winds and heavy seas. As a mammoth rescue operation swung into action, the *52-31 Newsbuoy* was launched, together with the Torbay lifeboat, the Severn Class *17-28 Alec and Christina Dykes* (ON 1255), and a Search and Rescue helicopter.

The Plymouth lifeboat, under the command of Second Coxswain Sean Marshall, was soon battling against winds that gusted to 60 knots (violent storm force 11) and a severe sea state. It took nearly three hours of concentration, deter-mination and discomfort before the *Newsbuoy* reached the casualty. The Search and Rescue helicopter, which had been the first of the rescue units to reach the scene, had to return to its base

due to a low fuel load. By this time the *Bothnia Stone* had regained power and was steaming for the comparatively sheltered waters of Torbay, now escorted by the Plymouth lifeboat.

The Brixham Coastguard reported that the 20-strong Russian crew refused a request to be taken off the freighter. However, the *Bothnia Stone,* which was listing some 40° to port, was rolling heavily and being swept by heavy seas, jettisoned 1,500 cubic metres of timber, which reduced the list to 20°.

After approximately one-and-a-half hours, the Plymouth crew were joined by the Torbay lifeboat, under the command of Coxswain Dave Hurford, which took over the escort duties, allowing Sean Marshall to set course for Plymouth, which was now nearly 60 miles distant and directly into the weather. At approximately 04.00 hours it appeared that the *Bothnia Stone's* list was worsening and the Plymouth lifeboat was requested to return to the casualty. The *Newsbuoy* was back 'on scene' at 05.20 hours and escorted the crippled freighter for the next hour assisted by the *Alec and Christina Dykes,* a Search and Rescue helicopter, a merchant vessel and the Coast-guard's emergency towing vessel, the *Far Sky.*

As part of the rescue operation, the Brixham Shipping Pilot, Rob Cumbes, was placed aboard the freighter. As the pilot approached the vessel

Severn Class 17-35 Sybil Mullen Glover *arriving at Plymouth, Tuesday 11 February 2003.*
DEVON AND CORNWALL POLICE, AIR OPERATIONS UNIT

Plymouth's Arun Class lifeboat, the 52-31 Newsbuoy, *sets out to welcome the* Sybil Mullen
Glover, *Tuesday 11 February 2003. Crew: Sean Marshall (Second Coxswain), Andrew
Redwood (Second Mechanic), Paul Jago, Andrew Thompson, Tony Giblett, T. Coombes.*

it was found that the *Bothnia Stone* was listing so much that he did not need a ladder to access her but merely stepped aboard. Rob Cumbes spent ten hours working with the ship's Russian master to stabilise the vessel before he took her into Torbay.

When the freighter finally reached sheltered waters, the Plymouth lifeboat was released from the operation and headed into Brixham to refuel. After refuelling, Sean Marshall once more set a homeward course for Plymouth, arriving back on station at 11.45 hours on Saturday, nearly 14 hours after launching. During this protracted and demanding operation, the *Newsbuoy* covered over 130 miles; this is thought to be one of the furthest distances covered on service by a Plymouth lifeboat throughout the station's history. The crew were: Sean Marshall, Tom Russell, Andrew Leigh, Andrew Redwood, Chris Hall, Jon West and Luke Tudor. At 12.30 hours on Tuesday 11 February 2003, the *52-31 Newsbuoy* slipped her mooring, with Second Coxswain Sean

Marshall at the helm. The lifeboat headed towards the west end of the Plymouth breakwater where at 13.00 hours she met up with, and escorted into the Sound, Plymouth's new £1.8M lifeboat, the Severn Class *17-35 Sybil Mullen Glover*, ON 1264, which was under the command of Coxswain Dave Milford.

The Severn Class lifeboat is designed to lie afloat and is the largest lifeboat in the RNLI's fleet. In common with the Arun Class lifeboats it carries a 'Y'-Class inflatable, which can be launched and recovered by a lightweight derrick and winch. The Severn shares the same hull shape as the Trent Class lifeboat.

Upon the completion of crew training, on Saturday 15 February 2003, the *Sybil Mullen Glover* officially became the operational lifeboat for the port of Plymouth, there to safely carry the men and women of her crew, as they continue to serve seafarers, in the long, proud and established traditions of the Royal National Lifeboat Institution's Plymouth Station.

The new Plymouth lifeboat, the Severn Class 17-35 Sybil Mullen Glover, *arriving at Millbay Docks, Tuesday 11 February 2003. Crew: Dave Milford (Coxswain), Sean O'Keane (Mechanic), Jon West, Dave Ellis and Tom Russell.*

18-01 on exercise, 1970.

The McLachlan Inshore Lifeboat A-509.

15

THE INSHORE LIFEBOATS

The 1960s were the golden years for the tourist industry of South Devon, with the traditional family seaside holidays being at their peak. These popular family holidays, together with an ever-growing number of foreign visitors and students visiting our resorts, saw a vast increase in the number of people using the coastline for recreational purposes. Often with little or no knowledge of seafaring, people took to the water in small fishing craft, dinghies, cruisers and yachts. Many of the more adventurous needed rescuing from the cliffs and rocks as they became cut off by the tide. Being acutely aware of these problems, together with the increasing and varying demands upon the service, the RNLI readily identified the need for a small, fast, shallow-draft craft that could be launched and manned by the minimum number of crew in a matter of minutes.

With these factors in mind, in May 1963 the RNLI introduced the first of its fleet of high-speed, inflatable Inshore Rescue Boats (IRBs), later to develop into the 'D' Class lifeboats, or ILB's (Inshore Lifeboats). The first IRBs were neoprene/nylon-hulled boats, 15' 6" in length, driven at 20 knots by a 40hp outboard engine. These small, agile craft, manned by a crew of two or three, depending upon the service required, met the design and operational requirements admirably. They proved to be able to operate in shallow water or confined spaces, into which the larger lifeboats could not manoeuvre, and were

Plymouth's first Inshore Rescue Boat cuts through the water, 1967.
Left to right: *Peter Plaice, Ivor Lovering, Dave Williams.*

ideal for other circumstances when the full service of the All Weather Lifeboat (ALB) was not necessarily required.

During the mid-1960s the RNLI introduced a number of these successful inflatable craft; the first to be stationed at Plymouth arrived in May 1967. The IRB, *No.130,* was housed at the old lifeboat house at the Camber, the house having originally been built for the lifeboat, *Clemency.*

This boat was followed, over the years, by a succession of craft, which were only actively kept 'on station' for the period April–October. Inshore Rescue Boats that performed services at Plymouth included: the Hatch-boat *18-01,* the McLachlans *A-506, A-507* and *A-509,* and the *D-123,* together with 'relief boats'.

The first recorded service for IRB *130* took place on Wednesday 24 May 1967 when, at 19.30 hours, whilst on exercise in Plymouth Sound near the Melpas Buoy, the crew saw a man aboard a motor-cruiser struggling to drag another man from the water. His attempts appeared unsuccessful. The IRB, which was manned by crew members Cotterell, Ashton and Baker, came up with the motor-cruiser in a south-south-westerly wind, of force 4–5, and a moderate sea. Crewmen Baker and Ashton were transferred onto the motor-cruiser and assisted in hauling the man aboard. It was established that the casualty had fallen from his own vessel, the yacht *Eskimo Nell,* when trying to recover the anchor. The man had been in the water for some time and, being unable to climb back aboard the *Eskimo Nell*, had attempted to swim to Drake's Island, but had been swept back by the tide. It was at this time that he was located by the skipper of the motor-cruiser.

The IRB proceeded on to the yacht, which was still under sail, a crewman was put aboard the vessel, the sails were lowered, the anchor retrieved and a tow-line was passed from the motor-cruiser to the yacht. *IRB 130* escorted the vessels into Sutton Harbour before recommencing the exercise at 21.00 hours.

In 1967 the RNLI introduced a new type of craft that was capable of being used as either an Inshore Lifeboat or a 'boarding boat', a boat used to take crews out to deep-water moored lifeboats. These boats were known as 'Hatch-boats' and, like the IRBs before them, normally had a crew of two. On 1 July 1968 the Plymouth Station received its first 'Hatch-boat', she was the 20' 0" wooden-hulled boat, *18-01*. The boat was driven by a Volvo 'Penta' inboard engine, with an outboard drive, which produced a top speed of 28 knots. She was kept afloat on a mooring close to the ALB.

The first effective service to be undertaken by the *18-01* took place on Sunday 8 September 1968, when she went to the assistance of the cabin cruiser, the *Ekco*. It was at 11.38 hours that Rame Head Coastguard reported having received the following message from the Penlee Fog Station:

Cabin Cruiser broken down off Penlee Point and a woman appears to be ill in the stern. – REPLY – Will launch Plymouth Rescue operating on Channel '0' V.H.F.

The duty crew were immediately alerted by telephone and *18-01* slipped her mooring at 11.45 hours. As VHF contact proved difficult between the IRB and the Coastguard, the Assistant Mechanic went aboard the lifeboat and opened up R/T communication with Rame Head and acted as a relay station. VHF communication between the IRB and the lifeboat was excellent.

The IRB came up to the *Ekco*, at a position approximately two miles south-south-west of Penlee Point, and quickly established that the craft was experiencing magneto trouble. A number of people aboard were suffering from seasickness. At the request of the vessel's owner, the *Ecko* was taken in tow by the IRB to a safe mooring at Oreston.

The *18-01* returned to her mooring and, following refuelling, was reported ready for service at 13.10 hours.

The *18-01* undertook her first night-time rescue on Saturday 5 July 1969, following a report being received at 23.55 hours from the Rame Head Coastguard that CRH Brixham had received a 999 call informing them of a vessel flashing SOS off Stoke Point. At this time the Yealm Coastguard was investigating the report. At 00.25 hours Yealm Coastguard confirmed the report, estimating the position of the vessel to be two or three miles off Stoke Point. Coxswain Peter White and Motor Mechanic Cyril Alcock were alerted and *18-01* slipped her mooring at 00.36 hours. On a fine night, with a calm sea, the IRB made full speed and came alongside the 20-foot cabin cruiser, *Kittiwake*, which had a crew of five men, at 01.07 hours. At this time the vessel's position was approximately three miles south of the mouth of the River Erme. The vessel had suffered engine failure.

The *Kittiwake* was towed to the River Erme, where she was moored, and her crew landed at 02.40 hours. Having returned to her station, the Hatch-boat was ready for service at 03.30 hours.

At 20.30 hours on Thursday 7 August 1969, Rame Head Coastguard reported that a Devonport Dockyard police launch was investigating a report of a dinghy, with two girls on board, being overdue at Kingsands. The Plymouth Lifeboat Station's Hon. Secretary, Ray Sainsbury, was requested to treat this report as 'anticipatory'. At 22.09 hours the Coastguard reported that the search, so far, had proved negative and requested the assistance of the IRB. The duty crew of Motor Mechanic Cyril Alcock and B. Puddicombe were alerted and were briefed with all known details. As they received the briefing, Longroom Signal Station reported that the Breakwater Fort was observing a red flashing light off the Shag Stone Rock. The *18-01* was launched at 22.17 hours and, off the eastern end of the breakwater, came up with a fishing trawler that was making its way to Sutton Harbour. The IRB carried on to the Shag Stone where she undertook a methodical search, which proved negative. Cyril Alcock was then instructed to return to Cremyll where he was to collect the Rame Head Station Officer and a portable searchlight, before commencing a search of the coastline towards Cawsand. At 23.48 hours, with the search remaining fruitless, it was decided to launch the ALB. The lifeboat joined the

IRB in Cawsand Bay at 00.30 hours and, with the assistance of two Royal Navy boats, commenced a detailed search of the eastern side of the sound.

At 01.43 hours, with all searches proving negative, and without firm confirmation of persons being reported missing, the search was terminated and both lifeboats returned to station.

Coxswain Peter White and crewman B. Puddicombe launched the *18-01*, in good weather and clear visibility, at 22.55 hours on Wednesday 13 August 1969, in response to a report that a yacht was in difficulty on rocks in the Sound and showing orange-coloured hand flares. On reaching the yacht *Raggamuffin*, which was towing the yacht *Coriolan*, off Drake's Island, it was confirmed that the vessels had fired the flares to mark their crossing of the finishing line in the Fastnet Race.

In July 1972 the *18-01* was replaced by the 18' 0" McLachlin Class, GRP-hulled, twin-engine ILB, the *A-509*. Crewed by Coxswain John Dare and Motor Mechanic Cyril Alcock, she undertook her first service launch at 23.40 hours, on Monday 24 July 1972, in response to a report of a small craft approximately one mile south-south-west of Rame Head, flashing SOS with a deck light. In excellent conditions the *A-509* proceeded at full speed, coming up with the fishing boat, the *Lady Mildred*, two miles

south-west of Penlee Point. The boat, which carried a party of six people, had suffered engine failure. The ILB took the fishing vessel in tow, returning her safely to Sutton Harbour at 01.45 hours. The *A-509* was on station and ready for service at 02.15 hours.

The harbour-master, Longroom, reported two people stranded on the breakwater at 20.37 hours on Thursday 17 August 1972. The duty crew of Coxswain John Dare, Keith Rimmer and K. Westlake were alerted and, four minutes later, at 20.41 hours, the *A-509* put out from Millbay. Upon reaching the breakwater, the ILB's crew located the two people and found their Belling Class yacht capsized in thick weed. Due to the thickness and length of the weed, the ILB had difficulty in approaching the breakwater. One of the lifeboat men went into the sea with a line and swam to the breakwater. The line was attached to each of the two casualties in turn and they were assisted to the ILB. The lifeboatman next swam to the capsized yacht, to which he attached the line before returning to the lifeboat. Coxswain John Dare towed the yacht into clear water where she was righted by the lifeboat crew. The yacht was then taken in tow to Millbay Docks, her crew being landed at Richmond Walk.

The type of rescues portrayed above are typical of those that became the mainstay of the services undertaken by the Inshore Lifeboats.

Left: *The McLachlan ILB, the* A509, *was placed on station at Plymouth in July 1972.* Left to right: *John Dare, Keith Rimmer, Clifton Andrews.*

Main: *Hatch-boat* 18-0, *on station at Plymouth from September 1968–November 1971.* Left to right: *D. Fowler, Danny Biscombe, Cyril Alcock.*

Above: A-509 *18' McLachlan which was in service at Plymouth from July 1972–June 1977.*
Left: ILB D-123 *with Fred Jackson (bow).*

Numerous calls were also received reporting 'swimmers in difficulty', 'persons cut off by tide', 'pleasure craft out of fuel'. Most annoyingly, the station received hoax calls.

The launch undertaken on Thursday 25 July 1974, by C. Alcock and K. Fitzpatrick, was performed in the Atlantic 21, *B-525*, which had been in Plymouth for the duration of the International Lifeboat Exhibition. The launch was made to search for a Firefly dinghy, which was overdue on a race to the River Yealm. The *B–525* set out to search the area from Jennycliffe to the River Yealm, but was recalled when the dinghy and crew were located, safe, in Plymouth.

The *A-509* set out from Millbay at 13.40 hours on Sunday 10 August 1975, following the receipt of a signal by the Coastguard from the FV *Ma Cherie* that she had a diver on board, whom they suspected was suffering from 'the bends'. The services of the ILB were requested to bring the man ashore for urgent medical attention. As Pat Marshall put to sea he was informed that the casualty had been transferred to the Coastguard vessel *Outrider II*. The ILB came up with the Coastguard vessel at 14.10 hours and the man was transferred to the ILB. Arrangements were put in place for the casualty to be landed at HMS *Drake*, where medical attention was at hand. The station's Hon. Medical Advisor had been made aware of the service, throughout which, via Rame Head, he gave medical advice to the crew for the casualty's care and treatment. The casualty was landed at HMS *Drake* at 15.00 hours.

The *A-509* was engaged on a protracted search for a missing skin diver, which commenced on Saturday 28 August 1976. The diving marshall at the Fort Bovisand Diving Centre requested assistance from the emergency services when the FV *Valdora* reported that a diver was missing from an inflatable. The vessel was approximately half-a-mile south-south-west of the Mew Stone. A helicopter was requested from RNAS Culdrose and at 11.08 hours the Hon. Secretary of the Plymouth lifeboat was informed of the incident. The ILB was under way within three minutes and arrived on the scene at 11.25 hours, where she was joined by the Plymouth lifeboat. It had now been established that a diver had run out of air and that a second diver had tried to assist him, but panicked and surfaced. The lifeboats commenced a search under the direction of Coxswain John Dare, who remained on board the *Thomas Forehead and Mary Rowse II*. The lifeboats were joined at the scene by the Royal Navy helicopter, *529*, and various small craft. HMS *Cutlass* responded to a PAN broadcast, and stood by one mile south of the Great Mew Stone, taking on the role of 'on scene commander'.

The search continued throughout the afternoon and evening; the IRB returning to station to refuel and to relieve her crew. The search having proved negative, at 19.50 hours, in deteriorating visibility, it was called off.

The *A-509* returned to her mooring at 20.00 hours and, after refuelling, was reported 'off station' for the night, as during the search damage had been caused to the propeller.

At 11.30 hours on Sunday 29 August the *A-509* returned to the search scene, as a precautionary measure, as 40 divers were reported to be searching for the missing man. At 12.01 hours the diving boat, the *Likely Lad*, reported that she had recovered a body. The deceased was landed at Millbay.

The *A-509* was replaced by her sister boat, the McLachlan *A-507*, between June 1977 and July 1979, although two consecutive launches, on 1–2 June 1978, were undertaken by the 'D Class' ILB, *D-123*. August 1979 saw the *A-507* replaced by the *A-506*, which remained on station until August 1980 when the *A-507* returned.

Anger and dismay was felt throughout the Plymouth Lifeboat Station when, in October 1982, the crew learned that the Search and Rescue Committee of the Royal National Lifeboat Institution had recommended that the Inshore Lifeboat should be taken out of service. The furious crewmen complained that they were only made aware of the situation when a notice was pinned on the station notice-board.

Speaking to the *Western Evening Herald*, on Wednesday 9 February 1983, with his interview being printed under the headline 'CREW FURY AS AXE FALLS ON LIFEBOAT', Les Vipond, the RNLI's Divisional Inspector of Lifeboats, claimed that the larger 44-foot Waveney Class boat, based at Millbay Docks, could fulfil all the tasks assigned to the ILB. Mr Vipond said that the 18-foot McLachlan inshore boat 'was getting a bit long in the tooth'. He added:

We had looked into this very carefully. Over the past four or five years tasks done by the McLachlan could equally have been done by the Waveney boat.

In Plymouth Sound there are so many boats we seriously wonder if there is a need for an inshore boat at all.

There are Ministry of Defence and Royal Air Force launches as well as ferries. And there is very little difference in speed between the Waveney and the inshore boat. There are

only four of these McLachlan boats left in Britain now and they are becoming rather expensive to maintain. Damage to one drive unit could cost up to £1,000.

The Divisional Inspector added that the only replacement boat was an inflatable – unlike the McLachlan that was glass-fibre – and one used on trials around Plymouth proved to be unsuitable for use in the Sound.

The anger felt by the crew was reflected in a letter to the *Western Evening Herald*, which read:

I am writing on behalf of all the men of the Plymouth Inshore Lifeboat crew, some of whom have been with the RNLI for 12 years or more.

The crews have been on duty every day throughout the summer months 6pm to 9pm weekdays and 4pm to 9pm weekends and Bank Holidays and all day if necessary for special events such as Air Shows and the Trans Atlantic Boat Race etc.

Each member had voluntarily put in a lot of time to keep this valuable service going, and you can appreciate what a shock it was for us to see the letter pinned up on the notice board in the Boat House.

No trouble was taken by the RNLI at Poole to advise our boys direct. This is the cold way we found out about it.

We are concerned about the people of Plymouth, who depend on the boat as they use the sea for so many leisure activities.

I hope the RNLI do not wait for lives to be lost before they see the need to keep this service going.

For obvious reasons I cannot give names of the crew, but we all feel the same about this and would like to know what the RNLI are doing for the sake of the price of a small boat.
Signed   Inshore Lifeboat Crew

The *Western Evening Herald* carried further devastating headlines on Thursday 24 March 1984, which read: 'CITY DOESN'T NEED 2 BOATS VOLUNTEERS TOLD' and 'RNLI SACKS 20 INSHORE CREWMEN'.

The uncertainty that surrounded the proposed withdrawal of the Plymouth Inshore Lifeboat had come to an end; the boat was to go.

At a meeting of the lifeboat crew on Friday 24 March 1983, crew members were handed a letter explaining the decision of the Committee, which

Gerry MacManus on board the McLachlan.

Members of the crew of 1982 on exercise.
Left to right: Barry Blewett, Alan Taylor, George Parker.

had the full backing of the RNLI Headquarters at Poole. The letter asked the crew to 'stand down' as it was felt unreasonable to ask them to continue to work on a rota throughout the summer, when the chance of a call-out was very remote. The letter stated that:

It is not money which precludes the provision of a further ILB in Plymouth, simply that the facts do not substantiate a need which can be met by a big boat.

The letter went on to thank the crew for their time and effort over the years and apologised for the 'unpleasant and regrettable decision'. The station's Hon. Secretary reported that the 12 to 15 men on the Waveney boat would crew whichever of the two lifeboats was needed – if the ILB returned to service for the summer.

On Wednesday 7 September 1983 the *A-507* was launched to assist two youths who were reported as being cut off by the tide on the Renney Rocks, approximately three miles south-

south-east of the station. The ILB launched at 19.00 hours, reaching the casualties at 19.30 hours, when it was established that they had intended fishing through high water. However, the youths agreed to be taken ashore. In the Return of Service for this launch, it was recorded that the handling of the *A-507* was 'unsatisfactory', problems having been experienced with the starboard drive. Electrically, the VHF radio signal had proved erratic. The ILB's crew on this occasion was Pat Marshall and Keith Rimmer.

This proved to be the last service at Plymouth for the *A-507* and indeed the final service provided by an Inshore Lifeboat of the Plymouth Lifeboat Station. The McLachlan was subsequently taken to Mashford's Yard, where it was to await repair. It was officially withdrawn from service at Plymouth on Monday 31 October 1983.

From the time of their inaugural launch in 1967, until withdrawal from the fleet, the IRBs and ILBs of the Plymouth station were credited with answering a combined total of 177 calls and saving 73 lives.

The end of the ILB at Plymouth. Certificates of service are presented to, left to right: *John Duke, Clifton Andrews and Ivor Lovering by the Lord and Lady Mayoress of Plymouth.* On the lifeboat, left to right: *John Dare, Cyril Alcock, ?, Ray Jago, D. Austin, Keith Rimmer.*

APPENDIX

Life Boat Regulations

The Committee of Management having given their earnest attention to the consideration of the Rules and Regulations necessary to be established for the government of the Society's Life Boat and their Crews, wherever such may come under their supervision, have adopted the following Regulations for the general guidance of the Local Life Boat Committees, or Honorary Agents.

They are however, aware that some of the Regulations may have to be modified, to suit the varying circumstances in the different localities.

They will therefore be prepared to consider any suggestions from the Local Committees or Honorary Agents, which they may see fit to submit, as in their opinion more suited to their immediate neighbourhood.

As a general rule, the Boats are to be built whale boat fashion, to pull short oars, double-banked, and to steer with an oar.

As the best Boat must be comparatively useless if not furnished with an efficient Crew, a Master, Second Master (when necessary), and Twelve Men, will be engaged for each Boat, in order to ensure a trained Crew of Eight Men on all occasions; and they will be required to sign Articles, to be approved by the Society's Legal Adviser, that they will obey such Regulations as may be laid down from time to time.

Each Man will be supplied with an Oil Coat, South Wester, and Life Belt, to be numbered from 1 to 8, and to be considered the Property of the Society.

The Pay and Allowances of the Master, 2nd Master, and Crew, will be as follows, viz:

	£.	s.	d.
Master, per annum	6	0	0
Do. going afloat to save life	0	5	0
Do. going afloat to exercise	0	2	6
2nd Master... per annum	4	0	0
Do. going afloat to save life	0	5	0
Do. going afloat to exercise	0	2	6
Crew, going afloat to save life	0	5	0
Do. going afloat to exercise	0	2	6

In cases where, the agency of the Life Boat, Money is earned as Salvage, or otherwise, the gross sum is to be divided as follows: Boat, one third part, which is to be paid to the General Life Boat Account of the Society; the remaining two-thirds to be divided into shares, of which the Master is to receive three, the Second Master two, and the Crew one share each.

The Life Boat Committee, or (if there be none) the Honorary Agent, will use their discretion in representing the conduct of the Crew, or any one of them, to the Central Board, when special cases of gallantry and risk in saving life occur, which may be deemed worthy of honorary or pecuniary reward.

The Crew are encouraged to wear habitually a Button appropriate to the Life Boat, to be provided by the Society, and a Medal, to be worn with a suitable ribbon, will be awarded in cases of extraordinary exertion to save life.

When authorized by proper authorities, the Boat with her established Crew may be used to render assistance to, or communicate with Vessels in bad weather, or to put a Pilot on Board. On such occasions, the amount of remuneration is to be settled with the Master, who will account for it, and divide it as in the case of Salvage. The Boat is not to go afloat, otherwise than to save life, without authority from the Life Boat Committee or Honorary Agent.

DUTIES

The Master of the Boat is to see to her efficiency for service, and report any defects to the Honorary Agent of the Society, or Local Life Boat Committee, if one be established, or, if not, to the Secretary in London.

He is to keep a list of the Boat's Crew, an inventory of the Boat's gear and apparatus for saving life, according to [a] list furnished to him, and see that everything is kept in the Boat ready for launching; he is to keep a Journal of every circumstance relative to the movements of the Boat, agreeable to the forms furnished to him from time to time.

He is to see the Boat placed in the Boat-House, immediately on her return from service; and that the Oil-Canvas Coats, Life-Belts, and South-Westers, are hung up in their places.

The Second Master is to take charge and command of the Boat in the absence of the Master.

Crew: A first and second boat's crew of six men are to be appointed, if possible, and in selecting them, if of equal ability, the preference is to be given to Members of the Society.

In the event of the boat being required, and any of the Boat's crew are absent, the men from the second crew are to supply their place, according to their seniority on the Master's list. If a sufficient number be not present to man the Boat, the Master is to select whom he pleases from volunteers present, who are to engage to conform to the established regulations, and are to be rewarded on the same scale as the regular crew.

Should it appear on inquiry, that any man belonging to the Boat was negligently absent, when required for service, he shall be discharged.

On returning from service, the Crew are not to separate until the Boat and gear are placed in her house, and their Oil Coats, South-Westers, and Life-Belts, are hung up in their places. In case of the Crew being much exhausted, the Life-Boat Committee will exercise their judgement in providing for the performance of their duty, and in making any other arrangements which may appear to them necessary, to meet the Boat on her return from any wreck.

It being of the utmost importance to the efficiency of the Boat, that the strictest obedience be at all times given to the Master, or whomsoever may be in command for the time being, any disobedience when on service, will involve the forfeiture of the whole or part of any remuneration that would otherwise be given. The merits of the case to be judged by the Local Life-Boat Committee, or otherwise referred to the Central Committee in London.

The Boat is to be taken afloat for exercise once a month, preference to be given to bad weather, at the discretion of the Local Committee or Honorary Agent.

In the event of any Local Associations joining the Institution, the Funds, Boats &c., which they may have, are to be transferred to the Society, and be subject to the general regulations thereof; the Local Committee, acting as a branch of the Parent Institution in London, to which all donations and subscriptions are to be sent, and from which all the necessary expenses, rewards, &c., are to be forwarded thro' said Local Committee or Honorary Agent.

LIFE-BOAT GEAR AND STORES

Anchor and cable (not too light).
One spare oar for each three oars the boat pulls.
Two steering-sweeps, two boat-hooks.
A good bow and quarter fast.
A small hand grapnel, with a line attaché, marked to use as a lead-line in case of fog, or to be thrown on board the Vessel for a hold fast.
A small sharp hatchet at each end of the boat.
Two small life-buoys with line attached, the inner end fast on board.
Spare grummets, and marlin-spike.
Telescope-boat binnacle-lamp, kept trimmed – oil-can matches, to be kept dry.
Lantern, and fisherman's white-light or port-fire.
Hand-rockets, for throwing a line on board wreck.
Hammers, nails, and chisel.
Life-belts, oilskins, and south-westers, for each of the crew.
Boat's carriage, if necessary, two handspikes.
One chest for small stores, on the boat-house.

The stores to be inspected from time to time, and replaced with new, if in the least degree doubtful.

ETERNAL FATHER, STRONG TO SAVE

Eternal Father, strong to save
Whose arm hath bound the restless wave
Who bidd'st the mighty ocean deep
Its own appointed limits keep:
O hear us when we cry to Thee
For those in peril on the sea.

O Christ, whose voice the waters heard
And hushed their raging at Thy word,
Who walkest on the foaming deep,
And calm amid the storm didst sleep.
O hear us when we cry to Thee
For those in peril on the sea.

O Holy Spirit, who didst brood
Upon the waters dark and rude
And bid their angry tumult cease,
And give, for wild confusion, peace;
O hear us when we cry to Thee
For those in peril on the sea.

O Trinity of love and power,
Our brethren shield in danger's hour;
From rock and tempest, fire and foe,
Protect them wheresoe'er they go:
Thus evermore shall rise to Thee
Glad hymns of praise from land and sea.

(William Whiting)